AFTER LIVE

THEATER: THEORY/TEXT/PERFORMANCE
Series Editors: David Krasner and Rebecca Schneider
Founding Editor: Enoch Brater

Recent Titles:

After Live

POSSIBILITY, POTENTIALITY, AND

THE FUTURE OF PERFORMANCE

Daniel Sack

UNIVERSITY OF MICHIGAN PRESS

Ann Arbor

Published in the United States of America by the
University of Michigan Press
Manufactured in the United States of America
♾ Printed on acid-free paper

2018   2017   2016   2015   4   3   2   1

A CIP catalog record for this book is available from the British Library.

ISBN 978-0-472-07286-6 (hardcover : alk. paper)

ISBN 978-0-472-05286-8 (paperback : alk. paper)

ISBN 978-0-472-12142-7 (e-book)

Contents

Acknowledgments

From California to Massachusetts to Florida and back again, I have been fortunate to call a number of extraordinary places home while writing this book. I am indebted to my current and former colleagues at the University of Massachusetts in Amherst, Florida State University, Amherst College, and Stanford University, as well as the many students who have inflected this project. Working groups at Stanford, Yale, and the Five Colleges have provided invaluable perspective, as have panels at a variety of conferences. This project also could not have been completed without a generous dissertation grant and postdoctoral fellowship from the Mellon Foundation, a research grant from Florida State University, and a publication subvention from the University of Massachusetts. On a smaller, but no less influential scale, I want to acknowledge John McBratney for modeling how individual arts support might work in a better world; a week's writing retreat at Percy Place in Dublin helped me through a difficult last leg of revision.

Amid brilliant interlocutors and friends too numerous to name, I have been especially grateful to those that read and talked through earlier versions of this work: Michael Hunter, James Lyons, Renu Cappelli, Matthew Daube, Kathryn Syssoyeva, Ciara Murphy, Rachel Joseph, Kyle Gillette, Rachel Anderson-Rabern, Florentina Mocanu-Schendel, Kris Salata, Nia Witherspoon, Freddie Rokem, Joselyn Almeida-Beveridge, Jenny Spencer, George McConnell, Aaron Thomas, Mary Karen Dahl, and Dominika Laster. The earliest iteration of this writing developed out of what were some truly glorious years of graduate study at Stanford University, where I found guidance from Pamela Lee, Branislav Jakovljevic, Alice Rayner, and Carl Weber among a host of others. Above all, Peggy Phelan remains an inspiration from the first days I considered this project; she has become a friend as it has drawn to a close.

I wrote this book in response to the many performances that have left me struggling for words or overflowing with them in late nights of ebullient discussion. Many of the artists responsible for my continued fascination with live performance have also been gracious with their thoughts, time, and materials: Francis Alÿs, Robert Morris, Didier Thèron, Rachel Chavkin and the TEAM, and the Edward Gordon Craig Estate deserve thanks, as do the photographers whose work I include in this volume. In particular, Matthew Goulish and Lin Hixson of Goat Island / Every house has a door and Romeo Castellucci and the members of Sòcietas Raffaello Sanzio have given me far more than I could articulate.

Brief selections from this text have been previously published elsewhere in different guises: a page from "Dramatic Possibility" became the basis for "The Brilliance of the Servant without Qualities: Bare Life and the Horde Offstage," published in a special issue of *Studies in Theatre and Performance* devoted to the playwright Howard Barker (November 2012); selections from the concluding discussion of *The Four Seasons Restaurant* in "Actualizing Potentiality" were included in "On Losing One's Voice: Two Performances from Romeo Castellucci's *e volpe disse el corvo*" in *Theatre Forum* (Winter 2014); and an earlier version of the discussion of the TEAM's *Mission Drift* in "Preferring Not to End" was published in an article from *American Theatre* magazine (January 2012).

I have been deeply impressed by the University of Michigan Press for its exemplary work on this project. The two anonymous reviewers of this text encouraged necessary adjustments to the argument both large and small, and brought insights for which I am grateful. I have admired the writing and editorial work of series coeditors Rebecca Schneider and David Krasner for many years and am honored to be included in their Theater: Theory/Text/Performance Series. Marcia LaBrenz shepherded the text from screen to page with grace, Mary Hashman prepared the index, and Richard Isomaki copyedited the book with admirable attention to detail. Whatever shortcomings remain herein are my entirely own. Finally, LeAnn Fields has offered steadfast support and faith from the start, and made the experience of preparing a first book a surprisingly pleasant one. It has been humbling and inspiring to work with an editor who has done so much for the fields of theatre studies and performance studies.

I think that our contemplations of what the future may hold are directed by our pasts, its lasting presences and absences. I could not have written much of this book without Sara, who for many years acted as the best of editors and friends, and who taught me that we must often end a world in order to begin another. A special thanks also to Wendi, Jen, Michael (again), and Kris (again and again) for sustaining conversations, food and wine, climbs and ziplines. Moreover, the tireless encouragement of my family—Cora and Rebecca, Robert and Deborah, and Quince—has kept me going and happily so. They remain my lasting home, no matter what geography's temporary divide. My interest in performance began nearly twenty-five years ago in two barns in Brookhaven, New York, where I took my first acting classes as a child. One still houses an acting school, but the other has since burned to the ground and become the site of a community farm. Both these places and the people that fostered them have marked me profoundly—Debbie, Robin, Mary, Diana, Michael, Jessica, and so many others. I offer these words to them and in memory of Betty and George, inimitable lovers of life's potentiality.

| # Introduction

The Futures of Performance

But how does one manage to represent the non-representable? How do you represent the non-representational and *not* represent the representational? It is all very difficult. Let us try at least to "participate" as little as possible, to dematerialize as much as we can, or else do something different: invent a unique event, unlike and unconnected with any other event; create an inimitable universe, foreign to all the others, a new cosmos within the cosmos with its own laws and consistencies, an idiom that could belong to nothing else: a world that could be nothing but *my own*, irresolvable but still in the end able to be communicated, substituted for that other world with which other people could identify themselves (I fear none of this is really possible).
—Eugène Ionesco[1]

During his tenure as secretary of defense in the administration of George W. Bush, Donald Rumsfeld's mastery of circumlocution achieved the highest states of obfuscation. Like carefully constructed koans, his statements gave the impression of an answer while holding any assignable meaning in reserve; an exhibition of power, they announced his potentiality to say many things without committing to a meaningful articulation. In a press briefing on February 12, 2002, Rumsfeld presented perhaps his most famous pronouncement:

As we know,
There are known knowns.
There are things we know we know.
We also know
There are *known unknowns*.
That is to say
We know there are some things

We do not know.
But there are also *unknown unknowns,*
The ones we don't know
We don't know.[2]

The "unknown unknowns" statement was variously hailed and lambasted internationally, receiving among other citations a 2003 "Foot in the Mouth" award from the UK-based Plain Speech Campaign. Yet for all its seeming obscurity and its politically nefarious ends, Rumsfeld's taxonomy of the limits of expectation pinpoints a very contemporary concern with how we comprehend future events. Here, the "known knowns" refer to that which one can already categorize as fixed and identifiable knowledge or experience. These are the things that belong to the past, have already been sorted and named. The more compelling distinction concerns the latter two future-oriented concepts. "Known unknowns" are future events that behave according to presupposed forms. One projects such defined knowledge into the future "unknown," colonizing its uncertainty as a distinct and stable entity that we could call a scripted *possibility.* Finally, the "unknown unknown" breaks with the expected orders of past and present to perform an indeterminate future without rational end or function—in other words, a boundless, unscripted *potentiality.*[3]

As one of the chief architects of the global state of emergency still ruling the day at the time of this writing, Rumsfeld formulates such *potentiality* in the darkest light, invoking it as the Terror that puts pressure on the habitual everyday in new and frightening ways. Here we face the threat that any individual may harbor motives beyond the seeming possibilities of his or her identity, carrying "suspicious" packages that contain who knows what toward who knows what end, that—following the 2001 anthrax scare—the very dust of matter coating the lines of our waylaid missives may affect bodies in catastrophic ways. Here the firm architecture of places that surround us may give way against all our expectations, the walls and floor falling out from under us. Framed in this manner, such potentiality stages a future *utopia* in the distinctly negative cast of the word as a "nonplace"; it implies the disappearance of our placement in the known world. And perhaps it is not so surprising that Rumsfeld speaks from, and on behalf of, a will to "secure" the future to the confines of his "known unknowns" and the dictates of what he deems possible. We might say that the brand of freedom so dear to his vision of the American Dream—and the international crusade perpetrated on its behalf—is a matter of possible advantages and positions, of using recognizable means to arrive at a recognizable future end: the new car, the new house, the new market, and so on.

But potentiality need not only promise Terror and annihilation, and it need not only belong to those claiming supreme authority. Another version of this same known unknown / unknown unknown distinction takes on a radically different cast in the first chapter of Henry David Thoreau's *Walden* (1854). While belonging firmly in the tradition of nineteenth-century American transcendentalism, Thoreau attributes his formulation to the ancient Chinese philosopher Confucius. Referring to humanity's tendency to interpret the future according to patterns established in the past—a tendency that I am calling "possibility" here and throughout the chapters that follow—Thoreau writes:

> This is the only way, we say; but there are as many ways as there can be drawn radii from one centre. All change is a miracle to contemplate; but it is a miracle which is taking place every instant. Confucius said, "To know that we know what we know, and that we do not know what we do not know, that is true knowledge." When one man has reduced a fact of the imagination to be a fact of his understanding, I foresee that all men will at length establish their lives on that basis.[4]

By acknowledging that "we do not know what we do not know" we make *possible* our *potential*; we take possession of our potential to become in an infinite array of directions from any momentary center. Thoreau depicts this realization as a miracle that announces the arrival of a new age, but it is a messianism that does not rely upon a particular messiah or a particular historical event; it does not, for example, await the second coming of the Son of God, as Christianity would tell us. It is no longer the province solely of those in power. Rather, such a new way of living becomes available to any one of a multitude of subjects in the fleeting present. To embrace and maintain potentiality is to realize the revelatory liveness "taking place every instant," and to disembark from known territories and subjections into the wide sea of the unknown. It is a project that cleaves close to the Jewish messianism explored by thinkers like Walter Benjamin and Gershom Scholem at the beginning of the twentieth century and recalls the earlier work of the seventeenth-century philosopher Baruch Spinoza, a doubly exiled Jew, who proclaimed an ethical and political project in exploring the hinterlands of "what a body can do."[5] This reverses Rumsfeld's conservative retreat from the Terror of potentiality to instead favor the pursuit of potentiality's many unknown futures. It is a progressive promise, a radical affirmation.

A last voice from the beginning of this twenty-first century, a voice from outside the American drama of freedom from or as security, should sufficiently locate these concerns as aesthetic problems as well as sociopolitical ones. For nearly three decades, the Italian philosopher Giorgio Agamben has pulled at the conceptual knot of such potentiality and its long history stretching from Aristotle to this new age of Terror and abandonment. In the two-page coda titled "The Last Chapter in the History of the World" that concludes his collection of essays *Nudities*, Agamben perhaps inadvertently echoes Thoreau's sentiment to say: "The ways in which we do not know things are just as important (and perhaps even more important) as the ways in which we know them. . . . The art of living is, in this sense, the capacity to keep ourselves in harmonious relationship with that which escapes us."[6] We have a tendency to approach the unknowable as a realm to be conquered, rather than protecting and sustaining our relationship with ignorance. For Agamben, this "art of living" with that which takes leave of our knowledge and makes for the future is the political project of the new millennium; to my mind, it refers not only to an art of living, but also to one of the essential aspects of a living or live art.

Over the past thirty years theorists associated with the (anti)discipline of performance studies have sought to articulate the meaning of live events in the midst of a world increasingly mediated by screen, speaker, or spectacle. These theories have generally framed the live event in terms of a repetition and reorientation of the past in the present (via interpretations of speech act theory and ritual studies in writings by Judith Butler and Richard Schechner, among others) and the loss of the ephemeral present (via the psychoanalytically inflected writings of Herbert Blau and Peggy Phelan).[7] They have, with occasional exceptions, overlooked that final dimension of temporality: the future. *After Live: Possibility, Potentiality, and the Future of Performance* regards live performance across a variety of disciplines as particularly suited to a revelation of a future in "real time." It sees its attachment to, and negotiation of, the time to come as one of the fundamental bases for performance's lasting relevance and reorients theoretical discourse accordingly.

How we experience the future of a live event and what we assume a body can do are not merely questions of aesthetic interest. To reference but one consequence of our approach to futurity, we might consider how debates on the ethics of embryonic stem cell research and what has been called the "culture of life" — deciding where the subject begins and ends — all demand a distinction between the human and its others based on what kinds of future are available to whom or what. In the history of Western philosophy, humanity's differentiation from the animal or material world has often been phrased in relation to potentiality, though which faculty identifies the appearance of the human has been a long-contested matter. Perhaps the most familiar version of this epistemological trope posits that humans are the only animals capable of speech, of language; we are the animals with the potential to say. In his *Grammars of Creation*, George Steiner offers an alternative conception of the human, proposing that the temporality of the future is humanity's distinguishing mark:

> The future tense, the ability to discuss possible events on the day after one's funeral or in stellar space a million years hence, looks to be specific to *homo sapiens*. As does the use of subjunctive and of counter-factual modes which are themselves kindred, as it were, to future tenses. It is only man, so far as we can conceive, who has the means of altering his world by resort to "if"–clauses, who can generate clauses such as: "if Caesar had not gone to the Capitol that day."[8]

This sense of the subjunctive "if" speaks loudly to the life of the theater as a site for staging alternative worlds and these clauses that human communities employ to harness the future. As the Russian director and theater experimenter Konstantin Stanislavsky noted, the theater demands that its participants invest in the full potency of the *"magic 'if'"* to propose alternative worlds of being and action.[9] Or, as performance theorist Richard Schechner puts it: "Performance consciousness is subjunctive, full of alternatives and potentiality."[10]

While it is doubtful that he meant as much, I would like to parse this last claim of Schechner's to discriminate between two modes of subjunctive becoming: one of "alternatives" — or, in my preferred terminology, "possibility" — and one of "potentiality." My usage borrows from philosophical conceits beginning with Aristotle and passing through Henri Bergson, Walter Benjamin, Gilles Deleuze, and Giorgio Agamben, among other thinkers. It should be emphasized, however, that the distinction claimed here is very much my own and any inconsistencies or faults therein should not be attributed elsewhere.[11] It should also be emphasized that I do not intend these as mutually exclusive terms, defining a strict binary, and one will often fold over into the other at its extreme or through a slight adjustment of attention. I propose them as tools, however unwieldy, for thinking through the particular affects of live events. Since performance is always happening now, these concepts speak of a present moment's outlook toward the future not as a relation with a divorced entity, wherein the future might represent a remote island of time, but as an extension of what is immediately before us. These futures belong to the present.

This will be explored in more detail in the chapters that follow, but let me take a moment here to sketch an outline. *Possibility* projects into the future an event or entity that resembles an already known actuality, a future designated by the terms and conventions of the past and used in the present. We recognize an object—a chair, say—and with that recognition arrives a set of uses or parts it may play in the future—a place for future sittings, a step on which to stand when changing a lightbulb, in dire straits a means to barricade a door or to fuel a fire, and so on. Likewise, recognizing an individual as a character determines what he or she may be capable of doing in the time to come. Possibility, therefore, plays with and amid our expectations for how time will evolve, with causes and therefores. This is to see the future as presenting (making present) a choice from among a set number of available possibilities. The predetermined rules of a world dictate a certain population of future forms, whether quotidian or fantastical, and their range of plausible expectations. Whatever lies outside these bounds must be characterized an impossibility, and this parsing of futurity into one category or the other is constitutive of its binary operation. I use the word "possibility" somewhat elastically to refer to these several distinct future ends (the possibility of having eaten this piece of cake) and the means toward these ends (the possibility of putting spoon, fork, or finger to mouth), and more loosely, for the perspective in which these means and ends coexist (a possible world). For, as I discuss in the next chapter, possibility conflates a means with its proposed end such that the two cannot be disassociated.

To a certain extent this orientation toward an expected possibility is bound up with the meaning of performance itself. The *Oxford English Dictionary* states that "perform" etymologically derives in part from the Latin *per*, meaning "thoroughly, completely, to completion, to the end." Framed as such, performance, we might say, implies the "completion" of a preordained "form": per(or pre-)form.[12] An audience's attention is often focused on the quality attached to that form, the manner in which it realizes its end. Richard Schechner regarded this repetition of an existing form as foundational, stating that "performance means: never for the first time. It means: for the second to the *n*th time. Performance is 'twice-behaved behavior.'"[13]

If past behavior exists virtually as a known entity presently available for use, looking forward in time will only reveal a future cast in relation to such behavior's presumed resolution. Likewise, when J. L. Austin first proposed the notion of the performative speech act as an utterance that does what it says, he would only imagine this act figured within a set of prior conventions and authorizations that it satisfied either "felicitously" or "infelicitously."[14] The felicitous performative would succeed insofar as it actualized the conventional intent of a named action. Infelicitous performatives, on the other hand, may do things—many things—but they do not realize the future named and expected; they are not possibilities.

Performance enacted in the economy of the possible trades in the currency of past actions. This outlook is most evident in the dramatic theater, that form of script-centric performance that developed in the West out of the Aristotelian tradition. Drama allows us to rehearse our encounter with an unknown event, gives us scripts to practice such encounters.[15] Thus, it makes sense to begin our discussion in the theater, where for more than 2,500 years of Western culture communities have gathered together to live through a common present and practice encountering a provisional future. In the next chapter of this book, "Dramatic Possibility," I look at how, in distinction from the larger landscape of nondramatic and postdramatic performance, traditional Western dramatic theater seeks to produce a future cast in legible terms. As Aristotle wrote in the *Poetics*, "The poet's job is not to report what has happened, but what is likely to happen: that is, what is capable of happening according to the rule of probability or necessity."[16] Aristotle refers to the tragic poet here, but his conception of the form as a revelation of what is predetermined possible greatly influenced subsequent writers and practitioners of dramatic theater at large. In these terms, tragedy stages the transformation of an impossible catastrophe into a dramatically meaningful possibility. Following theater theorist Bert O. States's rereading of the *Poetics*, I claim that if tragedy is a theatrical apparatus for processing a central catastrophic event into a socially legible meaning (designed to move an indefinite middle to a definite end), then the dramatic more broadly speaking similarly processes little catastrophes of "raw causality" into discrete and purposeful possible actions.

This is clearly a very partial reading of the Western dramatic paradigm, and I could be accused of constructing a straw man only to level blows at him; throughout this chapter and the larger book I suggest instances in script-based theater where the sense of potentiality repressed by the dramatic surfaces to complicate any absolute correlation between drama and possibility (Beckett and Shakespeare loom especially large). These works point out the potentiality that is always present in performance, even in drama that seems the most closed and absolute in its projected futures.

In one of the earliest theories to focus on an exposition of the future as central to the performing arts, philosopher Susanne K. Langer describes the drama as "form in suspense," always moving toward its completion.[17] According to Langer, while literature allows its reader to replay a virtual past, the dramatic medium (and here we must note that Langer excludes nondramatic performance and dance from this effect) directs its audience's attention toward the future completion of a form, or what she calls a "Destiny." In everyday life, we can only recognize causality through a retrospective superimposition. In the drama, everything that happens occurs as a part of a prearranged whole: "On the stage, every thought expressed in conversation, every feeling betrayed by voice or look, is determined by the total action of which it is a part—perhaps an embryonic part, the first hint of the motive that will soon gather force."[18] The present is pregnant with an imminent resolution; it acts as the guarantee of a possible end to come. Always passing out of itself and over into this future, drama is a profoundly transitive art: it lives for an end. If this is the case, it offers only so much hope for radical change and manages only to tell us, show us, or make us what has been authorized or deemed an acceptable contingency.

But what if we took Langer's attention to the futurity of drama and deprived it of its reassuring arrival at a destination? To put the question in other terms: how do we live through the present as it opens out into a future without the guarantee of a known end? In a small way, we encounter such an experience in the theater whenever we watch an actor forget his or her lines or an object malfunction onstage, the mistake tearing open a small catastrophe where the *potentiality* of this singular moment suddenly appears and we wonder what or who (character or actor or other) will happen next. Paul Virilio has suggested that the creation of every new technology anticipates the event of its accompanying accident: thus, the invention of the automobile simultaneously invents the car crash, electricity invents the blackout, and so on.[19] Thus, we might imagine that the technology of drama with its future-taming characters and plots presumes the advent of the accidental. Blocked or choreographed action presupposes the slip or the fall, scripted speech the stutter. No longer rehearsed or replayed as a form, the present reveals its capacity to become subtly or drastically different from itself, to do or make in ways that we cannot articulate, so that we in the audience, too, sympathetically gag or trip on the moment. By attending to such potentiality onstage, an audience may recognize its own potentiality to experience or to interpret. We discover our copresence in the imperfection of the present, in the departure of the present from the dictates of our expectations. Or, as Alan Read has argued, it is the capacity *not* to perfectly actualize our potentiality—to play with the impotential in a moment of failure—that marks theater as a human endeavor.[20]

In the above cases, however, the dramatic usually reasserts a possible end; actors are trained to reincorporate mistakes into the dramatic world, to cast this stuttering misapprehension as a Freudian slip or that broken vase as a symptom of their character. Indeed, we in the audience often applaud these instances of recovery as signals of virtuosic craft. We nod in appreciation when an actor gingerly takes account of the unexpected and does "not break character." I argue that, opposed to drama's tendency to cover up these sudden and gaping abysses, certain twentieth-century modernists of the stage and more recent experimenters working in theater, dance, and performance art—all those kinds of performance that Langer excludes from consideration—have sought to expose and isolate such appearances of potentiality and to hold them unresolved in suspense before an audience. My use of the term *potentiality* refers to a withheld realization, a possession of the capacity to do or develop. Potentiality "takes hold of" its faculties, displays them to the world or spectator without exhausting these capacities in an enactment. It is the blank page before the poet, the raw stone containing its many sculptures, the silence of the singer, the stillness of the dancer, the darkness of the theater. It is a medium communicating its mediality. It shows its power, but often through a kind of refusal to express that power: witness Rumsfeld's reserve of knowledge and the way in which so many of his press conferences revealed nothing so much as his preference not to reveal any information.

As if it could be, the conditional nature of potentiality locates its temporality between the present and many futures. Potentiality opens a medium wide and leaves it suspended on the threshold of figuration. This is to read Langer's definition of drama as a "form in suspense" as if the forming itself were suspended without arrival in a form, held back as the formative or even the formless. This is not a passive stance or form, although it may partake of a certain intentional stasis; rather the live event makes an unarticulated promise to keep promising, to keep setting out. In the language of speech act theory, this casts the performative as pure force or gesture. No act is named (for this would require a concluding identification), no thing is ventured, and yet the promise itself makes the fullest wager, the absolute commitment of a capacity to do. I promise that I will be here in the time to come, maintaining my capacity to say or do, though I will not limit myself to saying what it is I could do.[21]

For potentiality to retain its relationship to an indeterminate future, revelation must remain viscerally immanent. After all, what is potentiality without the pressure of an impending release, however extended that anticipation may be? Sitting with Vladimir and Estragon in *Waiting for Godot*, we in the audience are also waiting for an unknown deliverance from the masking of the offstage, not knowing when or how or what will come. Aware now that, to quote Vivian Mercier, "nothing happens twice" in Beckett's play, we forget the wonder and terror surrounding that initial encounter when, alongside the two tramps, we anticipated an arrival or hoped the boy or his brother heralded some other coming. We experience some inkling of this impending appearance in the moments before the curtain rises in the theater, or in the dark of the blackout before the first light catches on couch or character, when the theater holds its many worlds suspended on the verge of appearance. We hold our breath (to recall Beckett once more) awaiting the genesis of a new world before our eyes and ears. The pages that follow ask how one can hold that exhalation at bay. How can a performance sustain this sense of potentiality that grounds all live production? Or if the stage-world does begin, what kinds of future can appear within its frame? How do we stage a generative event before the (de) generation of a mimetic form? And how does such a staging affect those encountering its forces?

These questions are bound up with what performance theorists have taken to calling the "liveness" endemic to performance. For Herbert Blau, Peggy Phelan, Marcia Siegel, and others following in their footsteps, the fact of the disappearance or death of the performer present (both temporally and as a presence) grounds this sense of liveness. In outlining several universals of performance, Blau provocatively suggested that live performance is rooted in the unavoidable fact that the performer is dying in front of the eyes of a spectator—that we are dying together, as it were.[22] And in a frequently repeated formulation from *Unmarked: Politics and Performance*, Phelan locates live performance in an essential ephemerality, ontologically becoming itself through disappearance, such that it resists the logic of record and object. Her psychoanalytically inflected writings attend to the subjective affects of a liveness whose fleeting present is already haunted by the memory it will become; a future, then, but one forecast as to-be-lost to the past.[23]

While these conceptions of the live event have profoundly impacted subsequent approaches to performance and its ethico-political effects, rehearsals of the argument have at times focused on a reductive correlation between liveness and disappearance or loss, neglecting the complexity of both theorists' claims. Blau arrives at his conviction that "someone is dying in front of your eyes" in response to his imagined attendance at a performance by the great turn-of-century actress Eleonora Duse. Reflecting on her famed self-possession, he writes: "I have always retained (from I know not where) an image of her wholly alive in perfect stillness, then something passing over her face like the faintest show of thought, not the play of a nerve, *only thought*, and you would suddenly know she was dying."[24] A flickering thought that is no more than the appearance of a world passing, Duse's nerves show change in the most rudimentary and inarticulate sense: without qualification, without quality. That Blau sees this as a sign of death perhaps speaks as much to his preoccupations as it does to any ontological character of this most minimal of gestures. I would rather cling to the flicker of a stillness that maintains its capacity to think, a "*something* passing over" that cannot be named, and that opens out into the fullest potential of this—and only this—life becoming before our eyes, living. We will have much opportunity in the pages that follow to regard this minimal self-possession, particularly in the chapter "Withholding Potentiality" with its discussion of stillness in dance and drama. Elsewhere in *Unmarked* Phelan, too, focuses on the affirmative creativity of the ephemeral, writing that "performance is the art form which most fully understands the *generative possibilities* of disappearance. Poised forever at the threshold of the present, performance enacts the *productive* appeal of the non-reproductive."[25]

It should be emphasized that these theorists arguing for an ontological difference between the live and the nonlive acknowledge that not every performance overtly exhibits such poise at the threshold of leaving. For example, in the worst instances of mainstream professionalism, or what director Peter Brook has fittingly called the "Deadly Theatre," performance comes close to ossification in a reproducible text, so that the events onstage progress like well-oiled and unstoppable machinery.[26] This is perhaps the most repressive form of possibility, where the future experienced seems as decided as the past and we can see an end coming far ahead. In his argument against the ontological status of liveness, Philip Auslander points to the fact that the sense of the live as an unmediated event in real time only acquires meaning in opposition to mediation. He indexes the first usage of "live" in reference to an unrecorded event as occurring in 1934, when the advent of broadcast technology (radio) provoked a newfound uncertainty as to whether or not the performance one heard was prerecorded or performed in the moment. The appellation "live" only becomes necessary when it is possible for a performance to occur as "not live," as a record.

Yet, contrary to the conviction shared by both Auslander and Phelan in their initial forays, the live and the recorded are not mutually exclusive; indeed, both theorists have since complicated their claims.[27] In her book *Performing Remains: Art and War in the Times of Theatrical Reenactment*, Rebecca Schneider has cogently shown how, via the historic restagings of Civil War reenactors who "fight to keep the past alive," live performance can also act as a record of the past staged for the present.[28] The record, too, is live in the sense that it still affects the future-bound present both in scripted ways and in ways that may reclaim the past's undisclosed potential. And after Heisenberg's principle showed that the very act of looking changes the thing seen, it is difficult not to see the record as a live performer itself. If the reports of the death of the past have been greatly exaggerated, how valuable is the live as an epistemic for temporal knowing? Or can we not say that anything with a felt presence—object or subject, past or present—is inevitably live with the questions it raises for the future?

Bearing in mind this critique, I want to leave aside the debate about whether or not intermedial performance constitutes a live event and avoid pursuing some ever-receding province of unmediated contact between "not-dead" humans. For to consign the live encounter to a presence that, as Beckett puts it, is always already straddling the grave—giving birth as it takes to death—is to place its future in the most absolute of ends. Instead of presuming a stable ontological essence, then, how might live performance intervene as an expansion and troubling of what we mean by living in this new millennium, and who or what gets considered temporally and vitally live? This requires that we open our understanding of liveness to include some of its other connotations, to accentuate its sense of "aliveness" or "liveliness."

Quite a few different definitions of the word "live" precede the 1934 usage noted by Auslander, and it is my contention that these alternative meanings hold an unacknowledged significance for performance's exposition of futurity. In particular, the *Oxford English Dictionary* tells us that the live is "full of active power" or "containing unexpended energy. Of a shell, match, etc.: unkindled, unexploded," so that we can speak of a live cannon, live volcano, or live wire, each carrying a reserve of energy, prepared to alight at any moment. Shifting to such a perspective allows us to recognize the material or objectival as a live body alongside the human, or even the liveness of the situation as a whole, problematizing that other distinction between the live (subject) and the dead (object). This is akin to how Schneider speaks of the power of remains to remain effectual long after they have passed into the realm of the "dead" object.[29] In the theater, we can see how the full mise-en-scène—lights and sound, volume and surface—lives alongside whatever human performer may take the stage, if any does. The gallery, too, or any time or place framed as a live event, becomes a site full of animistic forces at work on the spectator's sensorium. This version of liveness corresponds quite closely to the terms with which thermodynamics describes potential energy. Framed accordingly, an entity possesses potential energy by virtue of its situation or state, an energy that can only be manifested through a changed condition. This change may merely be a matter of one moment moving into another. All materiality contains and maintains a reserve of energy prepared for release; all stands ready to perform a motion or expression. And that readiness itself can be a performance of a quite different character.

These senses of the live, normally repressed in the dramatic theater and marshaled in the service of its destined end, are as vital to our understanding of performance as any question of ephemerality, mediation, reproduction, or representation. Against the privation of the present that informs a certain mournful stance common to writing about performance in the late twentieth century and the beginning of the new millennium, I offer an affirmative gesture based on the material production of affect/effect. Yet this affirmation does not necessitate adherence to a purely optimistic or utopic understanding of the event. Live performance is not, by its nature, politically resistant or progressive. There is a great deal of danger and anxiety associated with live matter; it should be handled with care lest it go off at the slightest disturbance. The potentiality that the secretary of defense decried as a threat to national security prompted him to embody his own profoundly conservative potential, terrible in its own right. However reluctantly, my own writings contained here also perform an ambivalent power. At times, I enact the potentiality of the sovereign body and oppressive power, in order to show its affects. But I also explore how potentiality might be available to subjects excluded from the registry of normative and well-disciplined bodies. Live events that embrace potentiality may enact different modes of terrorism; their improvised explosives need not end a life, so much as hack or disarm the systems that determine the validity and invalidity of certain ways of life.

In this way, this book departs from some influential writing about performance from the last decade that considers its futurity in hopeful terms, where the present unveils a socially progressive community, however temporary that community may be. I believe that these claims, while intrinsically valuable for a rejuvenated politics of performance, do not fully address the ambivalent scope of futurity that may work through live events. Of particular note in this regard are Jill Dolan's *Utopia in Performance: Find-*

ing Hope at the Theatre and José Esteban Muñoz's *Cruising Utopia: The Then and There of Queer Futurity*, both important and influential books that have taken up the philosophy of Ernst Bloch and his magnum opus *The Principle of Hope* to explore a utopic dimension in the live arts.[30] In deeply personal writings that honor subjective experience as constitutive, both allow for a glimpse of the future in the present that does not reproduce the same, but imagines a time to come that might embrace subjectivities neglected, repressed, or fragmented by present normative culture and ideology. Both adhere, in divergent ways, to a political idealism that sees a better future at the edge or horizon of the present.

These are necessary projects, admirable and moving in their reclamations of the hopeful possibilities of performance, and they uncover an important source for theorists of the stage in the writings of Bloch. I want to diverge, however, from their joint investment Bloch's notion of directed hope as that which imagines and forecasts a future that we can qualify as "better" for particular, politically explicable reasons. Indeed, this is the nature of the criticality of the utopic: it challenges the official authorized line that dictates what *will* be in the future to instead imagine an end (however incomplete or unrealized) that *should* be in the future.[31] I agree that the futures Dolan and Muñoz strive toward *should* be, and I also believe that performance which expresses that desire for a particular kind of future in the present is very much alive. And yet, at the same time, I ask how live events negotiate what *could* or *can* become in addition to what they *should* become. How do we attend to futurity before it becomes *a* future? Live events can stage encounters not only with a hoped-for arrival, but also with the anxiety of the future in its unknowable plenitude. I want to trouble a tendency to view the live arts as inherently resistant, progressive, or hopeful that I recognize in much thinking about performance, a tendency toward which my own writing has often willingly adhered.

Part of this divergence stems from how Bloch himself conceived of hope as an "expectant emotion" available only to that forward-looking animal, the human. According to Bloch, all emotions look to a future, though a particular subgroup of expectant emotions rely on realizations that are not yet immediately available, chief among them hope and its opposite, anxiety. As an illustration, he recalls Marx's differentiation between the builder and the bee in *Das Kapital*. Marx writes that "what distinguishes the worst builder from the best bee from the outset, is that he [the builder] has built the cell in his head before he builds it in wax, at the end of the work process there is a result which already existed in the *imagination of the worker* at the beginning of that process, i.e. already existed *ideally*."[32] Bloch sees this conceptual building as analogous to the daydream, an ideally existent structure that the builder hopes to build in the future. As such, Bloch's directed future needs to be distinguished from the unqualified potential for difference taken up in the pages that follow. Approaching this question from a philosophical tradition inspired by Heidegger and Benjamin, Giorgio Agamben, for example, shows us how the builder's potentiality lies in his or her possession of the capacity to build without directing that capacity toward even an imagined end. The potential builder is *able to* and, more importantly, also is *able not to* propose a planned architecture. This potentiality extends both to the builder and to the bee as a faculty to do or make that each possesses. It is not solely a human propensity. Perhaps a more immediate image for the potentiality of the bee may hold if we think of its potential to sting. The slight pressure of a bee alighting on one's brow is most surely live with weighty and anxious anticipation, even if we know that the bee does not daydream of such an action. Yes, performance may instantiate the utopic thought of a temporary common project, but it may also allow a figure to retain its powers apart from scripting, apart from our hope that we may collectively establish a community. This book takes the first steps in a more willfully ambivalent approach to considering live futurity with and against the restraints of expectation.

This leads the writing that follows in some uncomfortable directions. If I write about a kind of radical isolation that may be engendered in performance, or discuss a nonanthropocentric or inhospitable ground of live futurity, it is not to neglect the important work of constituting community that we might find in the theater and related arts. Nonetheless, it seems necessary to invoke the *cruel* potentiality of performance—to recall Antonin Artaud's term—as a force that may be moved in political directions for better and for worse.[33] Some of the performance discussed herein stages an encounter with futurity that is terrifying, destructive, and that we hope might be avoided in the time to come.

Like the work of Dolan and Muñoz, this book traffics in personal memories and subjective terms, as an attempt at acknowledging my own inescapable perspective. In certain live events I, too, have felt myself a part of a community hoping for a certain future, or joined with others in the kind of aching pleasure of ephemeral belonging that Dolan has called "utopian performativity." I have lived briefly in these better times and I have longed to remain there. But I also believe that many of the senses of futurity I have encountered in live events—events whose forward-leaning pressures remain long past my attempts to name them as memories—have been singularly isolating experiences without the assurance of a common ground between myself and the others around me. These instances, aching in their own way, have haunted my writing and thinking for many years, stretching back to when I first discovered a love for the uncannily antiquarian, yet insistently contemporary, art of the theater. In the pages that follow I will often return to my distant memory of a child and his idiosyncratic patterns of behavior that play out again in these words so many years later. I remember being ten years old, for example, taking acting lessons in the attic of an old red barn—now burned to the ground—where, under flaking cabaret posters in faded French and alongside wildly foreign instruments, the sunken features of a small collection of hand-carved Indonesian puppets (I later came to know as *Wayang Golek*) stared out from the wings of this makeshift theater. These stilled bodies, gathered during the global wanderings of the couple that owned the building, were never taken up to play a part, yet they seemed to possess whole multitudes of other worlds in their smoke-tarred grooves.[34] Or several years later, perhaps at fourteen, I remember sitting alone one night in another barn-turned-theater just opened for the summer months—the Gateway Playhouse in Bellport, New York. The curtains of the small thrust stage had been lowered for the first time in decades, and the work lights left on behind the veil cast shafts of light through a tear or two in the fabric into the darkened, empty house beyond, where I sat staring. I knew the stage was empty, had seen its bare boards and walls, but felt an insistent desire to see what was behind the curtain, a desire coupled with as great a sense of terror about taking it up. So many worlds in that suspension, the theater was more live in its withholding than in the most spectacular extravaganza. Paralyzed, then, I knew that I could never approach the vastness of the medium as such.

For empty theaters are never truly empty. As Marvin Carlson reminds us in his book *The Haunted Stage: The Theater as Memory Machine,* past and future performances lie waiting in the wings, behind the curtains.[35] Furthermore, in every theater there is always the "ghost light," a bare bulb on a stand left perpetually alight during the nonworking hours, through midnights and morning hours, so that one will not trip over the gaping blackness of that unoccupied chamber. Across the world, thousands of dim beacons in theater houses together form a hidden constellation of dormant worlds gone past and signaling worlds to come. Before and after, the ghost light looks on, a truly unblinking eye on the potential spectacle of the stage. Muñoz marks a similar affect at work in Kevin McCarty's beautiful photographic series of empty performance venues: underground concert halls and clubs devoted to punk, queer, and minoritarian performance suspended in timeless preparation for a nightly gathering relieved of representation. For Muñoz, the spaces depicted in this photo series inspire personal reflections on past performances that transformed his world, particularly his contact with the experimental edges of punk culture that cleared space for his own explorations of queer culture as a teenager.[36] They also look out to the horizon of this present where other performances are always just about to happen.

The stories I have told are stories of the theater and work within and against its most conventional forms — proscenium frames imagined where there might be none, velvet curtains opening and closing on the scene — but a good portion of this book also explores the interplay between possibility and potentiality across other media. If the first chapter establishes the structure of possibility and adheres closely to dramatic texts and theory, the chapters that follow stage modes of potentiality in the live event at work in literature, dance, sculpture, and performance art. They ask: how does a figure or medium maintain its potential to say or to do ("Withholding Potentiality")? What are the effects that witnessing potentiality may have on its distanced beholder still caught in his or her web of possibilities ("Beholding Potentiality")? And can beholder and event experience a common potentiality ("Actualizing Potentiality")?

Much philosophical writing on potentiality has focused on the linguistic dimension of the concept even as the notion of a faculty incorporates senses beyond the written, spoken, or heard. The first of my chapters to address potentiality, "Withholding Potentiality," begins by looking at Herman Melville's short story "Bartleby the Scrivener" and considers how and why the famously reluctant copyist has held an increasingly prominent position in contemporary culture. It is my contention that this fascination derives in part from the story's literary manifestation of potentiality, an interpretation backed by Italian philosopher Giorgio Agamben's placement of the text as the centerpiece in his collection of essays *Potentialities*. The fictional construct of a life as tabula rasa, Bartleby retains possession of his capacity to write or perform a function by "preferring not to" do a prescribed action. Bartleby does not name what he will not do, but in preferring not to do the unnamed task, he remains able to do it. By opting out of the economics of normative representation, the scrivener writes a nonreproductive queer future that is live with the unwritten and that lies outside the possibilities presumed by narrative convention. I reconsider the inherently linguistic aspect of Agamben's theory of potentiality as an embodied practice, showing how performance thinks differently than philosophy and literature. In order to approach this embodied potentiality, the theatrical mise-en-scène must be pared of its lights, language, and scenery, leaving behind a lone stilled and silent figure, exemplified by the unmoving dancer who fully possesses the capacity to move or make any panoply of gestures. Here French choreographer Didier Théron's solo adaptation *Bartleby* (2006), which stages the word-bound protagonist as a virtuosic dancer intermittently frozen mid-movement, serves as the basis for an exploration of the effects of stillness and the gesture as displays of a faculty to do. I ask how this stillness differs from the stillness of the portrait or pose, so full of character. Bearing in mind the fact that stillness and silence often read as negation, the final section of the chapter investigates the stutter or gag as an affirmation of potentiality that does not arrive at a said statement or act. Beckett's protagonists in *Waiting for Godot*, unable to complete their vaudevillian gags, Faith Wilding's occupation of the meantime of *Waiting*, and the peculiarly adamant silence of the title character in Witold Gombrowicz's *Princess Ivona* offer concrete realizations of such affirmative potentiality.

Inspired by Branka Arsić's brilliant monograph *Passive Constitutions: 7 ½ Times Bartleby*, which delivers on its title's promise to offer multiplicitous interpretations of Melville's parable-like story, I return to several iterations of Bartleby throughout these middle chapters. In part my revisions derive from the fact that, even as I am thinking about live performance, I cannot escape from that same task of writing about potentiality that Melville's small world depicts. I, too, am playing the part of the narrator, retelling the life of the inscrutable scrivener. I also believe that the increasingly ubiquitous presence of Bartleby in Western culture at the turn of the millennium speaks to a contemporary concern with how to represent potentiality from without, and perform its power individually from within. In this way, Bartleby emerges as a kind of Virgil, guiding me through the abysses of potentiality. Arsić proposes a number of possible but ultimately partial interpretations of this enigmatic figure, as if he were a role put on again and again but never exhausted. I try something similar here, asking that we imagine the scrivener as an object both to our subject's gaze and, in a more literal sense, as a simple unarticulated form. In "Beholding Potentiality," I pick up the previous chapter's discussion of a figure suspending its potentiality and turn about-face to consider the experience of the beholder confronting such a deferred presence. What effects does an encounter with potentiality produce in a viewer? As the vessel for withheld gestures, the stilled body already approaches the position of the object. Looking to the minimalist art of the 1960s, which bear striking similarities to the actively passive form of Bartleby, one can recognize the sublimation of gesture into sculptural form.

I reread Michael Fried's seminal 1967 essay against theatricality and literalism, "Art and Objecthood" (arguably the most influential piece of contemporary criticism on the performance turn of the 1960s art world), through the critic's other art historical writings and his association with philosopher Stanley Cavell. Cast in this light, the minimal/literal object reverses spectatorial and performative roles, a reversal that sends the beholder into a kind of panic of actualization before the obdurate "gaze" of the potential object. Following Cavell's essays on *King Lear*, this lack of acknowledgment would be a tragedy, allowing me to read Fried's polemic as a performative expression akin to that of a ruler deposed from his throne and authority. To my mind, Fried's work remains an important example of how we (particularly as Americans) still try to rationalize the potential in human and moralistic terms, how we try to normalize its aberrant qualities or lack thereof.

We need not only rage against the storm—we may, instead, try to join in its tumultuous creation. "Actualizing Potentiality" returns to the theater to consider how beholder and event can share a common sense of potentiality. No longer based in the neutral ground, here I present an alternative model of potentiality, invested in constant and complete actualization, as exhibited in an event that stages the origins of a theatrical world—the mythical genesis before or after representation. In such performances of chaotic production or differentiation, a figure emerges from a ground at the same time that it becomes its own new ground for future emergence. The epigraph to this introduction, taken from the playwright Eugène Ionesco's notebooks, imagines staging the origins of a "new cosmos within the cosmos" of the theater, a universe without reference to known systems and without end. Ionesco recognizes the intensely private nature of this creation and the futility of fleeing from the representational in his parenthetical aside that ends the theoretical vision: "None of this is really possible." Likewise, I begin the chapter by reading an early and unrealized performance imagined at the beginning of the twentieth century by the modernist designer/director Edward Gordon Craig in which he prophesizes an impossible staging of genesis. This call is answered in a body of work spanning the turn of the millennium, that of the Italian experimental theater company Soçìetas Raffaello Sanzio and its director, Romeo Castellucci. I suggest that Castellucci's investment in iconoclasm, which attempts to release the forces submerged beneath the surface of a fully substantiated image, conceives of the theater itself as a constant oscillation between absolute creation and destruction, appearance and disappearance. This marriage of apocalypse and genesis expresses an affirmative and active sense of potentiality that departs from the suspended quiet of the still figure. It also points toward an inhuman future, where the individual is eradicated by powers that we might term the work of terror.

These chapters address live events as aesthetic productions, but occasionally signal consequences for nonaesthetic practices and "real world" situations. I will often ask questions of form and medium-specificity, though not to retain the illusion that the divide between art and life might still hold after it has been so thoroughly undermined in the aftermath of modernism. My predilection for the formalistic aspects of drama, and of performance outside the dramatic paradigm, arguably amounts to a continuation of the aesthetics of the avant-garde. This derives from an interest in work that intentionally tests the outskirts of its conventions and experiments with the chemical makeup of the live event. The histories of various media define the possibilities of their particular futures and therefore also define the juncture where those possibilities become "impossible," where the known becomes unknown. The intersections between various media or where a form rubs up against its outside or other become eventful sites for the emergence of potentiality. In order to speak of a field rich with the potential for differentiation we must also speak of the nature of this ground, some source or medium from which emergence may come. There is no emergence ex nihilo, or, as Lear would have it, nothing comes of nothing. (Though, in Lear's case, one might say that everything comes from nothing—the whole catastrophe of the future is contained in Cordelia's preference not to reduce the potential of her love to any number of possible florid phrases.) That being said, I recognize that there are real, material oversights attendant to such a perspective, not least of which is a cast of predominantly white Western artists who sit comfortably in a canon of experimental performance. Similarly, another book would take a more integrated approach to the labor and historiographical context of the futurity of artistic production.[37] I hope to write one such possible iteration of that book in the future.

For now, I can only promise in the final chapter that I am "Preferring Not to End." I set forth by recalling the last moments of *Let us think of these things always. Let us speak of them never.* (2010), a collaborative performance between the Chicago-based company Every house has a door and two Croatian artists, in which a series of enacted echoes delimit "where the theater ends." Mimicking this attenuation without conclusion, I present a series of short fragments that attempt to perform a means of production apart from the obligation to reach an end. These echoing fragments show some ways in which the issues raised in this book are at work in contemporary performance across a variety of media, focusing with some historical specificity on the white American post-World War II cultural land-scape. The central section, for example, reviews the conflict between possibility and potentiality in terms of an American obsession with the frontier myth and the dream of an infinitely transmissible free market capital. On one hand, capitalism continually feeds off the potentiality of another market, speculation, and the "futures market." On the other hand, potentiality may represent the multitude's capacity for unarticulated change. We saw this branded in Obama's first presidential campaign through the promise of "change" not as a series of programs, but as some-thing close to a formal movement. In the Brooklyn-based collective the TEAM, directed by Rachel Chavkin and fittingly called the Theatre of the Emerging American Moment, I find a theater that rehearses this apocalyp-tic moment in late capitalism again and again from within a dramatic id-iom. As with Sam Shepard's late twentieth-century revitalizations of char-acter and cliché from the annals of American history and popular culture, the TEAM replays a seemingly exhausted set of possible stories while a spectacularly catastrophic world erupts unseen just past the lip of their makeshift stage. They look out on a cataclysm that they cannot dramatize, a play of power that they cannot possess. Finally, I try to find myself fleet-ingly in a performance artist who seems to model a poetics of suspense that actively maintains the potentiality of an event.

It should be apparent that the following chapters wander through many territories and disciplines. These in no way represent a comprehensive sur-vey of the appearances of possibility or potentiality within performance, and, ultimately, these case studies offer only initial attempts at what I see as a promising direction for further critical thought and practice. While touching on the ways that performance affects the entire sensorium of the beholder, I have limited my discussion primarily to the visual and linguis-tic, so the most glaring absence from this theoretical foray into the perfor-mance of potentiality is the question of sound and music. Composer John Cage's work, especially his exploration of silence, would seem an ideal counterpart to the discussion of the choreography of his partner, Merce Cunningham, and subsequent incorporations of stillness in minimalist dance. Cage's 1952 composition 4'33", in which a pianist sits before an open piano for four minutes and thirty-three seconds of scored silence, is a case in point. The piece directs the attention of its audience not only to ex-tramusical sounds within and without the body in ways that announce the liveliness of the still body and surrounding event, but also provokes fasci-nating questions about the nature of the performer's potentiality.

As part of its *Art of Participation* exhibition in 2008–2009, the San Fran-
cisco Museum of Modern Art offered daily restagings of Cage's seminal
performance. In a subtle, but substantial departure from the original performance, the performers here were volunteers, and no musical training or
facility with the piano was required for their involvement. The performer
for the 1952 premiere of 4'33", David Tudor, or any number of musicians
who have presented Cage's score in the past, possessed a facility or even
virtuosity before their respective instruments. Their suspension of playing
exposed a vast and unfathomable potential to do: what Aristotle would call
an "existing" potentiality that the performer preferred not to enact in the
immediate future. This was clearly not the case in the SFMOMA reperformance, since an untrained performer sitting before an instrument possesses
a very different sense of capacity: a "generic" potentiality without a particular knowledge or faculty—it would require a decided change in kind
for him or her to be able to actualize a musical expression. These distinctions between "generic" and "existing" potential are explored further in
the chapter "Withholding Potentiality," but the differences between the
visual and auditory, as well as the divergent histories/conventions attendant to each, exceed the limits of this particular project.

A last word on divergent histories. Thoreau's reference to Confucius as
the source for his description of potentiality as well as Cage's indebtedness
to the I Ching and Zen Buddhism indicate that this work would benefit immensely from a robust conversation with Eastern philosophical and aesthetic traditions. Apart from a few asides, I, regrettably, do not possess the
"existing potential" to sufficiently realize this promise and to take account
of the incredibly rich field of intercultural performance in non-Western
contexts that would offer a great deal to these conversations.

As I attempt to signal throughout, my notions of potentiality and possibility occupy a common continuum that loops back on itself. There is
room for a good deal of overlap between the two concepts, and at the furthest extreme one seems to fold into the other. With all its attempts at building a world of possibilities, even the most conservative of dramatic theaters
contains prospects of potentiality within and at its limits. At the same time,
all of the theatrical performances I discuss are rehearsed and prepared
events (even if, in the case of a company like Socìetas Raffaello Sanzio,
there is room for adjusting duration and emphasis based on the contingencies of a particular performance). From the side of production—the backstage or artist's point of view—all are beholden to possible ends. With this
in mind I am strictly interested in looking at the live encounter between a
beholder and an event, where the sense of possibility or potentiality con-

fronts an individual audience member or gallery visitor. I do not consider the potentiality of actual catastrophes or improvised events, which may, in the case of improvisational comedy or practices associated with commedia dell'arte, maintain even stricter sets of possibilities. Again, my choices represent but a select few possible paths for future investigation; what I present here is merely a beginning.

Edward Said described a beginning as that which is always directed toward an end. In his *Beginnings: Intention and Method*, he describes how beginnings are historiographical demarcations applied retrospectively to mark the initiation of a chain of actions. They are "transitive" since they are "for" something in the same way that a means is devoted toward, and consummated by, an end. In characterizing the impetus or intentionality of a subsequent line of bounded activity, sealed with the perfect hindsight of actual occurrence, beginnings express not only how an individual intended to act at the time, but also how they *would* act in future occasions. In other words, beginnings also mark out what a future beginning could look like. Or, as Said writes, "Consciousness of a starting point, from the vantage point of the continuity that succeeds it, is seen to be consciousness of a direction in which it is humanly *possible* to move (as well as trust in continuity)."[38] Said explicitly sets out to supplement Frank Kermode's study of ends and the millenarian impulse, *The Sense of an Ending* (1967, revised in 2000), arguing that before an end can be determined, one must set forth an appropriate beginning.[39] But at the root ends and beginnings are two sides of the same coin; one requires the other in order to signify. I write these words at the end of the event, knowing this book's limits and course before inviting you to join me to begin along its paths. The future is set, its possibilities quite defined, though I imagine productive departures through the fields to follow, other beginnings and other ends.

If beginnings talk of possibilities, can we look to the other term in Said's study, the "origin," as the site for the efflorescence of potentiality? Where Said incisively pinpoints the essential characteristics of beginning, he struggles against the silence of the origin, approaching it obliquely again and again. This reticence is a product of the fact that the origin marks the boundary of language itself. Beginnings are full of names, transitive *for* something or someone, but the origin is intransitive; without determinant orientations it—like *Macbeth*'s weird sisters discussed below—does and does and does, though what it does, it does not say. The origin is a beginning of beginnings that ends itself as soon as it acquires a name, as soon as something determinant follows from it. This presents some difficulties for the writing of history.

So, too, my own constant returns and reconceptions evince a similar struggle with the difficulty in actualizing potentiality. It would be, as Thoreau notes, a miracle far beyond my means to recognize the infinite unknowns that radiate from this single point. And as Peggy Phelan characterizes the dilemma facing all those who stake words in place of performance: "In writing the unmarked I mark it, inevitably. In seeing it I am marked by it. But because what I do not see and do not write is so much more vast than what I do it is impossible to 'ruin' the unmarked."[40] So, too, it is my hope that these few and wayward scratches on the blank page of potentiality do not run too deep. I have reserved much space on the margins for others to remark and contest, in hopes of future encounters.

| Dramatic Possibility

A choice involves the anticipatory idea of several possible
actions. Possibilities of action must therefore be marked out
for the living being before the action itself.
  —Henri Bergson[1]

In the theater the audience wants to be surprised, but by
things that they expect.
  —Tristan Bernard[2]

If, as the poet Paul Valéry said, "one of the deepest, one of the most general
functions of living organisms is to look ahead, to produce future," then the
theater is arguably the most established aesthetic site for the human organism to play out such production.[3] The entire theatrical apparatus, from its
architectural support to its ceremonies of audience etiquette, comprises a
technology devoted to the revelation of what is to come. And the specific
manners through which the theater creates its actions and events determine the kinds of future available to its audiences. In the traditional Western dramatic theater the question of *how* something will happen (or in its
tragic form, the more direct question of how death will happen) comes
down to a choice from amid a set of distinct possibilities: Will Nora give in
to blackmail? Will Torvald find the incriminating letter? Even when Nora
leaves the stage and slams the door behind her to end a performance of
Henrik Ibsen's *A Doll's House*, the unseen and unspoken future available to
her after the curtain's fall seems to follow particular possibilities set up by
the world of the play.[4] Faced with an actual world comprised of inscrutable
events, the dramatic theater attempts to calm the anxiety provoked by the
unknown and unknowable by projecting a future cast in recognizable
terms; it rehearses our encounter with an event, gives us scripts to practice
such encounters.

As Gertrude Stein recognized in her own anxious relationship to this
kind of theatrical stage, drama is always bound up with the consequences
of past actions. For Stein, this nervousness derives from the disjunction that

separates the event onstage from the event experienced by the audience. One can only follow the drama through a kind of syncopated recovery, folding information already learned over the course of the performance into a future projection of what is to come in the plot.[5] While Stein does not explicitly say as much, this disjunction derives not only from the spatial divide between onstage and offstage, but also and even more directly from the particular kinds of action performed in the stage-world. Here, actions belong to and express a linear cause-and-effect relationship that determines the ends of both past and future events. In this chapter I will describe how drama relies on a seemingly comprehensive schema of plotting and causal actions in order to reproduce a knowable future—the possible. At the same time, I will keep troubling the seams and gathering places in this dramatic fabric to glimpse the great tracts of futures unforeseen at work in the most staid of theatrical productions.

Before continuing it will be helpful to define the term "drama" and set it apart from performance inside and outside the theater more broadly speaking. I borrow from Peter Szondi's *Theory of Modern Drama* in claiming that the dramatic refers to one strand of performance activity indebted to a set of historical conventions. According to this understanding, drama "stands for a specific literary-historical event—namely, the drama as it arose in Elizabethan England and, above all, as it came into being in seventeenth-century France and was perpetuated in the German classical period."[6] By the advent of the twentieth century such a notion of the drama had become the hegemonic form of mainstream Western theatrical practice. Here, dialogue is the defining force in the world of the play as it, following the means by which August Wilhelm von Schlegel differentiated drama from philosophy, influences character and changes opinion.[7] This emphasis on dialogue applies both to spoken exchanges between individualized characters, and to these same characters' relationships to the surrounding object world. At its extreme, as, for example, in the French neoclassicism of Racine, the object is excluded from the world of a play if it does not relate to a character (and, for Racine, in decorous terms at that). Live performance serves to materially reproduce or actualize a preexisting textual artifact, and elements of the mise-en-scène—such as the sound, lighting, sets, and costume, as well as corporeal movements extraneous to the progression of the plot—are of decidedly secondary import.

As is evident in the Greek etymology of the term ("drama" meaning "to do"), the Aristotelian marriage of imitation and action grounds this representation of the individual and his or her dialogues; drama represents the actual world as if it were a world of meaningful actions. We will explore below how this has a direct influence on the temporality of the drama. For, as Szondi writes, drama "generates its own time. Therefore, every moment must contain the seeds of the future. It must be 'pregnant with futurity.'"[8] Every discrete moment must contain the cause of a future effect and must, in turn, represent the effect of a prior cause. Such is the linear progression of dramatic action and the reason why Stein found herself split between looking forward and backward at the same time, trying to account for multiple causes and effects.

Thinking in terms of the dramatic allows us to identify a dominant principle while acknowledging that exceptions to the rule abound in alternative forms of performance as well as within play texts themselves. Looking back from a contemporary perspective, we can choose to read earlier plays as dramatic works—and most often today's practitioners and mainstream audiences alike do so—but such a choice would to greater or lesser degrees elide certain aspects of the performance score. Hans-Thies Lehmann's influential survey of more recent theatrical practice, *Postdramatic Theatre*, thinks through the limits of this drama (i.e., where the "dramatic" ends), proposing that there has always been a "theatrical" excess working as a counterforce on the stage and pushing at the boundaries of drama's mandate. For example, Stein's rejoinders to the dramatic—attempts at creating a "continuous present" through what she termed the *landscape* and *portrait* play—borrow from traditions of performance on the outskirts of drama but stretching back to at least the sixteenth-century stage in the *tableau vivant* or the masque, and arguably much earlier in the paratheatrical spectacles of the classical world. In fact, as Szondi argues, modern drama from Ibsen onward recognizes the form's failure to effectively construct a self or manipulate a world through dialogue and, I would add, action.[9] Working from within its constraints, many of the plays of the twentieth and twenty-first centuries expose the limits of drama's formal possibilities and thus allow for more complicated senses of the future to take the stage—what I will come to call "potentiality" in later chapters.

It would be a mistake, then, to say that all plays are irrevocably bound to reproduce a future constrained by what is assumed possible. Indeed, it is my conviction that to some degree all live performance, even the most restrictive form of drama, strains against such presuppositions through the vagaries of performance. There is always the threat that some mistake may break free, that the lights will not return after the blackout, or that someone or something unexpected may be knocking at the door to the kitchen sink drama. This pressure exerts itself in the dramatic text, too, in ways that this chapter will seek to expose. We may anticipate what is possible, but we do not know for certain what will come. Exploring how paradigmatic forms of drama seek to effectively tame the unpredictability of the future helps to disclose this same system's excesses and outsides.

A FUTURE OF MEANINGS AND ENDINGS

In *The Pleasure of the Play*, theater theorist Bert O. States extends Aristotle's *Poetics*, historically associated with a selective conception of classical and neoclassical tragedy, into a paradigm for the larger Western dramatic medium.[10] Chief among the claims of this expanded theory is the proposition that dramatic theater concerns itself with playing out what I have called "possibility" (States does not use the term) for the benefit of an audience of self-conscious individuals. According to States, dramatic action is "motion that makes sense," quite literally a motion that creates meaning.[11] This "making sense" of motion operates on both the macro level of the entire production (the arrangement of alogical events into a *plot*) and the micro level of moment-to-moment accumulation (the digestion of otherwise "endless" motion into a teleological *action*). We will first look at how possibility structures dramatic plot and then in the latter half of this chapter consider how possibility effects the ordering of dramatic action on a smaller scale.

For Aristotle, the plot of a drama, or its signature ordering of events, is the most important element in the construction of a play. The *Poetics* distinguishes between the *story* as a closed set of events and the *plot* that arranges these events into a progressive development. A number of plots may be formed from the same story. For example, classical Greek tragedy relied on myths whose final outcomes would have been immediately recognizable to its audiences; playwrights told and retold the same stories again and again, so the pleasure in watching this new version of Orestes/Electra lies in seeing what possible variations shape the landscape of this particular offspring while still belonging to the parent myth. The stories are identical, but the plot exhibits different possible means to the same or related end.[12] Plot, then, operates within a field of possibilities specific to the expectations of its story-world. As in a sports game, a kind of playing field of the appropriate delineates the bounds of the possible even before an individual action takes place, before its characters appear. Story defines the possibilities of plot; we could call it a "possible world" in which particular plots are actualized.

A preexisting myth may define the world of a Greek tragedy, but in States's expanded theory questions of form, genre, and author also define the territory of possibilities encompassed by a given stage world. Where Aristotle's theory of tragedy asks that its characters behave in a noble manner and follow a downward trajectory marked by plotted events, States envisions alternative fields of possibility based on different logics decided by author or genre: "Probability is what is possible, hence believable, either in the empirical world or in the play-world where, of course, different kinds of probability obtain."[13] To expand, Sophocles institutes a world in which a verbal prophecy can articulate a possible end—the Delphic prophecy determines Oedipus's fate in *Oedipus Rex*, while in *Oedipus at Colonus* the prophecies that Oedipus himself proclaims carry the weight of actual future events. Ibsen's domestic world of *A Doll's House*, on the other hand, transfers this supernatural prescience into a prophetic investment in objects—a letter, a gun. To paraphrase Ibsen's contemporary, Anton Chekhov, a pistol in the first act will make itself known by the end of the play, and, generally speaking, not too much earlier along the way. As Andrew Sofer writes in *The Stage Life of Props,* within the nineteenth century melodrama "a gun proved a tried-and-true device not only for driving home the moral (the virtuous triumph, and the wicked are punished), but also for bringing down the curtain with a bang."[14] In other words, the genre of classical tragedy institutes a world that allows for the possible appearance of a deity or a prophecy, while nineteenth-century realism must seek its deus ex machina in the secular or "natural" world.

Playing out possibilities or probabilities in recognizable patterns, drama stages worlds with what could have been, a kind of historiography for the future. Indeed, for Aristotle the articulation of a possible world becomes the basis for one of the fundamental distinctions between the poet-dramatist and the historian: "The poet's job is not to report what has happened, but what is likely to happen: that is, what is capable of happening according to the rule of probability or necessity. . . . the historian speaks of what has happened, the poet of the kind of thing that *can* happen."[15] This dichotomy relies only in part upon a temporal differentiation wherein the historian narrates the events that have already played out and the poet-dramatist narrates for the future. More importantly, Aristotle requires that the poet determine what the future of a said world is capable of producing, "what is *likely* to happen." The dramatist shows us a future that seems plausible according to our present frame of reference, though perhaps it is one that nonetheless remains overlooked enough to surprise us. Bernard's witticism quoted above deserves repeating: "In the theater the audience wants to be surprised, but by things that they expect." Bertolt Brecht made use of this disjunction between the possibilities of the historical and the poetical in plotting his epic theater as a means of prompting political criticality within his audiences. Ideally Brechtian spectators would recognize the limits of their own present possibilities by seeing them from the distance of a historicized situation (i.e., the Thirty Year's War in *Mother Courage*). Thus one could imagine alternative horizons for possible action in the present context.[16] Similarly, Augusto Boal's participatory theater, inspired in part by the Brechtian model, asks that its spectators intervene and perform other possibilities available within the world of the play.

Implicit in these formulations of probability, plausibility, and possibility is the role of the audience as a community of human mediators and arbiters of the appropriate. One can attribute this perspective on the dramatic at least in part to Aristotle's own approach to the event not as a practitioner, but as an educated spectator. The audience decides the validity of an event, determining whether it is believable and possible or, instead, fantastic and impossible, and thus a dramatic failure. For Aristotle, this opportunity to understand and categorize action provides a great deal of the pleasure in attending a performance.[17] In order to undertake this game of categorization, the audience must first recognize the world of the author, style, or genre and project such a remembrance into the future playing-out of the production. This recalls the notion of a reader's "horizon of expectation," where a text opens up a range of possible ends to a narrative that are progressively confirmed or diverted in the course of reading.[18] Depending on individual situation and background, each audience member provides his or her own horizon of expectation that may alter the production of meaning from the idealized result. The premiere production of Victor Hugo's *Hernani* in 1830, which so affronted the conventions of the day not least by having its actors turn their backs to the audience, could hardly be expected to have the same relationship to its field of plotted possibilities as would a production in Paris at the turn of the millennium, let alone in Gary, Indiana.

Let us look at a form of drama quite far afield from traditional Western theater, one that exemplifies this conception of plotted possibility as a bounded field or closed set. Founded in 1960 and still in operation today, the French literary group Oulipo (the Ouvroir de Littérature Potentielle) has devoted itself to the discovery and production of what its members term a "potential literature." In an array of manifestoes and theoretical essays, the group outlines a poetics directed toward the creation of new forms or structures of writing. Precisely what the various members of the group mean by potentiality remains an open question, but all share a common interest in creating new, and often esoteric, formal constraints as the basis for linguistic production; in the memorable words of one of its founding members, "An Oulipian author is a rat who himself builds the maze from which he sets out to escape."[19] Without wishing to shoehorn the sophisticated and multifarious play of its members into a unified misrepresentation, attending to what we may call a "strict" conception of the Oulipian endeavor is helpful to our cause. According to this canonical sense of the group, there is less interest in the content of an individual expression than in the display of a field of possible realizations particular to, and in correspondence with, a defined formal system. In the terms that I have outlined here, the Oulipo in fact elegantly represents an exploration of possibility.

Of course, I am not suggesting that Oulipo's definition of "potentiality" is *incorrect*; I say it exemplifies what I term "possibility" because the kind of future production proposed by the group emphasizes a choice between alternatives that are presupposed from the start. Many of the group's initial members were mathematicians, and their writings explicitly promote a mechanistic interest in uncertainty that is reigned in by a determined set, rather than an embrace of pure unmoored chance. This latter version of radical chance, or what John Cage would call "indeterminacy," holds little interest for the Oulipians.[20] Jacques Bens, one of the founding members of the group, states as much: "Make no mistake about it: potentiality is uncertain, but not a matter of chance. *We know perfectly well everything that can happen, but we don't know whether it will happen.*"[21] The particular iteration incarnated in each Oulipian piece, or in each performed reading of an Oulipian piece, sits against the larger background awareness of "everything that can happen" within its own set, an awareness shared by both creator and intended audience; one is meant to recognize the structure or set at play in the piece and how this particular present performance relates to the whole.[22] This last point is crucial: if the composition of the larger surrounding world were unrecognizable, the piece would descend into pure indeterminacy.

Each Oulipian literary act creates a system within which the parts of a language can come into being; each work constitutes its own possible world bound by its own logic and limits.[23] The prototypical Oulipian text requires its reader to recognize that his or her encounter is only one of a set number of other (presently inaccessible) possible interpretations. He or she chooses which plot to enact from the latent "story-world" of the text, while simultaneously maintaining a sense of this same latent structure.[24] How does this work in a dramatic form? In an Oulipian "combinatory" play by Paul Fournel and Jean-Pierre Énard, for example, the audience determines the action from amid a number of possible choices, so that the structure of the performance can be charted as a tree with a fixed number of iterations, replicating the standard linear direction of cause and effect.[25] The combinatory play operates under the sign of what Deleuze and Guattari call the arborescent (in fact, the Fournel-Énard piece is literally called "the theater tree"), its whole divided into parts branching off from the main "trunk" of the originating text.

Such combinatory plays remind me of long summer months as a ten-year-old spent poring over pulp fiction at the public library, where one section of the young adult shelves held particular interest. There must have been at least fifty of the *Choose Your Own Adventure* books lined up in identical spines, each with a colorful illustration on the cover, depicting another world: historical fictions, fantasies, a sci-fi dystopia, or dinosaurs roaming in thick jungles. A kind of preliminary hypertext, offering several actions at the end of each page that I—the protagonist of this adventure—could select to "perform." Each choice directed the reader to another page to take another step in the progress of the narrative. Each book contained a number of narrative paths, through a possible world not too unlike our own, but each had been clearly charted prior to my enactment as a reader. Impatient with this illusion of choice, I would flip pages ahead until my eye caught a particularly interesting juncture, then follow forward or fall back from there, only to flip ahead again, suspending the moment of arrival indefinitely in a constant state of beginning. Of course, I would always arrive somewhere, even if only at the climax of this particular cliffhanger or the choice between page 34 and page 67 that marked the conclusion of this segment: all variants on endings, parts within the whole.

My childhood refusal to arrive at an end presents a crucial mode for rupturing the network of possibility that spreads its root structure underneath drama. The work of Samuel Beckett is exemplary in this regard. To speak only of the longer plays, *Waiting for Godot* (1953), *Endgame* (1958), *Krapp's Last Tape* (1958), and *Happy Days* (1960), we can say that all are, in different ways, concerned with playing out various means toward an end that will not come. Metatheatrical to the core—or perhaps more accurately metadramatic—the characters here act like playwrights themselves, arranging and rearranging the unruly events of their story in the hopes that some possible conclusion will develop or reveal itself. Alas, it does not, and they can only, *must* only, go on. Many of the other plays that Martin Esslin gathered under the misnomer of "absurdist theater" (Arrabal, Ionesco, etc.) acquire their surreal or dreamlike persuasion from the way in which they intentionally interject otherworldly possibilities into otherwise mundane situations. They thereby interrupt the plotting endemic to one world of possibilities by splicing it with a second strain of expected futures. As soon as these foreign forms appear, they begin to assert their own plotted logic of possibility, but in that moment of transition some other kind of futurity makes itself felt.

Heart's Desire

I would like to consider for a moment a play that in some ways mimics the dance around alternative means without end that my childhood emphasis on "choosing" between adventures performed. One of British playwright Caryl Churchill's later short works, *Heart's Desire*, confronts this problem of a given world's assumptions by compromising the formal integrity of the play itself. Originally produced in a double bill with *Blue Kettle* in 1997 under the title of *Blue Heart*, the piece and its companion were described by Churchill as "anti-plays" written out of a sense of frustration with the dramatic medium.[26] Each begins in the world of traditional realism, albeit one that exhibits Churchill's slightly ominous stylistic characteristic of her later work, and becomes infected with a kind of formal disease that increasingly prevents its progress toward a plotted end. In this way, a field of contradictory possibilities overtakes the world particular to each play. As metadramatic propositions, they display and enact the logic of a system. But where an Oulipo piece typically exhausts and contains the set of possible solutions or enactments, here the pursuit reveals the inadequacy of that exhaustive effort to contain the plenitude of the live event and points to that which roils outside and offstage beyond a formal frame.

Heart's Desire repeatedly tests the boundary between inclusion and exclusion within the realm of the possible. The play exhibits all the trappings of a kitchen-sink realistic drama: a dysfunctional married couple in their sixties awaits the homecoming of their thirty-five-year-old daughter, Susy, who has been in Australia for the past seventeen years. The husband's quiet sister lingers about the kitchen, fidgeting and generally ignored by the bickering couple. Churchill's antidramatic virus infects the action right from the start. The play's first scene begins with Brian, the husband/father of the household, entering the room as he pulls on a red sweater. Two lines later and *"They all stop. Brian goes out. Others reset to beginning and do exactly as they did before as Brian enters putting on a tweed jacket."*[27] The same two lines and, again, a reset for Brian to reenter a third time, now putting on an old cardigan. Multiple possible outfits or configurations of the same scene are thus proposed, imagining parallel universes of the play proceeding along subtly different routes based upon the contingencies of a costuming decision. The next iteration of the scene underlines this sense of the multi-plicitous. Maisie, the sister, digresses into a speech about the wonder of the platypus as a variation upon other forms of life, reminiscent of duck, rat, mole, but wholly none of these: "It makes you think what else could have existed."[28] What other combinations of sweaters, cardigans, and tweeds could have existed in this world or its sisters?

Each time the scene will move forward a little bit further, then catch it-self going off on a diversion and return to a prior moment, restarting the engine once again. Many of these diversions unleash the clichéd possibili-ties of the kitchen-sink drama: the estranged wife packs her bag and leaves her husband, a sudden phone call announces that the awaited daughter has been in an accident, and—in the only possibility that recurs—a melancholic son intrudes on the scene in three separate occasions, each time visibly drunk and each time provoking the outrage of his parents. We could think of these as realizations of the character's subtextual possibilities or as ge-neric possibilities enacting likely alternatives to the path the plot unfolds. Other playwrights have used this formal device, rewinding the action to a prior moment in order to replay an alternative plot, but toward different purposes. For example, David Ives's *Sure Thing* (1988) spawns a barrage of revisions on a first-time meeting between a prospective couple, replaying variant possibilities whenever one or the other says something to disrupt their budding relationship, while Sheila Callaghan's *Lascivious Something* (2010) occasionally allows a scene to follow desires at the outskirts of the play-world's possibilities, before returning to enact a more socially accept-able continuation of the plot. In Churchill's play, it is as if we were witness-ing the playwright's creation of the drama including all its discarded pro-visional treatments. Every so often the entire scene is restaged from the beginning with a formal variation in delivery (i.e., everything double time, only the first or last words of each line with the accompanying gestures intact) reminding us what has come before and brought us to this point, but also how our perspective on the reality staged is necessarily partial. In at-tempting to "do exactly as they did before," the performers display the re-hearsed nature behind all of drama's future events, but also, against their will, they inevitably expose the slightest of situational differences between performances of the same scene.

Apart from these unsurprising articulations of realism's conventions, many of the play's variations reveal unexpected visitors lurking behind the door and entering the scene. Indeed, it is the ringing of the doorbell that mires the play's progression most fully and irreparably. This happens eight times in a row at the end of the piece before a final reset throws us back to start of the play once more and the lights dim out. Presumably the worlds of *Heart's Desire* continue stuttering along in the dark, even if we can no longer bear witness to their fabulations. Some of these intruders also comply with the expectations of genre: Susy makes her expected appearance a number of times, or another young woman appears at the door in place of Susy and reveals herself to be the absent daughter's partner. But other entrances open the form out in strange directions: a mob of gunmen charges on and kills everyone, a uniformed man barges in demanding everyone's papers, or a ten-foot-tall bird enters the room. The mystery of who or what waits behind the door to the offstage provides an underlying tension for a broad range of plays in the twentieth century, from Maurice Maeterlinck's Symbolist plays like *The Intruder* (1922)—where a sensed but unseen visitor looms outside a home and is eventually revealed as the spirit of death—to Eugène Ionesco's *The New Tenant* (1955)—where a pair of movers carry endless streams of furniture through an apartment's threshold until the stage is filled to the brim—to Harold Pinter's many menacing variations on the intruder plot.

These plays narrow into the frame of single doorway the encompassing pressure of the offstage space as the source of an outside seething with potential demonic intrusions, the vague "something moving" in and under the open field that drives Büchner's *Woyzeck* to madness.[29] *Heart's Desire* generally funnels these visitations through the conventional entrance of the doorway. But another iteration actualizes the potentiality that suffuses the larger theatrical space when a host of children suddenly bursts onto the scene. For the original staging, these little intruders all emerged not only from the expected mouth of the door, but from cupboards, closets, and ovens. In a play about parents awaiting the arrival of their child, the sudden flood does not feel entirely out of place. Yet it also signals an excessive procreation at the heart of the stage's life, investing all the objects and directions in this seemingly domesticated space with a kind of ludic vibration of the unconscious's potentiality.

But perhaps the most unnerving of the wayward possibilities in *Heart's Desire* occurs when the long-awaited doorbell rings and nobody moves to answer the door. The stage directions ask for a silence that lasts *"a longer time than you think you can get away with."*[30] The extended silence passes by its expected ends and stretches out into uncomfortable reaches as audience and performer wait for something or someone to act. Has something gone wrong in the performance? An entrance forgotten or cue dropped? What possibility lurks behind the door unanswered or in the next line that someone refuses to utter? The moment opens up a pure means without end, maintaining the capacities of the offstage through a suspension of its expected behavior.[31] The dramatic machinery that moves us toward a possible future has stalled.

When the play finally does rewind to start at the doorbell once more, it is the reticent sister Maisie who again offers a peculiarly perceptive digression. She describes lying awake at night in fear of her impending death, the absolutely unknowable and inevitable nature of that transition from conscious living to whatever follows. As in her comment on the platypus and its metadramatic interpretation of the variations of sweaters and cardigans, the speech illuminates the preceding version of the scene. Remember the terror of Maeterlinck's *Intruder* (death) pacing just beyond the threshold: is not death a meeting place of the possible and the potential? From without, the dead body looks as if it has achieved its most object-like state, stilled in the most absolute end to the means that we call life. But from within, for she who dies, death marks the limits of possibility and the beginning of a truly potential and unassumable existence so all-encompassing that it includes its own nonexistence as well.

Imagine sitting in the audience amid that awkward silence and stillness, after the initial titters of laughter have died down, and one hunkers down into the endless wondering of how the actors will take up a new possibility. The smallest of changes would set the performance tumbling forward on a new course, yet in this perfect inertia the field of available futures is so wide it disturbs all presuppositions. How would an actor begin to lay claim to one of these possibilities? This is no longer the question of a plotted end to the play at large, but the much more immediate question of how one determines a possible action, how one begins to act.

POSSIBLE ACTIONS

Just as possibility determines the course of the overarching plot for a drama, it likewise imposes an order upon the more immediate actions of individual characters. But how do we understand action as a discrete part within a larger plot? What determines whether an action is recognizable or not? In order to consider how this order asserts itself, I want to step away from dramatic theory for the moment and establish a clearer sense of actionable possibility through the philosophy of Henri Bergson.

In a body of work written between the end of the nineteenth century and the first half of the twentieth century, French philosopher Henri Bergson pursued an ontology of moving tendencies rather than the fixed and delineated states of classical thought. The quest for an essence of being, stretching from Plato down through the traditional canon of Western thought, is answered here by a philosophy of dynamic becoming and constant change—a philosophy of process. This processual approach characterized all of the French philosopher's wide-ranging oeuvre from investigations of the evolution of life across eons down to the foundational fabrication of individual experience. For Bergson, subjectivity exists in a present of ever accumulating and thickening past; as in Heraclitus's famous river of flux, "Consciousness cannot go through the same state twice. The circumstances may still be the same, but they will act no longer on the same person, since they find him at a new moment of his history."[32] Synonymous with this project was Bergson's theory of vitalism, which followed earlier post-Cartesian scientists and philosophers in proposing the existence of a living force common to all organisms, but beyond mere materiality.[33]

Bergson's enterprise implicitly deals with thought performatively rather than prescriptively. His philosophical practice does not rely on a consistent theoretical language, but instead seeks its means through a fluid process of thought particular to the situation at hand. Terms alter in response to the discursive terrain surrounding a given problem, so that, for example, the concepts grounding the discussion of temporality in Bergson's doctoral dissertation, *Time and Free Will* (1889), differ slightly from the humor theory of *Laughter: An Essay on the Meaning of the Comic* (1901) or the philosophy of science in *Creative Evolution* (1907). In other words, Bergson's written thought enacts the kind of tactical engagement with the world that his philosophy describes. Requiring subsequent readers to stage their own engagement with a concept or problem, philosophy becomes an overtly performative venture: the reading/saying is the doing.[34] My own conversation with this material, then, galvanizes certain submerged tendencies in Bergson's multifaceted project to articulate a strand of thought particular to the exigencies of performance rather than the domain of philosophy.

In spite of this principle of processual fluidity, a fundamental distinction runs as an undercurrent throughout Bergson's body of work, describing two modes of a consciousness's engagement with the world, or in our case, the staging of a world. On the one hand, the *intellect* oversees a world separate from the individual, composing its outside into a collection of objects or entities in stable states. Each of these entities claims a name and purpose while occupying a distinct place within a homogenous field of space and time. The intellect spatializes time by abstracting it into segments of minutes and seconds as if it could be charted on a stable coordinate plane. On the other hand, Bergson proposes that *intuition* approaches a world of constant flux and pure motion in time. It does not articulate distinctions between entities, but immerses itself in a holistic relationship with other forces, sharing insides with outsides, and thinking through time rather than space. The intellect belongs to human consciousness, while intuition is common to all living forms, human and nonhuman. The two perspectives provoke significant consequences for the staging of a world and how that world articulates its version of the future, both for spectators and for the performers within its purview: the intellect in terms of possibility and the intuition in terms of virtuality, or what, over the course of this book, I will come to call potentiality. In an elegant reformulation the Bergsonian concept of the possible, Manuel De Landa writes: "The category of the possible assumes a set of predefined forms which retain their identity despite their non-existence, and which already resemble the forms they will adopt once they become realized. In other words, . . . *realizing a possibility does not add anything to the pre-existing form but mere reality.*"[35]

In fact, the manner in which the intellect (and its mode of operation, analysis) determines the entities that populate the subject's field of perception depends upon the possible actions that these same entities make available for use. From out of the continuous flux of the material world the intellect excises an array of figures according to their expected function and sets them apart from a ground. Through this selection, it necessarily ignores myriad other aspects deemed "useless." Bergson writes: "The bodies we perceive are, so to speak, cut out of the stuff of nature by our *perception*, and the scissors follow, in some way, the marking of lines along which *action* might be taken."[36] Anticipated future action describes the shape of perception so that what we choose to perceive is what we may choose to *use*. An individual object belongs to a category of objects—and thus acquires its name—insofar as it represents a possible action, or range of possible actions, for the subject to perform.

Possibility not only casts its frame onto a spatial surround, but a temporal surround as well. It configures the future in relation to one's past experience with, and use of, materiality. Just as it carves the stable object from an inchoate surround based on the repetition of a previously known entity's shape, so it creates an image of future action that repeats the terms of the past.[37] This image is a tightly outlined entity, fixed and firm. Each possible action requires an anticipated length of time and will mark a segment of time between its initiation and its arrival at an end. Thus, the temporal placement of an action's end point coincides with the spatial placement of the object. Bergson writes of this coordination of abstract homogenous planes of time and space as follows:

Homogeneous space and homogeneous time are then neither properties of things nor essential conditions of our faculty of knowing them: they express, in an abstract form, the double work of solidification and of division which we effect on the moving continuity of the real in order to obtain there a fulcrum for our action, in order to fix within it starting points for our operation, in short to introduce into it real changes. They are the diagrammatic design of our eventual action upon matter.[38]

The "fulcrum" for the action, then, is projected onto a future arrival; the action's "starting point" is in fact the end point of the movement. One thrusts out a possible action toward a future end point, lodging its length of time and space into that fixed stopping place and then uses it as leverage to begin an action. This gives the false impression of a static point of climax where time and image meet in an action's end. I see a door that can open, a glass of water from which I can drink, a lamp to turn on. As such, *possibility separates the means of a movement from its ends* and attends to the latter as its defining element and its claim to certainty. According to States's update of the Aristotelian approach, the distinction between dramatic action and the pure motion of the natural world primarily relies upon the use—or lack thereof, respectively—toward which each is directed. Motion is thus reformed from both directions at once, casting a beginning (the subject and its intentionality) and an end (the completion and consequence) out of what was otherwise only an indefinite middle. In this respect it mirrors on a smaller scale the effects of plotting, which Aristotle sees as directing the undefined middle of an event toward a beginning and end. This conceptualization of change as bound within the brackets of a beginning and an end is artificially placed on movement so as to make it legible to a human interpretation.

I say human because the possible always refers to a common humanity's architecture of perception, what Jacques Rancière would call the "partition [or distribution] of the sensible."[39] We sense what is available to our acceptable use. Certain motions are included in the construction that we call the possible, and others are relegated to the inhuman outside. Just as possible actions determine the shape of the objectival world, so too do they determine the boundaries of the perceiving subject. One maps out possible actions upon the environment as if it were a mirror reflecting back the body, depicting the contours of capacity. As Bergson puts it: "*The objects which surround my body reflect its possible action upon them.*"[40] This carving of space works hand in glove with the possibilities of a specific organism and its specific faculties: the human.

Bergson's explication of this notion is most apparent in his *Creative Evolution*, in which he considers theories of evolution from the nineteenth century and the beginning of the twentieth century alongside his own notion of vitalism. The validity of the evolutionary model he proposed received criticism in the century that followed, but Bergson's conviction that the pursuit and representation of a possible world depends upon the particularities of perception finds support in more recent work in the biological sciences. In his lectures on *The Possible and the Actual* (1982), Nobel Prize–winning French scientist François Jacob describes how the sense organs of the human organism arrange perspective in order to make visible useful possibilities, a process almost identical to the one described by Bergson: "The external world, the 'reality' of which we all have intuitive knowledge, thus appears as a creation of the nervous system. *It is, in a way, a possible world, a model allowing the organism to handle the bulk of incoming information and make it useful for its everyday life.*"[41] Likewise, Jakob von Uexküll's famous discussions of the divergent worlds of various animals provide concrete examples of such an alternative experience of the environment determined by use. Indeed, if we think of a "world" as contained by a lifeform's perceptible use of its moving surrounds, biodiversity's multitude of ticks and birds offers very real evidence of other worlds existing alongside our own.[42] This multiplicity is not limited to the extrahuman, of course: the diversity of uses we make of our own environment based on individual history, acculturation, and physical capabilities suggests there is not one monolithic possible world belonging to all humanity.

Translated into an action, motion acquires a part to play. I mean "a part to play" in two different senses. First, teleological action acquires "a part to play" in that it becomes a part within a larger whole. One action incites a reaction, even a conflict, and thereby contributes to the accumulation of acts that taken together we call plot. This part-by-part nature of dramatic action surreptitiously translates the duration of performance into a spatialized entity.[43] Laid out across an abstract plane in this manner, the dramatic analyst can methodically separate the whole into discrete and measurable segments, like beads on string, or steps up the stairs of a narrative toward the climax and then down again on the other side during the denouement. The action becomes a discrete unit or building block in the construction of the plot.

Second, possible action produces a "part to play" in that it provides the scaffolding for the appearance of a fully constituted dramatic character. As the art of action, drama translates not only the motion of individuals, but also the disinterested motion of the world. It casts an event as the production of an anthropomorphized subject so that, in States's words, "what we experience in the presence of an action is a virtual personification of the world, as if events could think."[44] Considered as an action, the motion of the world or of a figure acquires a name and is placed in a social, legal, and moral context or representational system; as the effect of an intention it forms the basis for determining causality and, concomitantly, liability. An otherwise deaf and mute motion thus communicates by being cast as an action; it speaks in language we can understand. It is thus the modus operandi of the humanist theater, a theater devoted to the task of supplying an audience with an experience of recognition.

Rather than applying a predetermined quality to figure an onstage person, Aristotle advocates the creation of character through the actions and choices he or she makes. Oedipus is not a king unless he acts as one. This serves as the basis for the distinction between "character" and "thought" in the *Poetics*'s hierarchy of the six basic dramatic elements: "There is no character in that class of utterances in which there is nothing at all that the speaker is choosing or rejecting."[45] The class of utterances without an active purpose, "thought" is limited to abstract statements divorced from the translation of motion into meaning. It is perhaps with this distinction in mind that Walter Benjamin wrote: "Sophocles' Oedipus is silent, or nearly so. A bloodhound after his own blood, screaming with the pain inflicted by his own hands—he utters speeches in which there can be no room for thought, for reflection."[46] In *Oedipus Rex*, Oedipus's "thought" is silent as all his language pours into active utterances, or *actions*, staging a choice from among available options that allows the audience to determine the qualities of the character according to their evaluation of the decision. Actions reflect a moral position and define the part that the character plays, a part that is only fully comprehended at the conclusion of the performance through the accumulation of his or her many actions. As Aeschylus writes, "call no man happy until he is dead," or at least until the proverbial curtain falls. In sum we might say that in pursuing a possible action, a subject appears as a possible character or personality.

The commitment to creating a character through his or her actions rather than through the application of a preconceived quality has only received further ratification in the developments of mainstream theatrical production from the nineteenth century onward. Since the advent of modern actor training at the beginning of the twentieth century, the logic of possibility has formed the basis for the dominant model of acting technique first articulated by Konstantin Stanislavsky. It is certainly the case that alternative models of production embodied (and troubled) theatrical possibility in ways that diverge from the Stanislavskian approach and its subsequent incarnation in the American context as "the method." However, since Stanislavsky's work formed the basis for mainstream psychological realism to follow, it will suffice to pursue dramatic possibility through the channel of this broad tendency with the understanding that it in no way represents the full breadth of actor training.

In two books (three books in the abridged English translation) devoted to the foundations of acting Stanislavsky depicts a group of young actors as they progress through a training program lead by a director named Tortsov who strongly resembles Stanislavsky himself; in this textual performance Stanislavsky plays both student and teacher. While these writings do not represent the authoritative summation of the Russian director's investigation of acting technique—an investigation that lasted until his death in 1938 some thirty years after the period elaborated in these first pseudo-diaristic texts—it is clear that the conception of action relayed here triggered a paradigm shift with profound and lasting effects on mainstream acting in the West, particularly in regards to its effect on the burgeoning film industry.[47]

The first of the trilogy of books, *An Actor Prepares* (English translation 1936), begins with the fictional group's initial assignment before they have taken a single class under Tortsov's guidance: they are to rehearse and then perform a scene from the canon of Western drama. The untrained students' naive interpretations of the classic repertoire provide Tortsov with an anthology of failed approaches to acting, variously characterized as "forced acting," "over-acting," and "mechanical acting." All rely on an external approach to character portrayal that was popular in the Russian theater of the day, a presentation of his or her qualities rather than internal intentions. The narrator, for example, in his preparation of the role of Othello cannot break away from his preconceived notions of how a "savage" should behave and look, how he should "flash the whites of his eyes" and "bare his teeth."[48] In his subsequent judgment of these disastrous portrayals Tortsov states, "All of you began your work at the end instead of at the beginning"; they applied an affect/effect without tracing out the causal impetus through to its concluding realization.[49] "Don't act 'in general,' for the sake of action; always act with a purpose."[50] Acting stages an action that pursues an objective, tracing out a cause and arriving at an effect and a symptomatic affect, rather than displaying pure affect divorced from its provocation. In other words, it is an art primarily concerned with displaying a cause and its possible effects.

This intent requires that the actor approach her embodiment of the play text in a manner very similar to that of the discerning Aristotelian critic or spectator. In the beginning of Stanislavsky's chapter on "units and objectives," an older and well-respected actor compares the analysis of a play to the carving of a turkey. One breaks the organic whole down into progressively smaller component parts until a series of digestible pieces are laid out before the actor. Each digestible part, or unit, dictates a discrete action that the actor undertakes: his or her objective. Together, they lay out a narrative of set courses that in turn form an overarching "superobjective" for the play: in this case, to eat the turkey. Beholden to the discerning slice of an intellectual gaze, the role becomes a body divided into organs: a leg, a breast, or some other cut of meat. The role becomes the "body with organs" that Artaud so detested, a piece-by-piece consumption of what should be a holistic intuitive motion.

The dissection of drama into acting units requires a concomitant mark of the name. As Stanislavsky describes an actor's dramatic analysis, "it consists of finding the most appropriate name for the unit, one which characterizes its inner essence. . . . *The right name, which crystallizes the essence of a unit, discovers its fundamental objective.*"[51] The temporal is "crystallized" in an essential or idealized form, cut in sharp relief from the "plane of consistency" that is the unified performance event. The importance of picking the "right name" to capture the essence of the unit signals the desire to possess a grammar of available actions that remains strong to this day. For example, a publication from 2004, *Actions: The Actors' Thesaurus*, epitomizes the intercourse between writer/critic and actor, between the selection of an appropriately worded and embodied articulation.[52] Actors become writers, or analysts, seeking out an ideally worded action in order to perform their part eloquently.

Stanislavsky's theatrical explorations at the beginning of the century spawned numerous schools and reinterpretations in the intervening years, establishing the foundation for realistic mainstream theater and film acting, particularly in the United States. This genealogy has been traced extensively elsewhere, and for the purposes of our discussion a single example from the vast array of variously articulated and weighted techniques will suffice.[53] Under the auspices of New York University, actor William H. Macy, playwright David Mamet, and director Gregory Mosher led a group of students in formulating a straightforward acting technique they termed "practical aesthetics." The group would form the Atlantic Theatre Company in 1983 and presently continues its affiliation with New York University as one of the eight resident actor studios of the Tisch School of the Arts.

In 1986, the group outlined their acting technique in *A Practical Handbook for the Actor*, which has since become a standard textbook in acting classes across the United States. Of all the many revisions of the Stanislavskian method, practical aesthetics perhaps provides the least mystical of approaches, the most "practical" and purified of articulations; in a very short ninety-four pages the *Practical Handbook* pares the technique of the actor down to the play of possibilities.

Practical aesthetics emphasizes "physical action" as the basis for all forms of acting. The book begins with a definition of acting in complete compliance with the Aristotelian paradigm of dramatic possibility: "To act means to do, so you must always have something specific to *do* onstage or you will immediately stop acting. . . . an *action* is the physical pursuance of a specific goal."[54] This "specificity" is derived from the particular direction of the *doing*, hence the designation of the "physical" embodiment; *Physicalized* action disavows pure *doing* without a purpose and instead demands that the action pursue a definite and communicable end point. According to the *Practical Handbook*, one of the requirements of a "good" action is that it has a "cap" that marks its conclusion: "You must always have a specific *end* to work toward onstage."[55] Furthermore, the end in question must be accessible, literally possible, in the confines of the theatrical world. Here the *Practical Handbook* directly follows Stanislavsky, who wrote in *An Actor Prepares*: "You must do something more concrete, real, nearer, more possible to do."[56] The technique outlines a *practical* mode of performance, centered on a series of discrete tasks ("objectives") that one pursues by choosing from an array of proximate "tools," or actions. Here we see the actor as *Homo faber*, the crafter of action.

The book offers a sample analysis of Oedipus's first scene from *Oedipus Rex* that succinctly illustrates the system. The analysis of the scene reads the King's encounter with the blind seer Tiresias as an attempt at realizing the objective of "extracting an answer to a crucial question." In order to do so, Oedipus can make use of the following "tools": "to interrogate, plead, reason, level, demand, threaten, accuse."[57] These various tools represent an array of possible actions available to the actor, divergent means directed toward the same end point. Playing the scene, one chooses from among this toolbox the action appropriate to the momentary demands made by the actor playing opposite, or, in the terminology of the *Practical Handbook*, the action appropriate to "the truth of the moment." If in one performance Tiresias avoids his questions with humility, Oedipus may plead with the seer, "Oh speak, / Withhold not, I adjure thee, if thou know'st, / Thy knowledge. We are all thy suppliants."[58] In another performance, goaded by what he interprets as a mock humility in the seer, the actor may opt to threaten with these same words. Regardless which possibility the actor utilizes in the pursuit, the objective remains the same; the event is tamed.[59]

Tragedy: a tragedy

As the original form of Western drama, the classical tragedy translates the pure motion of an event in the broadest of strokes: the catastrophe is the central event in the play's world, a chaos of pure motion, which the tragic structure, in turn, harnesses and brings to an end. Catastrophe presents us with an emblematic realization of the problem of pure motion. The *Oxford English Dictionary* defines catastrophe as "a sudden and widespread disaster," but further qualifies the word's usage in regards to the dramatic form as "the point at which the circumstances overcome the central motive, introducing the close or conclusion; denouement."[60] Thus, catastrophe inhabits an unmarked time-space of open collapse that, through its dramatic representation, simultaneously instigates the marked beginning toward an end. As we saw above, this dual signification—as both unmarked and marked—derives from Aristotle, for whom the catastrophe represents the moment in a tragedy at which the indefinite middle moves to the end, enabling the passage and completion of a set history. The chance catastrophe of a highway accident in which several cars collide only becomes a true "tragedy" in the Aristotelian sense when its players are framed within a beginning, middle, and an end, when the accident ceases to be purely accidental and comes to serve an intentional purpose. Szondi places the restraint of the catastrophic at the core of the dramatic theater: "The accidental enters the Drama from outside, but, by motivating it, accident is domesticated; it is rooted in the heart of drama itself."[61] And States's description of a catastrophe devoid of tragic structure appearing as "an instance of raw causality rearing itself into visibility" equally describes the catastrophe of pure motion before a purpose informs it as an action.[62] If tragedy is a theatrical apparatus for processing a central catastrophic event into a socially legible meaning or product, to move an indeterminate middle to a determinate end, then on a much smaller scale the dramatic similarly processes little catastrophes of "raw causality" into discrete and purposeful actions. Tragedy, then, stands at the crossroads of possibility's incursion into both plot and action.

American playwright Will Eno's *Tragedy: a tragedy* (2001) reveals the impotence of this well-worn apparatus when faced with contemporary catastrophe and the consequences of this failure upon the actions available to characters. While the bankruptcy of the tragic form has been heralded throughout the last century, Eno's play is remarkable in its nearly exhaustive dissection of the Aristotelian mode; it stages, as the title suggests, a tragedy of the tragic form itself.[63]

A live television newscast covers a most improbable event: a day when the sun does not rise. John is in the field interviewing an exceptionally reticent witness, Constance provides updates in front of a nondescript and unoccupied home, and Michael the Legal Advisor occasionally reads missives from the governor and offers information on "the question of liability . . . to judge whether any of this was justified."[64] Finally there is Frank, the anchorman isolated in the studio, lodged in a chamber as inescapable as the noble house of Atreus, and trying to keep composure as the endless evening presses onward. All of the characters struggle, in the cadence and tropes of the twenty-four-hour news cycle, to relate an event that refuses to reveal a causal relation to the past or for the future.

The sun not rising is perhaps the most fundamental break with the expectations of the possible; it flies in the face of the most well-worn platitudes to the effect that "tomorrow's another day." It disrupts tragedy's aestheticization of the sacrificial ritual of death and rebirth that the Cambridge anthropologists of the late nineteenth and early twentieth centuries claimed as the root of the theatrical form, the cycle of yearly renewal through which one's sacrifice renews the world. And yet it is a logically possible proposition, for as David Hume wrote in 1772, "that the sun will not rise tomorrow is no less intelligible a proposition, and implies no more contradiction, than the affirmation, that it will rise."[65] We can conceive the event as an actuality, even if it breaks with our previous experience of the natural world's expected pattern of cause and effect. *Tragedy: a tragedy* stages the timelessness of the twenty-four-hour news cycle and its inability to project a possible future end.

Indeed, by losing its promise of an end, the whole mechanism of the dramatic has lost its hold on the theatrical world. The characters in a classical tragedy could rest assured that, if all else fails, the deus ex machina would knit the loose strands of the future into a contained text; here the characters continue to await a revelation or savior to guide them, "But there's no star, there's no manger, no blazing charioteer" (95). As the play progresses and—like a contemporary *Godot*—nothing continues to happen, the characters' attempts to cling to their authoritative role as television personae become more and more desperate. Eventually, all the subsidiary characters quit their posts, and the anchorman Frank is stranded in his efforts to maintain the broadcast's integrity. Exhausted and suddenly suffering from a heart attack, he too subsides into sleep, or perhaps death. In the final moments of the play, the unnamed witness that has lingered on the scene throughout tentatively takes up John's abandoned microphone and begins to tell his version of the event that he, too, lived through but missed. He tells a story without an end.

It is a premise that befits the world of Ionesco, but raises profoundly contemporary questions in the new millennium. *Tragedy: a tragedy* was written in the early months of 2001 and received its world premiere at London's Gate Theatre in April of that year, but, perhaps because of its uncannily prescient anticipation of that spectacularly terrible catastrophe, the American premiere was not until 2008. Satire seemed in poor taste for a country that had watched its familiar newscasters, normally so reassuringly confident in their interpretation of catastrophe, fumbling to replay the traumatically impossible event that they had witnessed live. In a brief preface to the published play, also written before 9/11, Eno remarks on the position of the newscaster as surrogate and as witness. The reporter "stands for us, somehow, standing there. He stands for us standing here wondering what we're standing here for. . . . Us, with only the early technology of our vocabulary, a tongue, trying to identify the rapturous trying to sum up the miraculous, standing right in front of it. Possibly" (75). Without taking (a) part, without taking action, the newscaster mediates an event to those of us who sit comfortably at home, at ease. Like the classical messenger, he or she may function as an onstage/onscreen version of the articulate witness, exemplifying how to narrate an event and translate an accident into an action. And like the messenger, the newscaster relates what we in the audience cannot see. For in Greek tragedy, and even more so in its French neoclassical descendent, the culminating event is almost always relegated to the offstage space, the unseen.[66] As Jean Genet writes in *The Blacks*: "Greek tragedy, my dear, decorum. The ultimate gesture is performed offstage."[67] The ultimate bloody gesture, the real spectacle, literally takes place in the dark in Eno's play, beyond the arc of footlights and floodlights. Which is to say that this overarching darkness is also the offstage. It is the unnamed and unnamable event that cannot be shown, cannot be enlightened, and remains forever ob-scene.

Fear of the dark is fear of the unknown. As Frank says: "From the beginning the first thing the first people were afraid of was the dark" (89). This dark is not a static or empty space; like Churchill's offstage it harbors instances and encounters outside the horizon of expectation. As the play progresses, bizarre intrusions puncture the otherwise uniformly uneventful darkness: a tandem bike passes on the streets, a hot air balloon overhead, and—in true apocalyptic fashion—a riderless horse wanders the suburbs. The newscasters are asked to interpret these events for the audience, to analyze the darkness that surrounds them. At one point they play a sound recording of the event, a sea of white noise with vague and distant sounds scratching at significance. They try to put a name to this motion, to cast it as the action of some recognizable entity or force, in order to humanize it, but to no avail. No illumination is possible, for the dark offstage surrounds the newscasters; wherever one claims a small piece of territory or shines a light on it to report its details, the darkness circles around behind.

Eno's characters are increasingly cognizant of their entrapment within an accident that refuses to conform to tragic processing. They mull over how to respond to car crashes, senseless accidents that proceed heedless of any possible response. Michael, the legal advisor, offers these words of wisdom: "While crashing your car, always steer into the direction of the skid. But now theory must be put into practice, and the stacks of books are pushed aside, as we career heart-first and bookless into the blackening night" (84). The characters keep trying to reestablish the tragic form throughout the play. The Governor, through his surrogate, Michael, is particularly concerned with reinstating the tragic as a way of making sense of the dark. He advocates a Bacchic panic, the celebration for the god Dionysus originally associated with the performance of Athenian tragedy: "Run wild across the world, lovely people, naked and wild, of flesh torn and spirit rash" (89). Constance, too, attempts her own Bacchic celebration of the earth to no avail. Furthermore, one could read the governor's ultimate abandonment of his office as an attempt to establish himself as the scapegoat for the community. For, in the interpretation of the tragic form promulgated by René Girard, among others, the crisis of a community is resolved by placing the blame on an individual scapegoat, regardless of his or her supposed responsibility.[68]

Likewise, the violence that does occur in the play is not the result of an intentional action—murder or suicide or retribution—but a kind of blind assertion of chance. For reasons she cannot explain, Constance throws a rock at the horse that approaches her in the night, hitting it in the eye and chasing it away. John inexplicably develops a nosebleed—the most inconsequential and senseless of bloody occurrences. And, near the end of the play, when Frank has a heart attack, it is arguably without cause and certainly not a consequence of an action taken or tragic error. It is the kind of quiet death, entirely internalized, that grabs one without reason.

But death is only the most definite and assertive of ends. There are also those possibilities that we think of as normal, accessible futures, actions that take account of an event by chipping away at the unformed block of its obdurateness to give it a likeness. The newscasters keep imagining various possible actions that offstage others could be taking at this moment, but which they (and we) cannot see. While filling the time, the newscasters repeatedly return to descriptions of what is available for present and future use at this moment. Constance describes possible scenes playing out: "We hear a voice, a father sitting down to eat, saying grace, or standing at a door, hat in hand, saying goodbye" (83). All such imaginings reflect some prior reference to normative behavior and a well-worn vocabulary. As John puts it, everyone is "stuck with saying, as everyone is, only the words they already know. Such as the words, 'I'm dizzy.' Or the words, 'I keep looking for something to look at.' Or, 'If I closed my eyes I know I would get sick'" (92). As the anchor for the program and for the identities of the others, Frank becomes the locus for a variety of domestic fantasies. Each of the satellite reporters confides that he or she has imagined Frank's return home from a day at work and the nighttime habits he would perform there. Each projection describes the anchor acting out different stereotypical behaviors associated with a lonely life—hand-washing the shirt he wears each day or listening to scratchy records of old speeches—and all imagine him sitting down to drink a glass of milk before bed. These clichés of the paternal figure playing his possible future according to type provide some comfort to the speaker, but Frank contradicts all of them.

So when the tragedy refuses to resolve the chaos of the unfolding event, the involved characters' whole sense of individuality splits asunder as well. As nothing continues to differentiate itself from the dark, the characters begin to spiral into an increasingly confused sense of their own identity and their own role. John is the first to recognize this problem: "In the interim, I, somewhat out of, out of I don't know what—character? Is that possible?" (91). He proceeds to identify the darkness with a life that is no longer recognizable as past biography or present surroundings. Frank responds with surprising acuity: "That was John in the field. John, out there, somewhere—reckoning. Trying like all of us to find some way of defining the evening we currently find ourselves in now" (92). John is, as his moniker suggests "in the field." The dark is where "we currently find ourselves" and to define our surroundings is to define ourselves. Recall Bergson's claim: "*The objects which surround my body reflect its possible action upon them.*" As newscasters asked to perform live, they cannot complete their action or realize their objective, because there is no news or role for them to cast.

To generalize greatly, in classical tragedy, the messenger delivers his or her description of the offstage event with the least diversion or inflection possible. He or she has no name, ideally, and arguably no character apart from the content of the message; the messenger does not appear onstage prior to this moment, nor stay beyond its calling.[69] The quintessential messenger is a person of no importance, with no ends, announcing his or her own mediality as message. He or she disappears into a means without end, a pure appearance of the medium without figuration, prophetic yet inarticulate. In the chapters that follow we will explore in greater detail this notion of life as a vessel that withholds the qualities and/or actions that would characterize an individual, as a vessel that sustains its potential for many futures. For the characters in *Tragedy: a tragedy*, the great tragedy is that there is nothing for them to report from offstage. Bereft of action or content, they appear as empty vessels adrift in the long, dark, and plotless night.

A POTENTIALITY TO "DO AND DO AND DO"

In the examples of *Heart's Desire* and *Tragedy: a tragedy* we've seen how contemporary drama approaches an indeterminate future by exhausting the mechanisms of possibility. Yet this exploration of the ends of dramatic action is not limited to theatrical work from the postdramatic era. Influenced by States's writings on action discussed above, Alice Rayner's *To Act, To Do, To Perform: Drama and the Phenomenology of Action* proposes drama as a laboratory for investigating the nature of action and its affects. If States follows Aristotle in seeing the theater as a medium comprised of actions, Rayner sees action as a medium in itself, which drama can illuminate.[70] Her work is decidedly bound up with the linguistic composition of drama and, following Kenneth Burke's theory of dramatism, employs grammar as a port of entry into the ontology of action.[71] It nonetheless offers a rich basis for an understanding of dramatic possibility and how it differs from other forms of performance that are more oriented toward the visual or physical.

Based on the taxonomy of action proposed by the Gravedigger in *Hamlet*, Rayner divides action into three related modes: acting, doing, and performing. The first of these refers to a notion of action very close to that which has been discussed thus far: it is a named and repeatable entity, made available to narrative. Such *acting* always functions on a figure retrospectively, as if the act cast a shadow in the shape of the subject behind it, outlining his or her intentions and qualities in ethical and moral shades. For Ophelia, the subject of the Gravedigger's rumination, the question of whether her death was an intentional act or whether it was the water's "intention" to take her life will determine whether she has committed suicide or not. The designation of the action has real effects, including the legality of the event and, subsequently, will determine her burial site (one could not bury a suicide in church grounds). *Doing* refers to what States would call the "pure motion" of the world. Here one encounters the "disintegration of the conceptual dimension; how the name dissolves in time and the subject cannot be identified as an object."[72] Doing resists appellation, pressing the figure into consort with inhuman motions and intensities. Figured grammatically, the verb "to do" names an action without quality, a word that nearly voids its role of designation, so that "while active, it has no particularities, only force."[73] Finally, *performing* invests a style or quality into the space between acting and doing, a performer's particular "adverbial presence" into the act and the fact of its doing. Like Barthes's "third meaning" or his "grain of the voice," Rayner sees performance as an erotic or pleasurable surplus in the dialectic between an act's meaning and doing's materiality.[74]

The notion of doing outlined here is divorced from the specifics of a verb or noun's possibility and instead points toward a kind of "potentiality to do" rather than a representable action. Doing breaks with the practical aesthetics dictum of always "having *something* specific to do" (my emphasis), of always having defined objectives, to instead offer a pure motion without clear orientation. It realizes Nietzsche's claim in *On the Genealogy of Morals* that "there is no 'being' behind doing, effecting, becoming; 'the doer' is merely a fiction added to the deed—the deed is everything."[75] Rayner leads us to the abyss that *Macbeth* inhabits between the doing of the thing and the thing done. Here, the First Witch's famous "I'll do, I'll do, and I'll do" stands as the utterance that most closely approximates the unnamable act, or rather the potentiality to do such an undetermined act. It is precisely the lack of a voiced possible action that makes the statement frighteningly potent, since "with no identification of what she'll do, there is no way to counter the act. And most particularly in the context of a nonhuman (i.e., nondialogic being), there is no way to speak back to her threat."[76] Figured in the heart of one of the great dramas of the Western canon, the witch's threat ruptures the possibility of dialectical exchange, of dramatic conflict, and stands as an anomalous assertion of unbridled potentiality. In early modern England, this expression, so divorced from human and political right, clearly evokes the supernatural and demonic power of the weird sisters and directs us toward the apocalyptic force of potentiality rather than possibility.[77] We need only glance back at Rumsfeld's warnings regarding the terror of unknown unknowns to see how the doable breaches all expected defenses. Such statements leave one with a seeming impossibility: characters within a drama who refuse to perform dramatically, who deny the dialectical structure that grounds the possible. We cannot know *what* these figures will *do*, what constitutes the ends of their motions, because they approach a world that operates in a drastically different manner from our own world with its investment in parts and intentions. Within the dramatic stage's world of possibilities, they stand as kernels of an inassimilable life, over which the intellect's gaze stumbles and tears open, gags on all its names and actions.

All of which leads me to ask: what of the motion that refuses to be named as an action? The chapters that follow consider work that attempts such impossible motions as expressions of a futurity specifically available to the live event as such, a futurity that eludes the skeletons of the past with their long reach into our looming possibilities. While I will look more closely at recent performances, it bears repeating that these concerns have haunted the dramatic theater for some while. As Rayner writes:

> To the degree that any action is a form of suicide because it eliminates possibilities, creates a past, and commits the actor to an identity, the reasoning may broadly serve to explain Hamlet's wider hesitations against action. To hold back means to keep possibilities open and to keep act and identity from becoming corpses.[78]

In other words, to keep the possible open—to keep one's potential to do—is to keep living. One retains the potential to become unfixed, to leave the corpse. But, even our man Hamlet must speak his indecision, display its parts and figures. His pure abstraction, what Aristotle would call his "thought," meets the hard flesh of spoken words and recalls distant figures and forms. In dramatic fashion, he appears and his words cause an effect.

Remember that Plato's injunction against the poet and excluding him or her from the ideal Republic holds just as true for the actor: the honest person can *do* one thing, but the poet/actor purports *to be capable of doing* many things. Before he or she takes on a specific role or speaks a part, the poet/actor is divorced from the performance of a single possibility or set of possibilities incumbent upon a stable identity. This protean capacity or "potentiality" would rupture the careful order of the Republic, where each has a part to play in the body of the state. This retention of potentiality has lasting consequences for our own contemporary disciplinary state, as well, in ways that I will discuss more fully below. As the ancient Greek rhetorician Lucian recognized in his exploration of the pantomime actor, "The Egyptian Proteus of the ancient legend is no other than a dancer whose mimetic skill enables him to adapt himself to every character: . . . he is what he will."[79] How might this multiplicitous protean maintain what he or she will? For, in performing a dramatic action, the actor masquerades as such an "honest" person and gives a face to his or her otherwise amorphous life. Here the actor performs according to the Platonic imperative to pursue "honest" possibilities, and if the performance convinces effectively, then the dramatic action "works" within the realm of that other possible world. But what of the performance that "honestly" displays the "dishonest" nature of the poet/actor, his or her capacity to do many things at once, but a preference not to do anything? What of the thing that refuses to act, and instead withholds and possesses its capacity to do? In order to pursue these questions further we must look beyond the dramatic paradigm or pick apart its seams, to face the body that suspends and exposes its capacity to do and not do without acting, its potentiality to move otherwise.

THREE | Withholding Potentiality

"Try to ensure that everything in life has a consequence." —
This is without doubt one of the most detestable of maxims,
one that you would not expect to run across in Goethe. It is
the imperative of progress in its most dubious form. It is not
the case that the consequence leads to what is fruitful in
right action, and even less that the consequence is its fruit.
On the contrary, bearing fruit is the mark of evil acts. The
acts of good people have no "consequence" that could be
ascribed (or ascribed exclusively) to them. The fruits of an
act are, as is right and proper, internal to it. To enter into
the interior of a mode of action is the way to test its
fruitfulness. But how to do this?
— Walter Benjamin[1]

I would prefer not to.
— Bartleby the Scrivener

To "ensure that everything in life has a consequence," that all labor bears
some fruit of knowledge, is to make everything an action progressing toward a certain end outside of itself. This prefigures the future, denies life to
motions and means that do not live up to our expectations. Echoing Benjamin, we might ask, how is one to "enter into the interior of a mode of action?" Is this not the dangerous ploy of Plato's performer-poet, possessing
for him- or herself the potentiality to become many things, many characters, to perform many actions? What happens when he or she holds that
potentiality in abeyance?

The fourth-century Taoist philosopher Zhuangzi offers an eloquent answer to these questions, here concerning the figure of the musician:

Emergence and, also, loss —
This is Zhaowen playing his zither.
Nothing emerging and nothing lost —
This is Zhaowen not playing his zither.[2]

We imagine Zhaowen sitting before us, fingertips just grazing the strings of his zither, poised on the verge of playing perhaps the most beautiful of passages, the most perfectly tuned chord, or even a single note, and yet holding back. We are not far removed from David Tudor as he waits at the open piano and chooses not to play for the four minutes and thirty-three seconds of John Cage's composition 4'33". Both musicians retain a potentiality that thickens the air with much more than a simple silence, if there were such a thing, or even the chance environmental sounds that come to our attention as we listen. François Jullien, in one of his several mappings of the interplay between French and Chinese philosophy that bear significantly on our discussion, glosses the above aphorism as follows: "In declining to play—that is, in refusing to participate in the play of individual beings, of separate entities, of 'for' and 'against'—Zhaowen maintains his position in the supreme state of musicality and of wisdom."[3] By not choosing to play a single note, Zhaowen and Tudor allow for a future replete with the plethora of sound; nothing emerges because the musician retains whatever could emerge.

This is not to advocate indecision or an enervated passivity before the world. I am told that at age six or seven I would stand in the children's room of the public library until closing time, paralyzed between the many volumes I could read for fear that I would not choose the best of possible worlds. Oftentimes, unable to make a decision, I would come home empty-handed in even greater distress. Those many futures relied upon an object set up "for" and "against" myself, to use Jullien's parsing, rather than the self-contained capacity that Zhaowen holds close. My childhood indecision derived from a fear of the possible as a reductive measure; nothing of my inability to make a choice belonged to me.

In order to think through some of the many dimensions of potentiality, and how that play of futures can be held close, the following pages circle what is arguably the exemplary literary realization of potentiality: Herman Melville's short story "Bartleby the Scrivener." The text describes an encounter between a figure that retains his potential for action in the midst of a surrounding world of rigorously defined possibilities. To the great distress of the story's narrator, the character Bartleby refuses to ascribe to the actionable. Instead, he willfully maintains possession of his potentialities through an increasingly attenuated behavior and, most famously, through his idiosyncratic formula, "I would prefer not to." As a short story, "Bartleby the Scrivener" shows us a form of potentiality discovered *through* language, and thus a potentiality *of* language. The story has been foundational to the Italian philosopher Giorgio Agamben's theory of potentiality, which will guide our own considerations as we flesh out the meaning of potentiality in the Western philosophical tradition.

But live performance thinks differently than its literary counterpart. By looking at a dance adaptation of the story in which the choreographer translates the verbal proclamation of Bartleby's formula into a moment of stillness, the second section of this chapter explores how a live figure may corporeally embody potentiality. Finally, in the third section I return to the problem of the dramatic and look at how stillness plays out in the theater and in living speech.

BARTLEBY THE SCRIVENER: LINGUISTIC POTENTIALITY

Written in 1853 and included in the 1856 collection *The Piazza Tales*, Melville's "Bartleby the Scrivener" has over the intervening 150 years prompted innumerable critical forays set on determining the qualities of its enigmatic central character. Even divorced from its character, the name itself has had a lasting legacy; consider the domain name of one of the first websites devoted to the free and open distribution of classic literary texts. Like its namesake, Bartleby.com ruptures the economy and legality of the written document.[4]

Let me rehearse the narrative in brief. The unnamed attorney that narrates the story works in a small office on Wall Street attended by three assistant copyists, each mildly remarkable in his regular vacillations through the hours of the day: one cannot work productively before noon, another can work only after noon, while the third functions as an errand boy mediating between the pair. Seeking a more constant presence in his office, the narrator places an ad that is answered by the slight and silent Bartleby. The attorney installs the new arrival within his own chamber, separated only by a green screen, an audible but invisible presence. At first, Bartleby is a model of consistency and diligence, working tirelessly through all hours. But one day, when the attorney asks him to look over a document, the copyist evenly states, "I would prefer not to." Thus begins a progressive accumulation of "preferences not to perform," until the copyist has completely removed himself from the functional operation of the office, instead spending his hours gazing out the window of the office at the brick wall opposite. The narrator-attorney's anxiety surrounding the presence of the obtuse Bartleby likewise mounts and he variously attempts to alter the behavior of his employee, even trying to fire him, but the scrivener prefers to remain in the office. Finally, the narrator decides to move his offices elsewhere, packing the furniture and leaving the reluctant copyist standing alone in the bare room. The reader is told that the lawyer who subsequently rents the office has Bartleby forcibly removed from the quarters, but that the scrivener still haunts the halls and passages of the building until eventually the landlord calls the police. Arrested as a vagrant, Bartleby is sent to imprisonment in "the Tombs," whereupon the narrator visits him and attempts once again to reason with the impassive subject to no avail. Bartleby says that he "wants nothing to say" to him. When the narrator returns to the prison some time later, he finds the scrivener in an enclosed courtyard, rigidly curled in the corner, once more and forever staring at the blankness of the brick wall with eyes frozen wide. Preferring not to eat, Bartleby has died.

In one of many plausible readings of the story, the conflict centers upon language's struggle to contain and maintain the character of an indeterminate life. How can one tell a story comprised of unnamable motions, how can one tell a life that performs no action? From the start "Bartleby the Scrivener" depicts a quest for the identity of its namesake, pursued by the attorney-narrator on behalf of his reading audience. The attorney-narrator initiates his tale by stipulating his difficulty representing the title character of the story, claiming that Bartleby eludes biographical history: "While of other law-copyists I might write the complete life, of Bartleby nothing of that sort can be done. I believe no materials exist for a full and satisfactory biography of this man. It is an irreparable loss to literature."[5] The unnamed narrator applies a name to the figure at the start of the piece (the only character with a proper name in a world populated by other office-workers called Turkey, Nipper, and Ginger Nut) as if in an attempt to pin that protean form down, to assign a legal mark according to the manner of his profession.[6] Whether the Bartleby in question refers to a first or last name remains uncertain, an ambiguity that displaces the scrivener from the certainty of both the historical reference to family hereditary line (via the surname) and present individuality (via the first name). He is a singularity.

As the narrator states outright, the story he tells seeks to repair a loss to *literature,* but not a loss to life. Bartleby is a literary creation, and his struggle presents itself within, and against, the demands of the logocentric worlds of language, law, and capital. To retain Bartleby in the realm of literature is to subject him to representation in each of these interwoven domains. If one takes the lawyer's rumor that introduces the epilogue as a truthful report of the scrivener's past, then it seems that Bartleby has arrived in the land of law via the land of letters—dead letters, no less. The rumor states that, prior to his stint at the lawyer's office, Bartleby had worked in the "office of dead letters," meaning the department in the post office devoted to those missives that had been misdirected, those communicative possibilities that had failed in their delivery. These were possibilities that had not reached the goals that defined/named them (for what is a letter without a recipient?), but rather were collected and consumed in a sealed and endless state.[7] Unopened, they maintained their potential articulations behind the veil or curtain of the effectively blank envelope. They remained offstage, unseen and unvoiced, like Caryl Churchill's abortive visitors discussed in the previous chapter. To be surrounded by mistaken possibilities is to mistake one's own possibilities, to respond in kind to those silent and weighty secrets; it is not surprising that the copyist dispenses his own obdurate voicings that have no end or object. And of course, as a literary construct, Bartleby's death itself quite literally stages the death of a collection of letters. The narrator symbolically indexes this connection between figure and page in describing the day he moves from the office, leaving Bartleby alone on the premises: "Throughout, the scrivener remained standing behind the screen, which I directed to be removed the last thing. It was withdrawn; and, being *folded up like a huge folio*, left him the motionless occupant of a naked room" (my emphasis, 28). The copyist remains as the excess of the folio-like screens that surround him, that are folded up and sent off, the spiritual remains of a manuscript held in suspension.

It is only natural then that Bartleby moves from the land of (dead) letters to this particular version of the land of law, a law fixed in scriptural demands and claims. For this lawyer-narrator does not hold forth in court, speak his speech before judge and jury in order to expand the limits of the system, its horizons of expectation, but rather he transmits the preestablished letter of the law in written form. His office is devoted to the reproduction and manufacture of multiple versions of legal pronouncements, distributing its determinations in triplicate. Unlike the courtroom, arguably the quintessential site for the performative utterance to instantiate legal action through speech, this office does not provide a stage for action, its diversions and perversions, merely reproduction to "the letter of the law." His imbrication within scriptural practice extends beyond his occupation as scrivener to the space of the office itself. The narrator encloses Bartleby behind a screen and within blank walls as if to sequester the copyist in the realm of the merely audible, or, more precisely, the verbal: "I procured a high green folding screen, which might entirely isolate Bartleby from my sight, though not remove him from my voice" (9).

Bartleby, then, lives in the heart of the reproductive/representational logos and progressively erodes its interior via his peculiar pronouncements. His verbal formula is a kind of self-immolating gesture, turned back upon the only means of reproducible communication available to him. We also see this in the fact that Bartleby is beholden to the requirements of the literary medium and must perform his presence in spoken terms even if his usage of these terms denies their very capacity to signify. An exchange between the narrator and the scrivener is emblematic:

> "Will you tell me, Bartleby, where you were born?"
> "I would prefer not to."
> "Will you tell me *anything* about yourself?"
> "I would prefer not to." (19)

He refuses to bring up a past, or any stable *thing*, to define his present; he uses a language evacuated of nearly all reference. Later, when asked what he would like to do with himself, Bartleby repeatedly turns down the narrator's list of suggestions with another refrain that threatens to become a new formula: "I am not particular."

Yet this disavowal of the particular does not necessarily imply a vacuity or inability on the part of the character. In fact, quite the opposite case holds true, for it is the copyist's possession of a capacity "to do something" that allows him to prefer otherwise. As his initial period of successful copying indicates, Bartleby is perfectly capable of writing (or rewriting to be more precise) and, in fact, exhibits a remarkable facility with the skill that the attorney, in a mixture of awe and repulsion, views as "mechanical" and inhuman.[8] Fully actualizing his capacity to do *something*, his capacity to produce representation after representation, the functional Bartleby who initially fulfills his obligations to work at the office amounts to an inhuman copying machine, a cog in the engine of reproduction (the materialist would say that he becomes "alienated" from his work). When he first arrives at the office, he fully translates his human life into productive time, into the purest form of labor, neutered of all qualities that may divert energy from efficacy. His production becomes quite literally a reproduction of the same.

Such a notion raises a rather strange question: does Bartleby become more human as he performs less labor? As he increasingly prefers to do less and less, and eventually moves toward a total refusal to do any writing whatsoever, Bartleby comes closer and closer to possessing his own brilliant capacity "to do." Rather than pass off his forceful creation into the digestible form of linguistic replication, he maintains his virtuosic performance for himself. Situated in this small factory of writing from the middle of the nineteenth century, Bartleby disarms the Industrial Revolution's mechanization of the human and instead posits a life outside of authorized quantification and qualification.

In other words, the peculiarity of Bartleby is a direct provocation to the social landscape within which he is situated, a landscape of free capitalism that was just opening up in the nineteenth century and would develop exponentially over the next century. We need only think of the most famous of many examples, in which Frederick Winslow Taylor's investigations into efficient human action at the turn of the twentieth century were used to streamline labor and institute assembly line production. Bartleby asserts his singularity in the midst of an industrial world committed to the production and reproduction of such a codified identity. Determining, defining, and regulating the individual as a set of traits—as a "character"—became the primary power relation in the period, a power relation that Michel Foucault termed "discipline."[9] Bartleby does not claim a discipline, vocation, or profession. In fact, with his signature phrase he defers the lawyer's suggestions to work in the office, but also all his other proposals of other possible careers Bartleby might pursue. His preference not to reproduce the same, not to copy the law of patriarchal order, disrupts identification and queers the very notion of a part to play (how can we call him "Bartleby the Scrivener" if he does not write?). Bartleby creates all kinds of affects but he most definitely does not procreate or replicate. This unplaceable appearance and inaccessible desire—or lack thereof—figures itself outside normative narrative logic.

Working against disciplinary social formation, then, Bartleby foresees a more recent mode of operation characteristic of the mid- to late twentieth century: free-flowing and infinitely translatable information. Writing about this new economy of subjectivity, philosopher Michel Serres claims that "the public man is unrecognizable; he is no longer a particular person. He is now only an operator for mimicry. He erases from his body every angle of singularity, he is moulded of smooth planes."[10] The scrivener, however, complicates Serres's view immensely, breaking down the opposition between the "particular" and the "operator." Bartleby begins the story as a man of mimicry—a copyist—and yet his disavowal of mimesis does not make of him a particular body. He retains his "smoothness" in a state of singularity. He is "unrecognizable" not because of an infinite transmissibility, but because he is illegible and intransmissable—he will not leave the premises. If, as James C. Scott writes in his book *Seeing Like a State: How Certain Schemes to Improve the Human Condition Have Failed*, "legibility is a condition of manipulation," then Bartleby's very blankness models a mode of escape from disciplinary power's manipulations.[11] Or, as Gilles Deleuze puts it, "Bartleby is the man without references, without particularities: he is too smooth for anyone to be able to hang any particularity on him. Without past or future, he is instantaneous."[12]

In this respect Bartleby epitomizes a trope that Deleuze recognizes in many of Melville's greatest creations and serves to illustrate what the philosopher calls a "singular" or "original" figure. He is an original figure that immediately and instantaneously possesses an inexpressible truth about life; he possesses this truth because in expressing it, the truth would cease to hold. The clearest example of such an original life would be the quasi-supernatural white whale Moby Dick from Melville's 1851 novel, published two years before Bartleby. In the stunning chapter "The Whiteness of the Whale," Ishmael/Melville ruminates on the color of the whale as the essence of its force. In that this whiteness evokes the sublime infinitude of creation ("the white depths of the milky way"), the speaker proclaims that the *original* is "of the *origin*," or as Deleuze would say "instantaneous."[13] Fixed within an eternal present of flux, the original lies outside of the doubling of re-presentation and its re-cognized qualities. The *Moby Dick* chapter goes on to propose that whiteness exposes the multitudinous colors of the world as mere surface fancy with the common field of white as the smooth ground beneath. The white whale appears as a figure that is itself composed of an open and indeterminate ground from which another world could begin anew at any instant. Originality, then, instantiates a plane without temporal or spatial differentiation, without referents as concrete anchors for language's mooring, but replete with the *potential to differentiate*. Bartleby's preference not to do or to name an action essentially unfastens his subjectivity and makes of him a "man without references," precisely because he does not ground his temporality in referential actions and their objective endpoints.

Imagistically, the blankness of the white whale finds a proliferating correlate in Bartleby's office surroundings. Many readers have noted the analogue between the series of undifferentiated surfaces that enclose the copyist in a kind of closet (the wall of the courtyard, the wall of the green screen interceding between narrator and copyist) and the blank sheet of paper before the pen's inscription that increasingly comes to stand in for the reluctant copyist. The blank sheet is also, of course, the tabula rasa, Plato's image of the wax surface before textual imprint. As a reusable writing surface, the wax template was a more popular means of quotidian inscription than ink on papyrus in fourth- and fifth-century Greece, so it becomes the classical counterpart to Bartleby's endlessly inscribable sheets of paper.[14] In *Timaeus*, Plato invokes the unmarked wax surface as the emblem of the *chora* (receptacle) since "that which is to receive all forms should have no form. . . . as those who wish to impress figures on soft substances do not allow any previous impression to remain, but begin by making the surface as even and smooth as possible."[15] The medium must be leveled to a pure ground without differentiation before receiving the content of an imprint. Devoid of history, Bartleby, too, does not allow any previous impression to remain, but presents instead a tabula rasa, a figure without written history or action, without particulars, laying bare the potential for inscription.[16]

Thus we may conceptualize *potentiality* as the appearance of a medium prepared for, but abstaining from, articulation; it is a circumscribed ground without figure, or a figure itself becoming ground, the white whale as the origin of a world, without which there would be no *Moby Dick*. In a passage from Book IX of *The Metaphysics*, Aristotle explains the relationship between potentiality and actuality through a series of analogies that make this same point. Actuality is to potentiality as is "that which has been shaped out of the matter to the matter, and that which has been wrought to the unwrought."[17] In this way, potentiality is not diametrically opposed to actuality and, in fact contains something of the actual within it: a field must be actually present in order to then express a future potentiality.

Potentiality changes character slightly when situated in a living being. In *De Anima* (*On the Soul*), Aristotle distinguishes between two types of potentiality: what he calls a *generic potentiality* and an *existing potentiality*. The former requires an alteration in order to be realized, as in the infant with the potentiality to learn a language or to become a piano virtuoso. The infant does not presently possess the ability to do these things, but may possess it at a later time, at a later age. In other words, generic potentiality's actualization is deferred to the *distant* future, requiring that the entity in question change from its present state before it can access an event or acquire a capacity. To say that one is a potential pianist is to say that one is not at present able to play the piano.[18] My use of the term is closer to what Aristotle understands as existing potentiality; it refers to one who already has the knowledge or skill to do something and, in possessing this capacity immediately and presently, may choose to *not*-realize it.[19] Potentiality in this second sense is the capacity *not*-to do something, a capacity reserved for one who already has the capability to do. As a zither player who does not play, Zhaowen's potentiality encompasses a range of futures quite different from the ones that I would face were I to take the instrument up in my hands. In opposition to generic potentiality's distant event that may or may not be available for actualization at some later point in time, in some possible world, existing potentiality could be actualized at the present moment merely by activating its passive capacity. It is the future at the immediate horizon of the present.

This second sense of the concept as virtually present mirrors the notion of potentiality used in thermodynamics. Such potentiality refers to the amount of energy stored in an object or structure readily available for consumption or use as kinetic energy, but only maintaining itself as "potential energy" in preserving its capability not to be used. Such potential energy is not a product of the thing in itself, but of its relation to the system of which it is a part and the work of which it is capable. In the gravitational field, we might think of a ball gaining more potential energy and more potential to "work" the further it ascends away from the surface toward which it could fall. Everything around us contains potential energy to do otherwise or create change outside of the expected uses or productive ends that a humanized perspective implies. A hammer may serve a certain purpose as a tool, but the materiality that makes up the thing we call a "hammer"—a shaft of wood and crosspiece of metal—possesses its own potentiality apart from its named ends. Breaking the hammer unleashes some of this potentiality, burning it would unleash it otherwise, and so on.

I do not mean to propose a one-to-one relationship between thermodynamics' potential energy and the conceptual potentiality at issue here. Thermodynamics is uninterested in the means by which an object arrives at its particular placement or how it utilizes its stored energy in a kinetic expression—its potential energy is the same whether the ball falls or rolls down a ramp or starts a wheel turning. For the potentiality at issue here, contrarily, the means is the matter of the event. Thermodynamics may attend to the quantification of power, but potentiality is more concerned with the qualification of that power. If all materiality is conceived as an interrelated structure, whether it be the arrangement of a piece of metal and a piece of wood or a temporary constellation of a set of elements on the molecular scale, thermodynamics helps frame potentiality not as the essence of an individual, but as a relationality. This relation may just be a matter of attention: think of how the potential gathering behind the door in Churchill's *Heart's Desire* is a product of the relationship between the object and the individuals waiting for it open, onstage and in the audience.

To speak of the potential of a living individual to "do something" is to refer to his or her capacity (as means) apart from any particular realization or action (end). One maintains one's potential to do by *not* doing a nameable thing, by *not* arriving at an end. Taking his cue from Aristotle's distinction and subsequent formulations of the same by medieval scholars, Giorgio Agamben discusses potentiality not as the display of a capacity "to be" but as the display of a capacity "not-to be":[20]

> In the potentiality to be, potentiality has as its object a certain act . . . ; as for the potentiality to not-be, on the other hand, the act can never consist of a simple transition *de potentia ad actum*. It is, in other words, a potentiality that has as its object potentiality itself, *a potentia potentiae*.[21]

Agamben denies that potentiality is the capacity "to be," because such a conception always implies a "something" accomplished as a definite action, while the potentiality "not-to be" relieves us of a definite conclusion to future motion. Translated into the terms I have proposed here, this transitive relation toward something's presumed conclusion is a possibility. On the other hand, the potentiality to not-be or not-do presents an objectless capacity for motion or making, an intransitive origin spiraling back upon itself toward its own continued sustenance.[22]

It is a cyclical and paradoxical statement, this potentiality to have potentiality/impotentiality. Only one who is capable of deciding not to do something—one who possesses an impotentiality—can be said to possess that decision. In an exemplary manner, Bartleby's formula gives voice to the fact that he is *able to* not do that which the law(yer) demands of him. Potentiality is, accordingly, "*the existence of non-Being*, the presence of an absence; this is what we call 'faculty' or 'power.' 'To have a faculty' means *to have* a privation."[23] The lack in this case is the absent, but immanent, figure encompassed by the ground, medium, or faculty. It does not connote a lack of energy or activity, but a gathering of one's resources and a preparation for what may come. To say that a figure possesses potentiality is to say that he or she exhibits a medium or means, a field prepared for action, unveiling his or her body as if it were a blank sheet of paper. Thus the figure becomes a ground.

Is Bartleby an original doomed to isolation in the Tombs of history, to the "loss of literature," as the narrator laments? Or do he and his formula announce the founding of a new time, a new community that the lawyer cannot recognize? Is his proclamation of potentiality merely a solipsistic gesture? Or does his presentation of potentiality show him to be a "medium" in both senses of the word: as the ground for appearance, but also in the prophetic or spiritual sense as a ground capable of announcing a future and giving body to voices from other dimensions, other worlds?

Melville's narrator ends his account with the highly enigmatic exclamation, "Ah, Bartleby! Ah, Humanity!" (34). Critical interpretations differ between considering the former as representative of the latter (Bartleby as Humanity) or the two as diametrically opposed (Bartleby against Humanity), and it is clearly this equivocal nature of the cry that makes it so compelling. Deleuze, however, sees the scrivener and all of Melville's originals (notably Billy Budd and Benito Cereno, two other eponyms from the author's collection of short stories) otherwise. He ends his essay "Bartleby: Or the Formula" by claiming that Bartleby stands as the messiah for a future community: "A schizophrenic vocation: even in his catatonic or anorexic state, Bartleby is not the patient, but the doctor of a sick America, the *Medicine-Man*, the new Christ or the brother to us all."[24] A schizophrenic statement itself, Deleuze's "vocation" hints at the "voca(liza)tion" of both the narrator's cry (split between the singular and the collective) and the scrivener's formula (in its directionless multiplicity). But it also more overtly refers to Bartleby's job, what he is qualified "to do," not as a singular and fixed occupation, but as a scattered attention capable of becoming whatever. As we discussed previously, in "preferring not to" Bartleby breaks with the basic tenets of industrial capitalism's sense of time and value, as well as the specific role of the laborer within the system of production. We see Bartleby as the man excluded from Plato's *Republic*: he is not the "honest," hardworking man devoted to his sole occupation, but, like the poet, like the actor, he is capable of performing many roles and many actions. Or, rather, this figure that is able to *not*-copy might be the performer before performance, still closeted offstage, presenting a version of (human) life without a preordained role to play on the stage of history.

In other words, by claiming that the copyist represents the "doctor of a sick America," Deleuze suggests that the formula's rupture leans toward a future time beyond Melville's nineteenth-century idiom, and into the twenty-first century. In an age where, according to performance theorist Jon McKenzie, we are told to "Perform or Else," Bartleby's ostentatious will "not to" perform bears careful consideration as a strategy for retaining a life that is not reduced to (re)productive actions or valuable statements.[25] The copyist hesitates on the edge of performance, resists action and inscription from without, and instead, to use Rayner's terminology, makes of *doing* a thing done, thinking a thing thought. He does not tell us what act it is that he would prefer not to do, and by the story's end his living is entirely riven from named and possible actions. Seemingly stilled forevermore, his life has escaped toward other potentialities that narrative authority cannot fathom or perceive.

This active passivity resounds loudly in the new millennium. The members of Occupy Wall Street, for example, have hailed Bartleby's means to profess without a profession, to occupy the future without adhering to a particular occupation, as the work of an important "anticipatory plagiarist" (as the Oulipians would have it) to their movement.[26] For, according to Agamben, the disruption of an ends-based economy of living is the fundamental political problem of our time. In a section of *The Coming Community*, a text that lays the grounds for an imagined future collective based in potentiality, Agamben locates the origin of all ethics in the realization that "there is no essence, no historical or spiritual vocation, no biological destiny that humans must enact or realize," for if this were not the case, "there would be only tasks to be done."[27] The moment of potentiality, therefore, actualizes the truly ethical position, because it displays that there is no particular directive that will realize humanity, no particular vocation that belongs to—or, more commonly, is dictated to—the subject. Excluded from the Plato's Republic of transcendent ends and parts, where an individual's future is fixed from above, the poet and the performer (in ancient Greece they are one and the same) of the coming community possess the potentiality for all vocations and characters.

Such a "preference not to" has direct consequences for an understanding of performativity derived from speech act theory. In its most basic terms, we might think of a linguistic utterance as an event placed in time and space that causes an effect—in other words, it *acts*—rather than a free-floating constative statement of truth/falsity divorced from the context of its enunciation. In his lectures that first introduced speech act theory, *How to Do Things with Words*, J. L. Austin requires that the performative utterance cite a prior term/name as the foundation for present being, drawing the past into current circulation through the iteration of an existing code. The speech act situates the subject and his or her utterance in relation to these prior behaviors and social forms, and in terms of its expected consequences.[28] As Austin writes: "With physical actions we nearly always naturally name the action *not* in terms of what we are here calling the minimum physical act, but in terms which embrace a greater or lesser range of what might be called its natural consequences . . . we do not have any class of names which distinguish physical acts from consequences."[29] Bartleby's preference not to perform dismantles this iterative system of physical and verbal possibility.[30] In order for an utterance to function performatively, it must recall a certain situation and reestablish its form in the present. Bartleby's performative act does not announce *what* it does.

In one of her "seven and ½" readings of Bartleby, literary theorist Branka Arsić describes the effect of his formulas as follows:

It is not referential. But it also fails to function as a speech act because it is often pronounced with no connection to the question Bartleby has been asked; neither, however, does it constitute or affect Bartleby himself (because it does not have an object, the indifferent repetition of the formula leaves the subject of the utterance undecided also).[31]

The formula disarticulates the normally interlocking linguistic corpus, the body that the speech act reciprocally defines. Recall that the naming of Ophelia's action in *Hamlet* had profound consequences for the determination of her dramatic character and its afterlife. "Preferring not to" submit to an intentional object or reference outside of himself, Bartleby performatively severs his being from language's law. Instead of directing his actions elsewhere, he turns endlessly upon himself. In a manner that surely speaks to his value to Occupy and associated protest movements, Arsić asserts that Bartleby tears open the social fabric woven of these citational possibilities and reveals a terrain for the excluded, the speechless: "If Bartleby had refused, he could still be seen as a rebel or insurrectionary, and as such would still have a social role. But the formula stymies all speech acts, and at the same time, it makes Bartleby a pure outside [*exclu*] to whom no social position can be attributed."[32] Of course, in his final imprisonment, Bartleby is indeed assigned a social position—he is a criminal—though this is a position emphatically outside society. The imprisonment acts in an almost indexical manner; it does not name a crime, it merely pushes him to the outside.

If the Law can only gesture at him, this is because Bartleby's announcement makes an affirmation outside of oppositional dialectics. It does not assert or contradict, but proclaims a force of will, a preference. In Agamben's evocative words, "What shows itself on the threshold between Being and non-Being, between sensible and intelligible, between word and thing, is not the colorless abyss of the Nothing but the luminous spiral of the possible. To be able is *neither to posit nor to negate*."[33] The whiteness of the whale is no colorless abyss, but the luminous spiral of all color, the demonic faculty to determine a color from out of the many-colored beast. Likewise, Bartleby's exposure of potentiality does not consider the veracity or falsity of a statement or state of being, but proposes a kind of aesthetic experimentation on the limits of truth and falsity, being and nonbeing. In this manner,

Bartleby's preference comes quite close to the disturbing promise of the Witch in *Macbeth*. What it is that she'll do, she'll do, and she'll do remains as indeterminate as what Bartleby would prefer not to (do). Even the copyist's negation (preferring *not* to) that seemingly sets the speech act of witch and copyist on opposite embankments gives way, slipping into the same indeterminate valley of affirmation. Both the utterances of Bartleby and the Witch become pure force without goal, in a Nietzschean sense, pure affirmation. Both figures stage feints, a linguistic proposal that sidesteps its meaning, for as stated in the previous chapter, the unnamed or unlocatable motion is impossible to counter or parry. Potentiality disarms the dialectical and the dialogic, leaving the narrator without a possible response, himself devoid of dramatic character: "It was his wonderful mildness, chiefly, which not only disarmed me but unmanned me, as it were" (16).[34] But must potentiality inevitably reference and return us to the realm of language? For is it not "his wonderful mildness, chiefly," rather than his befuddling formula, that "unmans" the narrator, displacing him from human communication and community? Which is to say, are there not other faculties or mediums that can display their capacity without realization?

BARTLEBY THE DANCER: LIVE POTENTIALITY

> FELDENKRAIS: In the motor cortex we have fixed connections, patterns; and the wide range of possibilities that were there from before are circumscribed and cramped. You have linked them into fixed patterns and that's that.
>
> SCHECHNER: So we're really talking about potentiality.
>
> FELDENKRAIS: That's it exactly. I want the neutrality only to free you from the inhibition of having one specialty.
>
> —Moshé Feldenkrais with Richard Schechner[35]

At times a warm smile flickers across his pallid features, lighting up some recollection or promise of intention, before he gazes off again, his mirth gently fading into that same impassive distraction. At other times, he physically teeters as if balancing on an edge between actions before resolving himself once more with the expected statement, "I would prefer not to." We find some clue to this peculiar distance later in the film, when our hero, the lawyer, discovers a photograph of an unnamed woman amid his employee's meager belongings: an estranged family member? Or perhaps a long-lost love? Some biographical past resides here, however inconclusive it may be.

As in other screen adaptations of the Melville's short story—no less than eight film and television versions in French, German, and English have been professionally produced in the last forty years—Jonathan Parker's 2001 film *Bartleby* fleshes out its title character with additions both endemic to the medium and additions more willfully appended. This Bartleby, played by the skeletal and truly idiosyncratic actor-filmmaker-performance artist Crispin Glover, does not reside behind a screen; he is entirely onscreen, visible to the assorted oddities that work in the office and to the camera's analysis. Taken together these suggest an interiority at odds with Melville's creation; every expression bespeaks a psychological character suffused with longing, however obtuse, whereas Melville's figure resolutely denies a place for desire through speech or gesture (or at least reserves this domain for the narrator's relation to Bartleby). The snapshot found in the desk, in particular, suddenly locates the scrivener in a heteronormative relation to a woman, thus eradicating whatever queer potential accrues in his written iteration. These misfired attempts at representing Bartleby pinpoint the difficulty with displaying the character as a visible entity. One cannot translate a thought from one medium into another assuming that there will be no consequences to such a shift. In live performance, too, Bartleby could not stage an appearance of potentiality by simply speaking his formula aloud. Some quality would adhere; he would give us too much of himself.

Let us imagine a Bartleby on stage, performing a potentiality disentangled from the performative speech act, from all speech. Such a thought experiment poses significant problems from the start. In *Macbeth*, any staged physical action, any dramatic possibility, accompanying the witch's promise of doing will weaken its demonic quality, give it a named intention. This is why depictions of the weird sisters so often leave something to be desired—the actors seem too small, too recognizably on our scale and of our element. They may proclaim to undertake "a deed without a name," but actor and audience will likely see an action in their motion. Likewise, any assignation of significance, even as simple as an appearance or pose, will inevitably diminish Bartleby's abyss of declaration. The witch must remain still or disappear entirely just as Bartleby's preference must withhold itself, affirm its own effacement. Perhaps he should remain offstage, screened in by the walls of his closet and free to resist showing up as normative action? As Martin Puchner writes of the closet drama, with its preference not to appear in person, "This acting out cannot take place in a real theater because it everywhere exceeds the limits of theatrical representation, especially its reliance on real actors, with real appearances and genders, as well as the presence of actual censorship."[36] The closet drama relies on linguistic figuration where embodiment falls short. Indeed, the preceding section of this chapter has shown how thoroughly the notion of potentiality laid out by Agamben and his philosophical predecessors deliberately concerns the linguistic faculty, whether in its grounding metaphor (the tabula rasa) or in the means of expression: for the scrivener and philosopher alike, it is the spoken/written formula "I would prefer not to" that captures the faculty of language.

A close reading of Melville's story suggests one manner of concretely staging the potential figure in performance. Perhaps as a result of the narrator's faith in the verbal before all else, there is very little of the text devoted to a description of Bartleby, but the few words that are shared suggest how the scrivener's performance extends beyond the linguistic. The lawyer repeatedly remarks upon the peculiar stillness of the young man, a stillness of both body and expression. This is, in fact, the first thing he notices about Bartleby and is the sole quality attached to the figure of the young man when the scrivener is introduced to the reader: "In answer to my advertisement, *a motionless* young man one morning stood upon my office threshold, the door being open, for it was summer" (8–9, my emphasis). Bartleby performs no prior action, but merely arrives at the door, motionless, as if he had always been waiting there. Once within the threshold Bartleby's constant and lasting presence, without beginning or end of departure, characterizes his occupation of the office as well: "As yet I had never, of my personal knowledge, known him to be outside of my office. He was a perpetual sentry in the corner" (12). And at numerous other points in the story the narrator remarks upon the "singularly sedate" aspect of Bartleby or "his great stillness, his unalterableness of demeanor under all circumstances" (9, 15). This quietude culminates in the discovery of the scrivener's corpse in the courtyard of the Tombs, the narrator declaring with an almost transcendent finality: "Nothing stirred" (33).

If Bartleby's formula acts as a linguistic "feint" that exposes the faculty of language, then I would like to suggest that his stillness performs a similar revelation of the faculty of movement, a potentiality of the living body as moving body. The text from Schechner's interview with the somatic practitioner Moshé Feldenkrais quoted above speaks to an active neutrality that frees a body "from the inhibition of having one specialty." As the art form most directly concerned with the essence of movement as medium, dance would seem an ideal site for staging the scrivener's profession-less profession in live terms.

At the Montpellier Danse Festival in 2006, French choreographer Didier Théron premiered *Bartleby*, a dance adaptation grounded precisely in such an investigation of stillness as potentiality. Over the course of the twenty-minute solo, Théron moves across the stage space, stringing together a series of incomplete motions, distended and suspended by unexpected expanses of stillness. He seems to fold into himself one moment, following and illustrating the presumed organization of his body's joints and junctions as an arm bends along its full range of motion or, straightened into a line, cuts an angular form from the space. He will stop and hold himself mid-collapse before embarking on a new and divergent path, which soon in turn meets its own premature interruption. Balancing himself diagonally off the ground on one extended arm, or catching himself at the midpoint in his descent into a squat, nearly all of these moments are held in isometric tension. This "holding" is not a passive stillness or resting place, in which the dancer declares that he "will not do," but an entirely active and exhausting passivity as if he were gripping the air about him or bracing himself against the pressures of gravity's demand to fall. He grabs hold of his *preference* in each muscular seizure. Not an action, exactly, but still an active stance in preferring, a difficult and almost virtuosic arrest. The distinction is particularly important, for here we clearly recognize potentiality as the affirmation of a capacity and not a passive negation.

A peculiar uncertainty lingers about the dancer's choreography. And even though the movement vocabulary recalls the pedestrian in its jagged walking lines and smaller gestures about the face and torso, each hazy recollection of the everyday meets the same obdurate repose, as if the dancer's body were collecting itself and forgetting itself at once. Théron, dressed in a brown velour bodysuit, clearly stands out from the black surround as a singular form—a figure set apart from a ground—but the articulations of his performance do not present as clear a figure-ground relationship. At the risk of oversimplification, one could say that in conventional modern dance (before Cunningham marked a threshold between high modernist abstraction and early postmodernism) pauses often emerge as organic "breaths" between the body's phrases. Strung together, these phrases form a part-by-part syntax of movement and create a sympathetic relationship between viewer and dancer where the two come to share a common organic rhythm. In conventional modern dance repetition and variation accumulate a formal vocabulary as the dance progresses, teaching the viewer how to read the dance as it evolves through the recognition of previous articulations. Théron's dance avoids both structuring principles to present a piece without a phrased arc of progress, without climax, and arguably without shape. The lights rise on the dancer midstride in the beginning of the piece and fall twenty minutes later just after he has embarked on another path. All the motion is at the same slightly rapid, but consistent, tempo. Instead of moving in phrases, the dancing body seems to gag on itself, stuttering out frozen gaps between divergent movements and indeterminate gestures.

While this movement vocabulary is not new to contemporary dance, it carries extra weight as an adaptation of Melville's story. Throughout his solo, Théron attempts to articulate the space in cipher-like curls and lines, both on the gestural scale, carving his immediate surround of face and torso, and across the larger field of the stage, cutting strokes along the horizontal plane. Bartleby's copying becomes quite literally a "choreo-graphy" (from the Greek *khoreia*, "dance," and *graphein*, "to write"), an attempt at incorporating the scriptural act into bodily performance. The illegibility and inconclusive nature of the dancer's marks coupled with their inevitable and immediate disappearance makes the dance a kind of self-effacing writing.

Théron's *Bartleby* thus epitomizes the disappearance of the gesture frequently mentioned in much writing about dance. Dance theorists such as Susan Foster, Mark Franko, and André Lepecki have detailed the struggle between the archival impulse and ephemerality that has haunted Western thought on the medium since early modernity. They direct our attention to the first great writers on dance, Arbeau in the sixteenth century and Noverre in the eighteenth century, who each lamented the loss of dance's present in the moment of performance and the loss of its past forms. In response to this perpetual disappearance, dance relies on choreography as a record of the past event and in order to stage future events. As Lepecki writes, "[Western] dance cannot be imagined without writing, it does not [exist] outside writing's space," even if that relationship to writing is one of opposition via an erasure.[37]

Some of the inspiration for this particular approach to the dance Théron locates in his study of Buddhism. Here he discovered the possibility of "a work without impulse in movement" that exemplified "Bartleby's quiet strength, the felt-like and polite intensity of his few acts."[38] I love this anomalous "felt-like" as a description of the copyist's quiet forcefulness. It brings forth a texture that, as Deleuze and Guattari remind us, is not comprised of the interweaving binaries of warp and weft, the strands of yes and no by which we might unravel his intensity.[39] Felt is a compressed tangle of matter without firm edge or organized coordination; it is all of a consistent piece, not to be picked apart. There is that warmth, too, that organic comfort with its echoes of Joseph Beuys wrapped loosely in his felt blanket while living with a coyote. In terms that are identical to our notion of potentiality, Jullien writes of how Chinese Buddhism celebrates a stance that is "not leaning in one direction more than in another, not characterized more by one quality than by another, but preserving, perfectly whole within itself, its capacity for action."[40] It is this return to the quiet possession of movement—the strength of Bartleby, as Théron puts it—that requires we look at stillness not as negation of motion, but as the affirmation of the potentiality for movement.

If the potential figure appears as a ground for future figuration/articulation itself—the dancer as a ground for future movement—against what ground or setting can this figure appear on stage? In *To Do, To Act, To Perform*, Rayner points to the great span between act 4, scene 2, and act 5, scene 3, of *Macbeth* where Shakespeare's protagonist is completely absent from the stage, to say that "doing" presents a major obstacle toward both textual and visual representation. Potentiality prefers to vacate the scene and undertake the impossible, far from surveying eyes of law and reason with which an audience is traditionally endowed. We've seen Caryl Churchill's fabulations charge the offstage with infinite proposed entrances (*Heart's Desire*), while Will Eno leaves the catastrophic event in the dark (*Tragedy: a tragedy*). Potentiality prefers to remain unnamed and undetermined, working its demonic power from the offstage.

In fact, it could even be argued that it opposes the very existence of an onstage set, since such a set forms a concrete counterpoint and pivot—an objective correlative to use T. S. Eliot's term—to the possible action.[41] The visual correlates presented in the Melville text—the blank walls and green screens that surround Bartleby—reinforce this evacuation of description. The courtyard wherein the scrivener is found dead also displays an analogue for the character, but one that raises his enigmatic presence to the level of the sacred and otherworldly:

> The yard was entirely quiet. It was not accessible to the common prisoners. The surrounding walls, of amazing thickness, kept off all sounds behind them. The Egyptian character of the masonry weighed upon me with its gloom. But a soft imprisoned turf grew underfoot. The heart of the eternal pyramids, it seemed, wherein, by some strange magic, through the clefts, grass-seed, dropped by birds, had sprung. (33)

Here, in the heart of "the Tombs," removed from the common world of both citizen and prisoner, springs a nonhuman life "by some strange magic." This is not the expression of a sentiment or situation, but the removal from such. The courtyard is the most fully realized reflection of the life that it contains. If anything, the objective correlative seals the figure of Bartleby within a pyramid inaccessible to the excavations of linguistic ax or shovel, external sound or sight, eternally timeless but still vibrantly alive with secret shoots.

In performance the most logical realization of such a setting would entail an empty stage, the tabula rasa of the black box theater. But Théron's adaptation presents a far more enigmatic set. The extreme upstage corner of an otherwise empty stage is occupied by a gigantic inflatable rabbit at least twice the height and many times the breadth of the wiry dancer—no features on the towering form, just a massive beige balloon in the shape of a rabbit. Throughout the performance the figure watches Théron dance, watches the audience, perhaps, and waits. It is a radically "other" presence, only animal in its iconic suggestion of a shape, unnervingly oversized, and far too still for comfort. The fact that it is inflated with air, possessing a fragile buoyancy that evokes the lifelike in its suggestion of withheld breath, only accentuates its uncanny heft. There is no reference to a rabbit anywhere in Melville's story, in fact, apart from those wayward seeds and shoots in the Tombs, no reference to the "natural" world in this most urban of stories. Assigning a role to the form, a character, then, presents a difficulty akin to the narrator's attempt to identify the scrivener. And yet it demands to be answered: What does the rabbit signify? Whom does it represent? Standing there in its unfazed stupor, the rabbit's interplay with the plane of being divorced from speech might be a surrogate for the lawyer, reduced to speechlessness. He is dumbfounded, full of hot air, and unable to act upon this stage where the impassive scrivener of the story can finally write (choreograph) the indeterminate, the unwritten. Or, perhaps I have this all wrong and it is the dancer who represents the lawyer, babbling before the yawning abyss of the inhuman Bartleby, here cast as a grotesque exaggeration and mutation of the statue the narrator references throughout. After all, isn't this rabbit, like Bartleby, "a perpetual sentry in the corner"? Finally, perhaps the rabbit and dancer together form Bartleby as a single field of presence displayed before the uncomprehending lawyer-mind of the analytical audience, a singular relationship shared between the two figures under surveillance. Dancer and sculpture wear the same beige-brown color as if to underline their kinship and common heritage. I've suggested elsewhere in reference to another theatrical rabbit that the animal

Fig. 1. Didier Théron, *Bartleby*, 2006. Photo Courtesy Didier Théron.

stands as nature's symbolic representative of mass (re)production, which here would suggest a kinship with the copyist.[42] Dare I say that, in their stillness, both are tumescent with procreative potentiality?

Designed by Donald Becker, this is not so much a "set" as it is a fluid relation between the dancer and the inert monolith, a duet between almost-human and almost-animal (for we must remember that this *is not* an actual rabbit).[43] They diverge from one another as the dancer moves, his gesticulations even more human when set against the inert sculpture, but then, in the dancer's moments of stillness, the two hang together with bated breath. A shared ground opens up between them as they together announce an interstitial community, a shared existence in the gray zone between human and nonhuman, communicative and noncommunicative. Théron's other dances at times stage a similar relationship to the material world, one built on the interplay between forces and the between-ness of subject and object.[44] For example, in the 2007 *Democratic Combine*, a duet with Keith Thompson, the dancers don suits that greatly expand their physical dimensions to create "bio-objects" that blur the line between object and body. In her *Relationscapes: Movement, Art, Philosophy*, Erin Manning conceptualizes dance as the mutual construction of body and surrounding space in helpful terms:

> The not-yet takes form through the intensities of preacceleration that compel recompositions at the level of both strata, the body and the room. What this means is that both body and space are experienced as alive with potential movement. . . . The body-room stratum is therefore neither object nor form, but infinite potential for recombination.[45]

Thermodynamics speaks of the suspension of a form as a relation taut with potential energy; so, too, the body-room-rabbit assemblage allows Bartleby to appear at once in one form and to retreat in another. As Manning's impressive book argues, this establishment of an interstitial community between the moving and the not-yet moving is a characteristic of postmodern dance at large, which has often been called an art of mediation or indexicality.

Théron's *Bartleby* bridges traditional dance grounded in fictions of character and narrative with more experimental work that investigates the epistemological, ontological, and phenomenological dimensions of the art. The move toward stillness has a rich history in dance of the last sixty years, stretching back at least as far as Merce Cunningham's willful inclusion of stillness alongside scored movement as equally interesting to the choreographer.[46] To a large extent Cunningham's interest in stillness responded to a modernist pursuit of the essence of the dance medium. More than a decade before Clement Greenberg defined the modernist tendency as the search for the essence of an artistic medium/form, dance critic John Martin wrote of the beginning of modern dance as a shift of attention away from ballet's focus on narrative content to a more direct investigation of movement as such: "This beginning [of the modern dance] was the discovery of the actual substance of the dance, which is found to be movement. . . . With this discovery the dance became for the first time an independent art."[47] Movement became the essence of dance, the distinguishing feature by which one could differentiate it from the anything-goes intermediality of the theatrical. While Cunningham has traditionally been credited with incorporating stillness into dance, André Lepecki has argued that even in the early days of twentieth-century modernism, well before Cunningham's explorations, stillness stopped being considered the antithesis of dance and instead became the site for the origin of movement. Choreographers and spectators alike recognized the still body as a kind of dancing body. For example, in an essay on Nijinsky's *Le Sacre du Printemps* written concurrently with the premiere of the piece in 1913, Jacques Rivière wrote that "in the body in repose, there are a thousand hidden directions, an entire system of lines that incline it toward dance."[48] For these early modernists, however, the still dancer possesses this panoply of directions and movements *prior* to the beginning of the dance, in the moments before the curtain rises or the music's first chord, but never within the performance itself. One of Merce Cunningham's revolutionary acts, then, was to bring this site of original impulse into the composition itself and to include it as a form of movement in much the same way that his collaborator John Cage sought to include silence within the realm of musical performance. In both cases the term normally perceived as the negation of the art's essence (sound in music and movement in dance) came to represent a texture in its own right.

In the 1960s, as part of a larger project critiquing representation, choreographer/dancers such as Douglas Dunn and Steve Paxton of the Judson Church in New York created work that verged on the absolutely immobile and flirted with the dancer as sculptural form. This next generation of choreographers (many of whom trained firsthand with Cunningham and/or Cage) explored stillness as a conceptual experiment upon movement rather than as an additional, albeit equal, color on the choreographer's palette. In her landmark survey of these postmodern choreographers, *Terpsichore in Sneakers*, dance scholar Sally Banes describes Dunn's *101: A Performance Ex-*

hibit (1974), in which spectators discovered the dancer lying prone in the midst of a massive labyrinthine installation, as an experiment that "carries to its logical conclusion the notion that not moving is still dancing."[49] In the installation-performance Dunn choreographed the audience's available movement by articulating certain paths and possibilities, but left the actualization of a particular passage to the individual viewer. The spectators moved through the construction, performing on a "stage" that filled the entire gallery, to arrive at last at Dunn. Like some Minotaur at the center of his maze, Dunn presented the monstrous proposition of a dancer who does not dance, or at least does not seem to dance. In fact, for Banes, watching the living figure ripple and throb with the change of breath and of blood, the immobile body revealed the lie in the notion of an absolute stillness: "Narrowing the movement down to zero only emphasizes the fact that there is no time during which our bodies are not in some kind of motion; in *101*, Dunn's heart still beat, blood still flowed, thoughts still continued. There really is no zero point in motion, only asymptotes."[50] In the same way that Cage's silence is not an absence of sound, but an invitation to those noises normally excluded from music proper, the stillness pursued here draws attention to the infinitesimal movements of the body in repose, frames it as dance. Cage famously recounts entering an anechoic chamber (a room sealed so as to be completely soundproof) and still hearing two sounds—the hum of his neural system and his circulatory system. The body is always making music, always becoming, just as it is always dancing.

In similar terms, Lepecki speaks of Steve Paxton's conceptual dance/exercise "the Stand"—a self-explanatory piece of choreography that asks its participants to attend to and perform their own stance—as an example of how stillness is a kind of dance in itself. A spoken text describes the relaxed standing body as performing a "small dance" composed of the slight adjustments and fluctuations of the musculature supporting itself upright. Paxton's text was read during a workshop he led in 1977, while the participating artists enacted its instructions; it functioned as a part of a larger practical exercise rather than as a performance for a viewing audience. In other words, "the Stand" is a pas de deux that the dancer watches his or her own body perform with and against the force of gravity, as if it were a living partner.

When it comes to the question of the still body, Lepecki argues against the live figure as a stilled figure, instead proposing that it performs a "micro-scopic dance" akin to Paxton's constantly readjusting stance as the force of gravity and the vibrations of musculature provoke a subtle instability.[51] The fact that the body of the stilled dancer performs a "microscopic" dance of organic shudderings and fluctuations, as Banes, Lepecki, and Paxton claim, does not discount the potentiality in this inertness. If anything, these slight palpitations of the skin trouble the notion of a faculty as a uniformly consistent and stable field that forms a figure ex nihilo. If dance's expressive body is the intentionally moving body, then the intentionally unmoving body possesses its own potential for action in a manner akin to the wax surface's possession of the potential for inscription, backed by a tensile pressure of mounting expectation. Such stillness lingers around what Manning has called the virtual state of "preacceleration" that vibrates through all actual bodies, the many not-yets that will proceed from this one present stance.[52] The microscopic dance of blood flow and breath proves that the body in question still lives even though it does not act.

This dance of the nerves is remarkably close to the flicker of thought that Blau imagines passing over the brow of the great actress Eleonora Duse, a flicker not only referencing her slow death right now before our very eyes, as the theorist would have it, but her possession of the potential to think forward in time. Of course, Blau could not have seen Duse's stillness dancing across her face—she had actually, permanently, died in 1924, two years before Blau was born. In the essay in question, he says, "I have always retained (from I know not where) an image of her in perfect stillness, then something passing over her face like the faintest show of thought."[53] The image is the work of the critic's imagination in more ways than one, for there are no images of Duse in action as a performer. Technological constraints regarding the length of exposure time mean that any photograph of Duse at the time would have been posed, a difference that is signal to our understanding of liveness and potentiality.

Without delving too deeply into the extensive literature on the pose, we might recall Roland Barthes's account of striking a pose before the camera:

> I instantaneously make another body for myself, I transform myself in advance into an image [so that] I am neither subject nor object but a subject who feels he is becoming an object: I then experience a microversion of death (of parenthesis): I am truly becoming a specter.[54]

The future is foreclosed for the posed, decided as a fixed image with determined possibilities in two senses: first, it defines the present in relation to the past, and, second, it makes the present moment a past moment. In the first case, the pose reiterates a legible image of the subject as a recognizable identity, donning the mask of a character consistent with past representations of the self and establishing a relationship with an environment com-

posed of actionable and accessible parts. In the second case, the posed image is immediately ensconced forever within the past, deferring the present
for a later time. Barthes suggests that the photograph indexes a moment as
if to say "it was but is no longer," and the pose is the subject's preparation
for this entombment within the "no longer," the subject becoming "spec-
ter." The "click" of the camera's shutter may capture the subject as (dead)
object, but the pose anticipates and prepares for the transition from living
to lasting (as final, remaining index).[55] Craig Owens's important essay
"Posing" (1985) extends Barthes's argument in psychoanalytic terms to address the increasing number of artists throughout the 1980s and afterward
who employed the photograph and the pose to trouble notions of stable
identity, gender, and representation—artists like Cindy Sherman, Nikki S.
Lee, Eleanor Antin, and Adrian Piper, among many others. Owens contests
the still as sole possession of the photographic medium by attending to the
pose as a performed action prior to the "click" of the shutter. Mimicking
Barthes's first-person account of sitting for a photograph, he writes: "Still,
I freeze, as if anticipating the still I am about to become; mimicking its
opacity, its still-ness; inscribing, across the surface of my body, photography's 'mortification' of the flesh."[56] In performing the pose, one encounters
oneself as an object. However, Owens would suggest that this allows the
invisible and unrepresentable subject to come into being apart from his or
her fully constituted appearance.

   Much performance theory has found the notion of theater and photography's bind with death particularly compelling in conceptualizing liveness as loss and disappearance, and the pose clearly stands at the crossroads of these intersecting media. I do not deny the convincing nature of
much of the writing and art that has pursued this line of thought. However,
it would be mistaken to approach all performance as ontologically bound
solely to dead possibilities or all forms of stillness in performance as
trapped within the confines of the pose. In an argument that significantly
reconfigures the relationship between performance and the photographic
medium, Rebecca Schneider suggests that Barthes's interpretation of the
pose (as well as the body of performance theory that employs a similar
logic) unnecessarily privileges death as the primary force in the dyad of
presence and absence staged in the still. She argues against understanding
stillness as enthrallment to the past, and shows that the still image or pose
projects liveness into its future reception, where it lives again, or continues
to live. The images of Abu Ghraib, in her account, continued to live and ir-
rupt through their circulation and to require witnessing long after the
grisly and theatrical poses had been dismantled in the far reaches of Iraq.

Playing off the dual meanings of the word "still," she writes: "Thus the future subsists not only in the photographic moment of the shot, but in our complicities in encounter with the *still*, or *ongoing*, or live mode of return."[57] Thus, Schneider contests the common perception of the still and liveness as terms in opposition to one another and proposes that neither belongs solely to performance or photography, which both intermingle and circulate productively across media. It should be noted, however, that whatever live potentiality the still-posed image casts into the future, it is made available to the viewer who encounters it in the days to come. Like the generic potentiality of the infant, the image itself must await the arrival of another or the change in its own relationality in order to activate the potentiality of the exchange.

On the other hand, stillness is very much alive with potential in embodied performances that invoke the rhetoric of the pose to critique its tendency toward objectification. We might consider the Native American artist James Luna's performance *Artifact Piece* (1987), staged at the Museum of Man, San Diego, in which the artist lay still within a vitrine while dressed in a loincloth, his personal belongings and documents arrayed in adjacent glass cases, posing as if he were a specimen or object on display. Or his *Take a Picture with a Real Live Indian* (1993), where Luna offered to pose for photographs with visitors while dressed in costumes that confirmed or contested stereotypes about Native Americans. Both performances referenced practices of exhibiting Native peoples in Western museums and public spaces—live, dead, or via effigy—that originated under colonialist and imperialist regimes but which persist in diluted form today.[58] These performances and others that explicitly reference the history of the pose as a technology of control gather no small part of their disruptive power from the copresence of the live artist in the gallery space. Whether returning the direct gaze of the beholder, or just attentively present, such a live presence demands that the beholder acknowledge his or her participation in the circulation of forces that consign certain individuals to object-like status and allow others to disappear into disembodied spectatorship. Encountering "the artifact" in a present that is unavoidably activated by the prospect for change, we know that "the future subsists . . . in our complicities in encounter with the *still*, or *ongoing*, or live mode of return," a return that involves a history of subjugation and dehumanization that lives on. And yet, even as he dons the trappings of a stereotype, Luna is pointedly performing his capacity to escape such confines. Whatever possibilities we spectators attach to the pose are our own projections; Luna still retains his potential.

We can further clarify the distinction between the pose with its legible possibilities and stillness's access to potentiality in actual performance practice by looking at Russian director Vsevolod Meyerhold's grammar of theatrical action. Developed in the 1910s and 1920s as part of the approach to performance he termed "biomechanics," Meyerhold divided theatrical action into a three-part structure of *intention, realization,* and *reaction.* The third term referenced a kind of suspension of action between distinct intentions, a place of readjustment, of reorientation.[59] This suspension in action could be likened to the apex of a pendulum's swing, a kind of breath between two trajectories holding them together. Meyerhold termed these moments of stilled linkage *raccourci,* after the French word for "foreshortening," with the suggestion that the entirety of the previous and future action were somehow compressed into these transitional images. In the *raccourci,* one sees a line connecting the means of action toward its possible end (and possible beginning). The great film director Sergei Eisenstein, one of Meyerhold's students, turned this theory toward the cinematic and made this the basis for a further distinction between the *raccourci* and the *tableau vivant*'s pose: "A *raccourci* is the arrangement of the body for maximum expressiveness of the movement being mechanically made acute. A pose [as in the *tableau vivant*] has no relationship to the general movement, it is static, contained in itself and for itself, an end in itself, complete, nonutilitarian."[60] Building off of Eisenstein's suggestion, we may say that, as an instant's pause between two actions, the *raccourci* perfects the expression of a means toward an end outside itself (back to the action it completes and forward toward the conclusion of a future movement that it is just beginning). On the other hand, the pose is self-contained as an end in itself, an expression like the constative statement artificially removed from its context and frozen in the past. In the flash of an instant, the pose contains its possible end in itself—for Barthes the end of death—and is legible as such without further movement. But the nonobjective stillness of potentiality we have been describing requires a third term, one that does not orient itself toward an end either in itself (à la the pose) or outside of itself (à la the *raccourci*). We seek a means without an end.

GAGGING ON POTENTIALITY: GORDON, GOGO, WILDING, AND IVONA

> We are led to find a superior ease in the movements which can be foreseen, in the present attitudes in which future attitudes are pointed out and, as it were, prefigured. If jerky movements are wanting in grace, the reason is that each of

them is self-sufficient and does not announce those which
are to follow.

    —Henri Bergson[61]

How do I describe the way this body falls short of itself, how it insistently decomposes the edge of every motion? The young man balances on the outer sole's cusp or the knuckle of a protruding toe; he flutters between stances. The air around him is filled with a panic of gestures. Though seemingly sound of body, even fit and muscular, physical and psychological wounds have left this veteran from World War I unable to complete the simplest of actions: to stand, to sit. He occupies a space and time between ends.

In *10ms-1* (1994), video artist Douglas Gordon reworks archival medical footage of an unnamed soldier caught in his attempts to negotiate a body that refuses to let him stand upright.[62] And yet this incapacity to act also shows a capacity to do: all the space between the horizontal and the vertical becomes available to potential movement tragically bereft of the possibility of simple action. Slowed down and looped endlessly on itself, Gordon's video literally becomes a version of a means without end, the grim sight of a body in purgatory. Even after watching the video over and over several times, it is not clear what will come next in the man's gesticulations, how the logic of this time will play out. The ceaselessly struggling soldier exhibits the mediality of a motion, the interiority of an indeterminate action without consequence. In this respect he is not so far removed from patients suffering from Tourette's syndrome who, as described in Agamben's "Notes on Gesture," "can neither start nor complete the simplest of gestures . . . the whole musculature is engaged in a dance (*chorea*) that is completely independent of any ambulatory end."[63] What is this *gesture* but a suspension in motion? Not an action in suspension, or stopped, but a motion withheld from action's name; a suspension that moves, that "still-acts."

To arrive at an understanding of gesture, Agamben takes us on the philological tangent that I will recount here. In *On the Latin Language*, the Roman scholar Varro delineated a field of action between "making" (*facere*) and "acting" (*agere*), using the poet/playwright who makes the text, but does not act it, and the actor who acts a text, but does not make it, as examples. Varro derives these two terms from Aristotle's *poiesis* and *praxis*, respectively, as outlined in the *Nichomachean Ethics*: "For production [*poiesis*] has an end other than itself, but action [*praxis*] does not: good action is itself an end [in other words, the praxis itself is the entire end]."[64] In our sense, both pairs of terms—acting/*praxis* and making/*poiesis*—fall under the umbrella of the possible. This is because making/*poiesis* subsumes an action within a presupposed end or object that explains and outlines the movement from without. On the other hand, acting/*praxis* performs a predetermined role that in itself is prewritten; it makes of the subject a characterized object, a possible personality. The action, as Aristotle would have it, makes the man or woman.

Set against the pairing of *poiesis* (*facere*) and *praxis* (*agere*), Varro suggested a third term, exemplified in his text by the general or statesman who neither acts nor makes, but "carries on" or "supports" (*gerere*) a burden or responsibility. Agamben interprets this third term as the *gesture*:

> What characterizes gesture is that in it nothing is being produced or acted, but rather something is being endured and supported. . . . if producing is a means in view of an end and praxis is an end without means, the gesture then breaks with the false alternative between ends and means that paralyzes morality and presents instead means that, *as such*, evade the orbit of mediality without becoming, for this reason, ends.[65]

Gesture reveals a means without end, a pure mediation without external direction. One can hear the echo of the characterless messenger—the man without qualities of the classical tragedy as well as Bartleby of the mislaid letter—resounding in this appearance of a medium undisturbed by intention's inflection or listener's receipt. In other words, as one shoulders the faculty of doing or saying; one becomes the carrier of the ability to communicate. Gesture supports an experience as if it were a burden—something that both empowers the carrier and weighs heavily on him or her. Think of Coleridge's ancient mariner harrowed and hallowed by the experience that he alone has the capacity to relate. Or think of the soldier's body in *10ms-1* carrying the burden of its living motion while never arriving at an end or even defining itself in relation to a recognizable end.

We can also think through a related form of gesture at work in language, akin to the manner in which Richard Blackmur claims that "when the language of words fail us we resort to the language of gesture."[66] Elsewhere in his writing, Agamben finds an analogue for the gesture's suspension in poetic *enjambment*. Occupying a position that looks both forward and backward at once, enjambment asserts a line break in the midst of a single line of motion or thought, separating it from itself. Like Bartleby's formula, every instance of enjambment is the same (gap), but different in its feint away from its instantiated context of language. While Agamben does not make such a claim, it seems that the gesture thinks through a stillness that is neither a pose nor a frozen instant between actions (a la the *raccourci*), but a living pause vibrating and indefinite, where forward and backward lie endlessly in every direction. The gesture holds a hesitation in place, it mediates between places.[67]

In a proposal that offers a productive basis for the lived gesture, Agamben writes of how, when faced with a roughness at odds with the clear cuts of possible perception, the "inoperative" presents itself as an indigestible morsel that possibility cannot swallow—a *gag*. Characterized as such, gesture's potentiality no longer appears as the failed reaction to an active force, with a problematic negation at its root, but instead asserts its own positive presence as a visible behavior. Not a subsequent effect, it can be a beginning. Several valences of the word *gag* resonate here: (1) the material thing that withholds articulation (a piece of cloth that restricts the mouth); (2) the figure's articulation of a suspension of speech or breath (the "stutter"); and (3) in performance, the improvised comic routine as in a slapstick repetition or the many *lazzi* that Italian commedia dell'arte employed, in Agamben's understanding, to cover for a forgotten line or action. The last of these refers to a performance structure that traps the plot in a repetitive form that keeps time still while still moving in time.

In the same way that the gag occupies both a positive materiality (in its first sense) and denotes an absence (in its second) Henri Bergson writes:

> If the accomplishment of the act is arrested or thwarted by an obstacle, consciousness may reappear. [Consciousness] was there, but neutralized by the action which fulfilled and thereby filled the representation. The obstacle creates nothing positive; it simply makes a void, removes a stopper. This inadequacy of act to representation is precisely what we here call consciousness. . . . consciousness is the light that plays around the zone of possible actions or potential activity which surrounds the action really performed by the living being. It signifies hesitation or choice.[68]

Rather than projecting the future as a web of linear possibilities, true consciousness, in Bergson's terms, forms an undifferentiated zone or halo of futurity around the hesitating or stilled figure. This introduces a strange reversal of conventional thinking. As opposed to seeing the obstacle as a negation of a positive possibility, something that blocks and cancels its line of futurity, it is the possible action that is here portrayed as a "stopper." The obstacle removes or voids this possibility in order to reveal a potentiality that beams out like a light from an unshuttered lantern. At the moment of indecision, when the world starts from its expected path or in passive contemplation of this dislocated haze, consciousness asserts itself as potentiality.

Returning to the theatrical form, Alice Rayner sees something akin to a gestural burden that must be endured by Didi (Vladimir) and Gogo (Estragon) in Samuel Beckett's *Waiting for Godot* (1953). "The tragic suffering of Didi and Gogo is specifically related to a form of action in which suffering takes on its more archaic meaning in the sense of experiencing or letting something happen. To suffer is to bear the weight of experience—a weight that deforms and defines the particularity of an identity."[69] Throughout much of the drama, Didi and Gogo let actions play out their course upon or over their bodies. In these instances, as opposed to Varro's hypothetical general who shoulders the burden of his gesture as a means without end, the named action asserts itself upon the suffering figure and "deforms and defines the particularity of an identity"; without an intention of their own to define their character, Didi and Gogo acquire the action's identity. As in other works by Beckett, they literalize the manner in which a dramatic action disciplines the body of the performer and makes of him or her an object. The means becomes an end in itself and forecloses the future.

Yet there are also moments in *Waiting for Godot* where the action cannot be actualized as a named possibility because the world asserts itself differently, thrusts up an obstacle to prevent fulfillment of a preordained future action. The shoe does not fit, the pants do not stay up, the man cannot sit down. With the failure to complete an action the machine of possibilities breaks down and the figure is left midair: there Pozzo stands hovering over a stool he cannot access, desperately hoping someone will return to script and ask him to sit down. The action appears as a means onto itself without hope of end; it becomes a burden to carry.[70] "Nothing to be done" is the refrain the two tramps pass back and forth: no point of arrival, no acceptable response, no name to the doing at hand that must be done.

In *Waiting for Godot*, then, the gesture appears as a scripted routine, a *gag* in all its varied senses. The moments where Beckett's characters try to negotiate a world at odds with their possibilities play out as vaudeville acts and draw attention to the fact that such routines represent a means laboring to find an end. If the comic routine is an exposure of a means, it is only insofar as it tries to set in motion possibilities that have been disrupted by the gasp/gag of laughter or the forgetful actor. (It is worth noting that the actor who forgets his or her lines is referred to as the "corpsing" actor, as if to once more reassert stillness as a dead end rather than as a productive disruption in the dramatic order of scripted actions.) The routine is a framed habit that jump-starts action when it has stalled. Beckett's characters thus find their way back into the possible, usually through a humorous return to mechanistic behavior, but in each instance a hesitation overflows the edges of the dramatic fabric. Set against the thesis of Bergson's famous essay on *Laughter*, where the philosopher argues that humor results from recognizing the mechanistic behavior of a world and its characters, we see that the vaudeville *gag* excessively attempts to reassert possibility to cover over an otherwise gaping hole of potentiality. An actor keeps slipping on the same banana peel (recall *Krapp's Last Tape*) as he replays a possible response to the potentiality of the accident.

Beckett's characters have their momentary gag when the world breaks from possibility, but they soon return to the task at hand or play out a routine to staunch potentiality. They circle through a routine until, like some well-worn cog slipping by on a spinning gear, something catches and they can move a possibility forward a little further. *Waiting for Godot* is essentially an engine of possibility that keeps stalling out, working its way in short gasps and starts across the wide expanse of the future. All of which leads us to the question: how does one sustain the dislocation of the gesture, of the gag? Does the gag only appear as a flash or flicker of unassimilated potentiality within the regular flow of representational speech?[71]

The overtly performative version of the gag as routine plays out as a moving "still-act," repairing the damage done to an ends-based order of representation. Yet the first two senses of the "gag"—as a material object that blocks the mouth and as the subject's active expression (or lack thereof) when confronted with that object—fold back on each other to form another kind of performance that could be called a gesture of stillness. One gags on a gag in much the same way that one thinks thought or makes doing a thing done. Subject and object join to become one endless network or circular relation; nothing to be done or resolved except in its cessation or release. The gag gets stuck in a rut, it stutters on itself. Before routine restarts the engine and has us moving again in a familiar direction, the gag takes possession of the body against the subject's will. We might think of Théron's dance catching on the massive obstacle of the rabbit like a gag in the wide maw of the theater. To remain in this gag is to let a halo stream out from the stilled interruption, projecting its light in the present and outward toward some future to come where a motion, a sound, will begin a progressive time once more.

Writ large, waiting, too, is a kind of gag in time, a hesitation to begin in earnest that may be sustained indefinitely. On one hand, the uncertainty of Godot's identity, and whether or not he, she, or it will arrive, frees the tramps from a definite end. On the other hand, this Godot damns them to

a life determined in relation to a distant other, an absence enacting its oppressive power from afar. In her 1972 performance *Waiting*, the artist Faith
Wilding presents a similarly ambivalent case of suspended time. She sits in
a chair rocking back and forth, repeatedly declaring herself "waiting" for
various events in the normative lifeline expected of a heterosexual American woman. The text spoken begins:

> Waiting . . . waiting . . . waiting . . .
> Waiting for someone to come in
> Waiting for someone to hold me
> Waiting for someone to feed me
> Waiting for someone to change my diaper.[72]

The videotape of the performance shows Wilding sitting on a chair draped
in red, a setting recalling the presentational frame of a plinth or a theatrical
curtain. She is like a character out of Beckett, isolated in the fact of being
seen. Indeed, Wilding was inspired by Beckett's *Happy Days* (1961) and its
earthbound Winnie passing her time in quotidian drudgery, and the performance presages the playwright's *Rockaby* (1980) with its lone woman in
a rocking chair passing back and forth, in and out of light, in and out of
sight.[73] But Wilding is not in the darkened abyss of the theatrical space as
Beckett would have placed her; she sits in the well-lit living room of Womanhouse, the feminist installation space where the piece was originally
staged, in public view of an attentive audience of women.

Are they witnessing her becoming a particular kind of woman, narrowing her future into the most circumscribed of courses? She is presumed to
exist only in relation to these many expectations, most often configured
around an impending male presence ("waiting to wear makeup . . . waiting
for him to tell me I'm beautiful . . . waiting for my wedding day"), without
ever seeming to occupy a place in the present. This tragic interpretation of
the piece is in line with the second-wave feminist critiques shown and performed at Womanhouse and yet, in waiting for the thing or event, she is not
doing the action: she is living in the meantime. Judith/Jack Halberstam has
read Wilding's performance alongside Yoko Ono's *Cut Piece* as an act of
"radical passivity" that amounts to "an anti-social way out of the double
bind of becoming woman and thereby propping up the dominance of man
within a gender binary."[74] Wilding's text may enumerate specific predict-
able futures in her prospective biography, but each of these named possibilities is preceded and occluded by the affirmation of the present "waiting" into the future. Such a waiting takes up the time-space between what

is now and what one would prefer not to do or become. It prefers not to acquiesce to whatever it names—or, rather, whatever society names. This is the "anti-social way out" that the piece enacts à la Bartleby, not by relying on reactionary defiance but by waiting out its claims on the subject. Wilding's many expected courses keep stalling or gagging on the word "waiting." It is a gesture that is both physically embodied in its stuttering back and forth motion and verbally stated with rhythmic insistence. Putting weight on the waiting, the meantime rather than the end, Wilding's performance might be read as her announcement of a preference not to arrive.

The fact that this waiting is both done and said at the same time deserves attention. For tellingly, much more than the stoppage of living breath, of the living body, Agamben's gag is a stoppage of speech. The gesture ultimately returns us to a preconceived linguistic community by displaying the potentiality for language without the instantiation of an actual statement. This is confirmed by the conclusion of "Notes on Gesture," which defines gesture as the

> communication of a communicability. It has precisely nothing to say because what it shows is the being-in-language of human beings as pure mediality. However, because being-in-language is not something that could be said in sentences, the gesture is *essentially always a gesture of not being able to figure something out in language.*[75]

In spite of the seeming corporeality of the "gesture," then, the gag always references an obstruction in the linguistic means to an end, once again returning to the question of an utterance. Even if it is a physical motion, its suspense is one of the speech act only, of the performative wrestling with its own impossibility to articulate motion. It takes place on a ground already prepared for speech, in which speech is already a possibility, even if that possibility belongs more to the observer than to the one who gags. For, while Agamben does not say as much, the gag only acquires meaning from the witness of another, or from the speech that returns after the gasp. The potentiality of such a figure always refers back to the question of the human, to the community that can speak on its behalf. This is particularly evident in Agamben's reading of Primo Levi's story of the child Hurbinak. In his harrowing account of his time in the extermination camps of World War II, Levi tells of a lone child encountered after the camps were liberated who could only speak the word "Hurbinak," over and over again. None of the other prisoners could determine what the word meant, whether it referred to the child himself or belonged to some lost language. None knew the origin of the child, and it soon died, only living on through the witnessing of Levi himself. The word "Hurbinak" stands as a gag in language, the expression of an impossibility of expression, but only for Levi as witness. The child itself did not possess the capability for speech.[76]

Taking a more literal tack and seeing the gag as the stoppage of voice or breath, we find what could be called a gestural force at work in silent characters that appear throughout the dramatic tradition. Preferring not to speak in a world that relies on the dialogic to build the kinds of architecture described in the previous chapter, we keep waiting for these occasional figures to speak, and when they do, we expect their voicings to carry significance far beyond the mundane. To return to *Godot*, there is the silent Lucky who delivers upon this promise when he finally lets loose the torrential flood of his pent-up thought. In the earliest moments of the Western dramatic canon, one might think of Cassandra's silent presence in Aeschylus's *Agamemnon*, when the captive prophetess appears but says nothing for more than two hundred lines of text. As a number of classicists have written, her divine ability to speak the future makes this gag an increasingly powerful deferral.[77] Or, later in the trilogy, consider the disturbingly silent friend of Orestes, Pylades, who says nothing throughout *The Libation Bearers*, until Orestes falters before the matricide of Clytemnestra. Pylades's short three-line reminder that the murderous deed is the will of the gods spurs his friend on not only because it references a divine purpose, but because the gathered potentiality of his silence has invested this one enunciation with an almost superhuman power. It is not coincidental, then, that both of these temporarily silent characters do in fact act as vessels for divine power. In plays where, apart from the mass of the chorus, at most three characters would be onstage at one time, the presence of a silent figure may obtain a significant potentiality.

Witold Gombrowicz's play *Princess Ivona* (written in 1934–1935, first performed in 1957) cuts to the heart of the gag's uncanny power in the dramatic medium.[78] The prince of the realm becomes fascinated with the commoner Ivona, in part because she is alleged to be extraordinarily homely, but more pointedly because she does not speak a word in response to any entreaty or cruelty directed her way. (The original version of the text had Ivona speaking twenty-five short lines, but Gombrowicz progressively cut her lines in subsequent versions until she was rendered completely mute. This textual genealogy reminds us that however silent she may be at present in whatever production, the character can speak.)[79] Some distant cousin to Bartleby, Ivona's impassiveness inspires the most atrocious behavior from the royal family and court as they explore all possible provocations to force a response.

As the prince puts it, "One can do whatever one likes with her." Each in turn begins to believe her the sole witness to his most denigrating secret, her silence some attestation to a profound power to know made more manifest by her preference not to reveal herself. The other characters see their own transgressions figured on the blank surface of her silence: Ivona becomes a kind of veiled theater withholding the spectacle of the King's rape and the subsequent death of a young woman many years ago; the withheld recitation of the Queen's terrible private poetry, and so on.

Psychological drama often relies upon the spoken revelation of a secret past to arrive at its future end (Chekhov's gun transubstantiated into a traumatic event). While Oedipus's revelation of his identity offers a template for this shaping of time, the nineteenth- and twentieth-century inheritors of such an analytical structure were often women "with a past," a past that dictated a future resolution to their troubles that the play sought to supply. Elin Diamond has convincingly shown how this directly relates to the coeval development of psychoanalysis such that psychological realism stages the analyst/analysand relationship in casting the audience as the silent analyst, listening as the analysand recounts her past. A paternal male character often acts as the audience's surrogate, inquiring into the hysterical female character's past. In this system of representation there is, to quote psychoanalyst Sarah Kofman, "no crime worse than silence, for it covers woman's sex with its 'thick veil,' renders it inaccessible, indomitable, implacable."[80] The silent character frustrates this contract with every unanswered question and reverses its attention; like Bartleby before the narrator's analysis, her preference not-to asks the inquirer what he would prefer to do. We will return to this matter in the next chapter.

In Gombrowicz's play, the entire operation of the kingdom, the assurance of role and reign, stalls upon the princess's silence. According to the prince, they "speak in order to not let her silence speak." Eventually the King and his councilor decide that the only solution to the standoff is to murder Ivona—not by committing some violent action themselves, but by *letting* her choke to death. As if cognizant of theories of tragedy that warn of the contagious nature of violence, they choose to expose her to death rather than actively force it upon her; they abandon her as Oedipus was abandoned on the mountain of Cithearon, as Antigone was entombed within a sealed cave to waste away. They resolve that her secret silence, so rich with their own pasts, will be made to last. Though Ivona will die, in a very real way she will be buried alive, with her potential to reveal all veiled for eternity. At the great banquet concluding the play, they need merely suggest that she be careful not to choke on the bones of the pike she is eat-ing and suddenly the princess seizes up, gagging her way to the grave. If this were an Ibsenite psychological drama, the silence would have been the symptom of some trauma that the course of the play would reveal. All the other characters fear that their transgressions are indeed the inassimilable kernel upon which Ivona gags throughout the play. By suggesting that this indigestible event is literally a gag—the mundane accident of a bone in the throat—they stop up the many futures she could reveal; providing her with an action that explains her silence ("to choke"), they direct her toward an end. The play, too, concludes almost immediately after Ivona's death with a solemn ceremony as, like the tragic hero of old, the princess is sacrificed to heal the corrupt nation-state and restore social equilibrium. The bone in the throat has provided a possible cause for Ivona's silence and a possible future in which she continues to say nothing.

With Beckett's play, we witness the figure's endurance of a gesture as his suffering before an impersonal world, a world that will neither deliver a properly functioning shoe nor the long-awaited Godot. Bartleby's realm of dead letters, suspended in their secrecy as written gestures, lends itself to a similarly bleak outlook. The dead letters, those messengers without recipients, that come to represent the scrivener have "forgotten their goal" and are now lost in transit and lost to the world. It is this forlorn consignment that allows the narrator to indulge in what he sees as noble Christian pity befitting the tragic idiom, and allows him the cathartic release at the end of the tale that he portrays: "Ah, Bartleby! Ah, Humanity!"

But perhaps it is the audience's faith in, and desire for, the dramatic form and its subsequent disappointment that contributes to whatever tragic suffering we might find in a play like *Waiting for Godot*. After all, Didi and Gogo do momentarily call themselves "happy" and only rediscover their despondent predicament when they ask, "What do we do now, now that we are happy?"[81] In other words, it is only in the demand that they reassert a need for *what* may be a possible end that they discover their disappointment—a demand placed on them by the presence of an audience requiring an event. Otherwise, they might persist in the nirvana of doing happily but not needing to do *something*. Ivona, too, seems perfectly content in her silent state; it is the court full of spectators that finds her gagging so unsettling. The many ends of Wilding's waiting are scripted by the society that interpellates her. And perhaps it is not Bartleby himself but the narrator of *Bartleby* who casts a pall over the office scene. Perhaps the frustration of the lawyer's faith in the literary-historical form and of his desire for a self-righteous "humanity" projects a larger unhappiness across Wall

Street. Who can say what Bartleby does on the other side of the office screen? Who can say how bright his halo glows? We, the audience, are still on this side of the narrator's telling or this side of the proscenium arch, listening to one possible story or watching another possible dramatic event. We want the gag released and some definition to our future.

In other words, the role of the audience or author facing potentiality remains a provocative worry. Through the form of the solo dance Didier Théron conducts what he describes as an experiment upon himself and upon his own field of subjectivity that supersedes any relationship with or for an audience.[82] In the *Bartleby* piece, the dancer encounters his own potentiality and we, the audience, only regard the appearance of such an exposure. Aren't we forced to play out the role of the narrator in Melville's story, endlessly attempting to access the inscrutable motion of the figure before us, to translate it into our own parameters of possibility? As long as I see that other subject as a discrete human likeness, beholden to my own sense of possibility and as a being-(already)-in-language, I can only approach such experimentation from without, wondering alongside our man of the Law how to write or speak of this life that refuses all actions. This is to say that the private lived experience of potentiality, which is revealed in the gesture's dislocation of means from ends, differs from the experience of observing another body performing the gesture. Agamben's potentiality always shows itself to a human observer who—no stilled dancer him- or herself, no Bartleby in waiting—remains bound to the possible and configures the stilled in reference to his or her own possibilities.

In the next chapter, I will look beyond the limits of the audience as observer of the potential, to see if an encounter with potentiality can bleed over the lip of the stage that divides seer from seen, doer from done, and infect the viewer, all the while attending to the consequences of such a meeting. In order to do so, one must overstep the bounds of the (human) figure and its utilities. One must eradicate the line between audience and actor and step into the white cube of the gallery to stage an encounter with one's own potentiality.

FOUR | # Beholding Potentiality

Whoever fights monsters should see to it that in the process
he does not himself become a monster. When you look long
into an abyss, the abyss also looks back into you.
—Friedrich Nietzsche[1]

The following is a "prologue" from an unwritten TV
"spectacular" called *The Tribulations of Michael Fried*.
—Robert Smithson[2]

Who am I to witness or write of potentiality and its many futures? Who can
look long into the abyss without becoming a monster, a fool, or a caricature?
    Consider once more how the stilled stance and formulaic statements of
the eponymous copyist from Melville's "Bartleby the Scrivener" produced
a peculiar effect upon the lawyer telling his story, how they, to repeat the
narrator's words, "disarmed me and unmanned me" (16). However histrionic such a claim may be, the dismemberment and dehumanization (or,
alternatively, emasculation) described here refer to a significant suppres-
sion of the actionable: a tool carries no use and no possibility to one deprived of hand or arm, to one deprived of a human conceptualization of
utility. Bartleby's exhibition of potentiality, his announcement of a preference not to do dismantles possibility and reflects all such expected futures
back upon the human subject who encounters it. Here and throughout
"Bartleby the Scrivener," the exaggerated self-dramatization of the lawyer
reveals the importance of his own role in the performance of the narrative.
This chapter will show how contact with a life suspending its potentiality—a life withholding and displaying its capacity to perform without acting upon such a capacity—can provoke the beholding subject to perform
him- or herself, to take the stage while that obdurate other seems to look
on. To put it somewhat differently, I will look at how the potential object
becomes an audience facing the beholding subject.

Before doing so let me look a little more closely at Melville's story, but this time turning away from the obtuse scrivener to observe the figure of the narrator. Throughout "Bartleby the Scrivener" the narrator variously tries to engage the copyist through the terms of what I have been calling possibility, in socially formulaic behavior played according to the rules of what Wittgenstein would call "language games."[3] As the previous chapters have discussed, possibility projects a network of representable actions forward in time, taming the future's unruly indeterminacy into a set of predetermined paths toward predetermined ends. In Melville's story, the narrator weighs the merits of each available gambit in relation to an expected response that, of course, Bartleby does not offer up.[4] As a result, he is driven to produce actions himself in order to incite a reaction on the part of his subordinate. After one of Bartleby's preferences not to, for example, the lawyer invests his response with an accompanying display of unspoken emotional significance: "'Very good, Bartleby,' said I, in a quiet sort of serenely severe self-possessed tone, intimating the unalterable purpose of some terrible retribution very close at hand" (14). Elsewhere his passion overcomes this performance of restrained aggression: "'Will you, or will you not, quit me?' I now demanded in a sudden passion, advancing close to him" (24). Beyond these and similar examples, there are also moments when the narrator explicitly indulges in sentimental outbursts of pity or humility, culminating in his cry "Ah, Bartleby! Ah, Humanity!" (34).

These performances become increasingly melodramatic as the story progresses, provoking the otherwise mild-mannered lawyer to indulge in the extremities of expression. They reach a climax of sorts when the lawyer recognizes himself on the verge of committing a "fatal act" against his placid subordinate: "I was now in such a state of nervous resentment that I thought it but prudent to check myself at present from further demonstrations" (24–25). Note the fact that the lawyer refers to his expressions as a form of display ("demonstrations") as if watching his own behavior unfolding from a theatrical distance, his double performing up on stage. His attempts at instigating a response inevitably act upon the lawyer himself, setting in motion a vicious cycle of action and reaction centered upon his own personage that accumulates to excessive proportions. By instituting an action with "feedback," he inspires his own hysterical performance. If Bartleby refuses to perform, then the lawyer comes to compensate for what he sees as an "increasing" lack of action. In fact, the narrator only manages to enforce a separation from his employee by actively deciding to move his offices elsewhere:

"Stationary you shall be then," I cried, now losing all patience, and for the first time in all my exasperating connection with him fairly flying into a passion. "If you do not go away from these premises before night, I shall feel bound—indeed I am bound—to—to—to quit the premises myself!" I rather absurdly concluded, knowing not with what possible threat to try to frighten his immobility into compliance. (30)

The narrator has reached the limits of all "possible threat" and, quite "absurdly," all logical causality. Rather than forcing the "stationary" figure to remove himself from the space, he removes the space from the figure. Or rather, he performs the action that he desires of his companion.

Taken together, these demonstrations of the narrator offer a peculiar image of the subject beholding a figure of potentiality. The beholder is forced to produce action upon action in order to find a response or future possibility in the object of attention that will confirm his or her own action's ends. The narrator, in essence, must confront the question: If that other will not acknowledge my actions as possibilities (as defined future end points), then how am I to know my possibilities, to recognize myself? Otherwise, I, too, risk falling into the abyss of potentiality. The narrator in Melville's story, for example, recognizes Bartleby's affect spilling over into his surroundings when that odd word "prefer" begins to surreptitiously and inadvertently insert itself in the office life and into his own speech; even when merely added as supplement to a statement—as when the narrator states, "Mr. Nippers, I would prefer that you withdraw" (20)—it casts a shadow of hesitation before the most resolute action.[5] These hesitations could accumulate to become Beckettian gags or stutters, preventing a means from ever reaching its end; one could "prefer to prefer to prefer . . ." ad infinitum. As Nietzsche writes in *Beyond Good and Evil*: "Whoever fights monsters should see to it that in the process he does not himself become a monster. When you look long into an abyss, the abyss also looks back into you."[6] In facing the abyss of the potential, the beholder confronts his or her own potentiality to act or to see. One encounters and, in turn, becomes an abyss without objects or orientations. The behavior of the narrator is emblematic of an audience unwilling to depart from the shores of humanity and descend into common indifferentiation, desperately grappling for footholds and handholds of possibility. He seeks some future place to anchor his action's resolution and thus project a consistent subjectivity forward in time.

In this context, the narrator's endless and increasingly frantic actions are guided by a need to confirm the humanity common to Bartleby and himself, for the scrivener's refusal to abide by social convention problematizes the humanity of both characters. In order to combat this threat to his very personhood, the lawyer sets out to assert his humanity in two senses. First, he attempts to reclaim the system of social and economic relations that he understands as expected and acceptable human behavior. These possibilities are determined by various overlapping unspoken codes of conduct or language games based on office hierarchy (informed by position, tenure, and the like), conventions of the trade (as he puts it, "To comply as far as may be with the usages of this office" [19]), and codes of civil gentlemanly exchange more broadly conceived. Second, in an ethical register, this assertion of humanity attempts to confirm a Christian sense of responsibility toward a lacking other. It is this second interest in humanity-as-humane-behavior that inspires the imagined dramatic monologue that the lawyer performs for himself intermittently throughout the story. In order to affirm that his approach is reasonable, the attorney refers to and relies upon the writings of the eighteenth-century American theologian Jonathan Edwards and the subsequent writings of Joseph Priestley (apart from the businessman John Jacob Astor, the only references to personages who exist outside the fictional world of the text) and their conception of rational expectation. Of particular interest is Edwards's theory of assumptions as outlined in his most popular work, *Freedom of the Will* (1754), a text that repeatedly contests the meaning of the word "preference."[7]

The reference holds significance not only as a frame for the narrator's understanding of the ethics of the social contract, but also in relationship to the larger story I hope to tell here. Jonathan Edwards was one of the leading Protestant thinkers of early America and arguably the greatest philosophical theologian in the history of the United States. His formative encounter with the empiricism of Locke and Newton at a very early age inspired among other ideas a reconceptualization of action and the notion of the will. In this regard Edwards's revision and extension of his predecessors is of great interest to our project of determining potentiality. As Branka Arsić writes in her investigation of the connection between the theologian and Melville's story,

The will, says Edwards, is the power of acting, the power of actualization of the potentiality to act. The will is always faced with at least two possibilities but prefers one. Thus, being the power to elect one thing rather than another the will is, in each of its acts of preferences, both the power of affirmation and the power of negation.[8]

This does not diverge greatly from Locke's conception of the will, except that for the earlier British empiricist, a slight but significant difference splits the will from the preference: one may prefer that which one cannot will and one may will that which one may not prefer. For Locke, preference or desire interjects itself as another force between the will and the act, complicating any attempts to determine the authentic intention behind an action or lack of action. Edwards, reading Locke on the other side of the Atlantic and from within a theological frame that required authentic belief/conviction behind prayer or "good action," sets out to eradicate the difference between the preference and the will. He claims that the one is identical to the other: the preference is the will is the enactment.[9] In Edwards's phrasing: "The very willing is the doing; when once he has willed, the thing is performed."[10] According to this most wide-ranging conception of the performative, all thought, all willing, and all action are always already actualized. To say or to think is to do. In order to contend with the problem of the still body or body in repose—the figure who, as I argued in the previous chapter, embodies the potentiality of his or her field of (in)action—Edwards deems perception itself as an action of the will. Since one cannot elect to survey a scene all at once, the moment of perception as a selective attendance to sensation is itself an actualization with no space for preference between one glance of an eye and the next. A lustful glance is tantamount to a lustful action. Arsić explains that the attorney, inspired by Edwards, reads Bartleby's "preference not-to" as an active decision to resist, a willed refusal to act rather than a suspension of willing.

This notion of the will derives directly from the theories of potentiality and actuality that we have discussed heretofore. In *The Philosophical Theology of Jonathan Edwards*, Sang Hyun Lee describes how the central ordering principle in Edwards's ontology, habit, is inspired by a reconceptualization of Aristotelian metaphysics. Remember that Aristotle distinguishes between two manifestations of potentiality: generic potentiality and existing potentiality. We speak of the former when we say that an infant could become a pianist (requiring any number of changes or passages of time before actualization); we speak of the latter when we say that a pianist can decide to play the piano (a presently possessed capacity that could be actualized at any moment—as long as a piano is available). Edwards reinforces and redefines this second sense of potentiality, existing potentiality, as the law of nature by casting its tendency to become as a *necessity* to become. He calls this operating principle habit. Habit is a "real possibility" in that, even if it has not yet been realized, it "would *certainly* be realized if certain conditions are met. On the basis of such a tendency, one *predicts* that a certain event would occur if certain conditions are met."[11] It may sound ludicrous, but if one has the habit of playing the piano, one cannot choose to do otherwise once seated at a piano. We can see how readily (and, in its strict interpretation, absurdly) this affirms the sense of an immutable character or set of qualities attendant to an individual, the damned habitually willing to do wrong, the righteous habitually willing to do right.[12] We can also see how, by removing the element of choice or preference from the category of the potential, Edwards has converted it into a form of strict possibility. Even if it has not yet been actualized, habit exists halfway between actuality and potentiality, virtually in the world as a real expectation; it predetermines the future in exactly the same fashion as possibility. The habitual can always be interrupted through miraculous intervention, but God alone possesses true potentiality to do and not to do.

Edwards's theory may seem to solve the "problem" of the figure suspended in potentiality by transforming him or her into a subject enacting a willed actualization, but this same figure also opens an irreparable rift in the fabric of the theologian's plan of a coherent world. For woven into Edwards's notion of the will is the assumption that two wills exposed to rational argumentation will operate in agreement, willing a commonly understood good. The willing subject always determines his or her future actions according to prior events, cleaving rigidly to the best of possibilities. Accordingly, a strict form of causality based on common assumptions emerges for the human subject and his or her community; there is no room for a will that contradicts this common sense. Likewise, there is no space for accident in a world in which every action is willed.[13]

The fact that Bartleby's behavior departs from the ground of assumptions, then, undermines the entire picture of consistent causal relations that Edwards advocates. The threat such a disruption poses to the ethical and theological groundings of the rational human subject perhaps begins to explain why the narrator's response takes on such a zealous—nearly religious—tenor. Melville's performance, however suggestive in regards to this matter, is a fictive enterprise akin to the narrative account of a performance. In order to more fully comprehend the workings of the potential figure's effect on an audience, we need to look toward an account of an actual encounter with such a form.

MINIMALISM: A THEATER FOR THE OBDURATE MASSES

Michael Fried's Disappearing Beholder

In what may initially seem a mere coincidence, Edwards's writings also serve as significant inspiration for the art critic and historian Michael

Fried's famous 1967 essay on minimal art, "Art and Objecthood." Fried's text opens with an epigraph that borrows from Edwards's description of divine presentness, according to which a comprehensive and complete view of the world is made visible in an instant, and concludes with a similar call to a transcendental present as the goal for all "serious" and "advanced" art. In the interceding pages, the art critic outlines an attack on minimalism, a loosely defined movement of work from the mid-sixties concerned with reducing or purifying sculpture to a prime or essential form (a definition that, as we will see below, is unsatisfactory for a host of reasons). Above all else, Fried's polemic depends upon the relationship that such work establishes with its viewers, or, as he terms them, "beholders." Where the modernist painting and sculpture that Fried champions here and in his contemporaneous art criticism seek to eradicate the presence of the beholder, to subsume his or her presence under the influence of the artwork, the minimal (or "literal," in Fried's preferred terminology) stages its objecthood to foreground the beholder as a subject in time and space in a manner that he derisively terms "theatrical." This conflict of effects prompted Fried to famously claim that "the literalist espousal of objecthood amounts to nothing other than a plea for a new genre of theater, and theater is now the negation of art," or, in an even more inflammatory manner, that "theater and theatricality are at war today, not simply with modernist painting (or modernist painting and sculpture) but with art as such."[14]

Since its publication a substantial body of critical response has variously contended with the argument of "Art and Objecthood," but it is generally agreed that Fried's articulation, while casting minimalism as a negative development from high modernist art, nonetheless signals some of the movement's essential characteristics.[15] Indeed, the tendency toward time-based, intermedia art centered upon the experience of the beholder that Fried collectively names "theatricality" would characterize much of the art of the following decades and arguably represents minimalism's greatest impact on subsequent postminimal movements or approaches to art making (including earth art, conceptual art, and installation art, to name a few). It is beyond the scope or purpose of this chapter to explicate the larger debate around Fried's essay, a book-length endeavor in its own right, as is the complicated unraveling of the knotty concept of "minimalism." Both are matters that others have considered eloquently and effectively.[16] Rather, over the following pages I will show how the issues that Fried sees at work in his notion of the minimal object bear a striking resemblance to the effects of potentiality. Moreover, it is the exaggerated, even melodramatic, response of the critic to these works of art that will ultimately serve as the focus for our consideration. Here we find a more theoretically self-aware reading of the confrontation with potentiality than Melville's story. I mean "theoretically" in two senses: first, to signal a concern with conceptual operations and, second, to acknowledge the hypothetical nature of such a claim to self-consciousness, for we will see how it also masks a certain blind spot in the critic's engagement with the work of art. Fried's histrionic tone did not escape the attention of previous readers, many of whom were affronted by the moralistic register employed by the critic. But, in a letter to the editors of *Artforum* soon after their publication of Fried's essay, the conceptual artist Robert Smithson took a more playful stance, stating that "in a manner worthy of the most fanatical puritan, [Fried] provides the art world with a long-overdue spectacle," a spectacle in which the art critic himself is the starring player.[17] It is this performance that I want to draw out over the following pages.[18]

But first let me circumscribe this endeavor even more clearly. As Richard Meyer has convincingly argued in his historical overview of the movement, *Minimalism: Art and Polemics in the Sixties*, minimalism does not offer up a consensus definition or canon so much as a multitude of variously related practices and critical conceptions that at the time established themselves in relation (often in contradistinction) to one another; a "field of differences" in Meyer's phrasing.[19] More pointedly, the minimalism that Fried attacks in his essay as "literalism" exemplifies only one such selective and subjective definition; for example, it amalgamates explicitly opposing projects like those of the artists Donald Judd and Robert Morris into a single body of work, based on pseudo-morphic similarities between their work but disregarding diverging theoretical claims by the artists themselves. Furthermore, the essay focuses almost exclusively on minimal work that exhibits a unified singular wholeness—in Morris' words a *gestalt*—while ignoring the broad range of work also termed minimalism that explored multiplicity, illusionism, and other qualities.[20] Long since canonized and ensconced in museums around the world, these artworks may not confront the beholder in the quite the same manner after years of familiarity. In order to retain the impression that the affects at issue stem from a historically specific response to a subset of minimalist artwork, I will henceforth employ Fried's term "literalism" throughout this chapter when referring to the work as read by the art critic and his preferred term, "beholder," when speaking of the relationship between a subject and the literal object such a concept entails.

To appreciate more fully the issues at stake in this notion of theatricality, it is important not to read "Art and Objecthood" in isolation from the author's larger oeuvre, even if much of this work follows the publication of the 1967 essay. Most glaringly from our perspective, a great frustration for theater and performance scholars encountering Fried's "Art and Object-hood" on its own is that he never clarifies *which* theater he means by "the-atricality."[21] Fried, himself, supplies an answer in an oblique manner through his other texts. As opposed to Fried's art criticism that focuses on contemporary artwork and treats the theater as an ahistorical unified entity, his subsequent art historical texts occasionally (but only occasionally) frame this characterization of theatricality as a particular aspect of performance, dependent on particular modes of production, that in no way remains constant throughout history.[22]

Soon after the publication of "Art and Objecthood" in 1967, Fried would devote nearly all his attention to an extensive art historical investigation into the origins of modern painting in eighteenth- and nineteenth-century France, a project that stretches over three main volumes—*Absorption and Theatricality: Painting and Beholder in the Age of Diderot* (1980), *Courbet's Realism* (1990), and *Manet's Modernism: or the Face of Painting in the 1860s* (1996). It was as if the performance "Art and Objecthood" had completely exhausted him and his involvement in the contemporary scene; he would retire from the stage. Apart from occasional articles on select contemporary artists, Fried focused on this earlier chapter of art history until the publication at the end of 2008 of a full-length study on photography from the 1960s onward. Through all of these texts, Fried has sought to establish the binary of theatricality/antitheatricality and their divergent relationship to the beholder as foundational to much painting leading up to the beginning of modernism in the late nineteenth century and beyond.[23]

Beginning with *Absorption and Theatricality*, the first of these volumes, Fried directs our attention to certain French painters and contemporaneous art critics from the middle of the eighteenth century who began to privilege work aimed at defeating theatricality. In the simplest terms, here and throughout the rest of Fried's art historical oeuvre, theatricality implies an "awareness of being beheld."[24] Much of the painting from the rococo period established a theatrical relationship with the beholder by indexically recognizing his or her presence before the canvas, usually by depicting a direct gaze crossing the bounds of the painted world and meeting the gaze of the beholder. Beginning in the 1730s and becoming a widely approved approach to painting by the salons of the 1750s, painters like Jean-Baptiste-Siméon Chardin and Jean-Baptiste Greuze "defeated" this awareness of being beheld by presenting figures "absorbed" in a task and oblivious to all around them both within and without the painted world. A boy is shown building a castle

Fig. 2. Jean-Baptiste-Siméon Chardin (1699–1779), *Boy Building a Castle of Cards*. Oil on canvas. Galleria degli Uffizi, Florence, Italy. Bridgeman Images.

out of cards, another blows a soap bubble from a straw or tube, while many other paintings depict figures engrossed in the act of reading a book, even painting a canvas. Such work achieved what Fried calls "the supreme fiction that the beholder did not exist," supreme in that painting ontologically relies upon a frontal engagement with the beholder; it needs him or her to look it in the eye, even as it pretends to remain unseen.[25]

This absorptive quality was not only apparent in portraiture. On a different scale, the painted tableaux of the period presented groups of figures absorbed in events, multiplying the singular figures from Chardin's domestic scenes, engrossed in their solitary games or actions, to a much larger gathering of individuals. In these paintings a group of people collectively attend to an orator or event, and the pull of this internal draw is palpable across the surface of the canvas; for example, Greuze's *La Piété filiale* from the salon of 1763 depicts an old man on his deathbed with several generations of his family gathered around him, all directing their attention (and the beholder's) inward; even a pair of dogs in the corner of the canvas seem fixated on the scene of the ailing patriarch.[26] The tableau stages a stillness that reveals causality's chain by encapsulating both prior action and future action in a single comprehensive view. Such stillness strongly resembles the 'breath" between two actions that Meyerhold calls the *raccourci* (discussed in the previous chapter). In Greuze's painting, it is, perhaps, the ailing man's dying breath that the tableau holds in perpetuity.

In order to show that this is not merely a theory arrived at in retrospect, Fried relies on a selection of art criticism from the 1750s and 1760s, focusing on the French philosopher and art critic Denis Diderot's writings both on the theater of the period and on the salons in which many of these paintings made their first public appearance.[27] Much to Diderot's chagrin, the theater of his time approached the proscenium frame as a porous threshold, indicating the presence of its audience in much the same way as nonabsorptive painting indicated the presence of its audience. Audience members were often seated on the downstage corners of the stage and others were seated in boxes within the proscenium. Without the possibility of directed light afforded by the gas lighting that would be installed in these buildings a century later, the entire theatrical house had to be illuminated as well as the stage. In order to further isolate the scene from the beholder, Diderot proposed the then-novel idea of actors constructing an imaginary fourth wall between stage and auditorium, mimicking the effect of the canvas's surface within the absorptive work of art: "Whether you compose or act, think no more of the beholder than if he did not exist. Imagine, at the edge of the stage, a high wall that separates you from the orchestra. Act as if the curtain never rose."[28] Diderot's ideal theater would thus construct its own "supreme fiction" to defeat its ontological reliance on the presence of a watching other by depicting its characters absorbed in the drama at hand, still living behind the obscuring curtain.[29] To further absorb the beholder in the fiction of a temporally complete onstage world, he would also advocate the onstage embodiment of the painter's tableau, asking that actors hold still at the apex of the dramatic action, their characters posed in transparently meaningful positions.

Of course, as Fried notes, within a few short decades the condensation of action into a single comprehensive tableau would itself become a highly theatrical device, its overt artifice pointing directly to the viewer for whom it was staged.[30] By the same token, Diderot's dream of actors performing behind a fourth wall and subject to the gaze of an audience of invisible voyeurs has since become standard in the mainstream dramatic theater, the very thing that Fried rails against in his denunciation of the art form. So, too, many of the paintings that the critics of the late eighteenth century celebrate for their eradication of the presence of the beholder today seem to us the height of artifice, constructed for, and directed to, the viewing subject. Over the course of two subsequent studies of Courbet and Manet, Fried traces the struggle against theatricality in order to ultimately claim that the crisis embodied in the work of the proto-modernist Manet had precisely to do with the obsolescence of absorption as a means of defeating theatricality.[31] If absorption remains a potent marker for denying the theatrical presence of the beholder, it is because the subject represented on the canvas is fixedly involved in a recognizable action and attends to a future that the beholder can project forward satisfactorily. This is, of course, the briefest of glosses on a nuanced historical narrative, but it serves to suggest Fried's conviction that the strategies utilized by artists throughout history to "defeat theatricality" have varied extensively and, at times, even employed approaches that we would retrospectively term theatrical.

While the Jonathan Edwards of the transcendent present that "the fanatical puritan" (to cite Smithson's epithet) Fried invokes as bookends for his essay is not exactly the Jonathan Edwards of rational assumption recalled by Melville's narrator, the two facets of the theologian overlook a common ground. For Edwards, the distinction between divinity and humanity relies precisely on the instantaneity of the former and the temporal duration of the latter. And it is willed action with its consequent sense of causal procession that places the earthly firmly outside the eternity of God's single glance. Fried opens his essay with a quote from Edwards, excised from the final pages of Perry Miller's intellectual biography of the theologian that obliquely explains this matter:

> Edwards' journals frequently explored and tested a meditation he seldom allowed to reach print; if all the world were annihilated, he wrote . . . and a new world were freshly created, though it were to exist in every particular in the same manner as this world, it would not be the same. Therefore, because there is continuity, which is time, "it is certain with me that the world exists anew every moment; that the existence of things every moment and is every moment renewed." The abiding assurance is that "we every moment see the same proof of a God as we should have seen if we had seen Him create the world at first."[32]

On one hand, Edwards's notion of the instantaneous destruction and re-creation of a world would seem to suggest a kind of radical potentiality by stating outright that this renewed world would nonetheless be different, indeed this is close to the claim I explore in the next chapter. But the single difference that Edwards references in a world that is otherwise exactly the same is time itself—in other words, a time separated from spatial difference—as if the epiphany in question were the extraction of temporality from the process of the world. Edwards's genesis and apocalypse are presented as snapshots of an identical entirety, with time as the only interceding element. God's ability, according to Edwards, to contain the entirety of the world in a single instance of grace lies outside of time, and does not belong to history, because it is every moment renewed. Thus, "There is a crucial difference between God and man: God is by definition a Being who perceives not separate entities in succession, but the totality of being in a single, eternal glance."[33] Put otherwise, Edwards's conception of the human will as embodied and temporally situated perception stands opposed to the instantaneous survey of the divine moment where all holds as a tableau with its mortal actors completely absorbed. As movement, the will takes, and thus becomes, time. Placing this version of Edwards in conversation with the Edwards that Melville's narrator invokes, one could argue that Fried's frustration with the literalist object stems at least in part from its refusal to comply with the ordinances of rational assumption and relation determined by expectations about how an art object "works" effectively or produces meaning. Fried desires an art that gives access to a divine appearance outside of his temporally invested/infested body. He wants a work of art that, like a church, provides the architectural support for a moment of eternal transcendence.

Bartleby the Literal

The citation of the American theologian is not the only common thread linking Melville's story and Fried's essay. In fact, when set alongside one another a much more consistent and extensive correlation emerges, wherein nearly all the primary characteristics that the art critic recognizes at work in the literal form are reflected in the narrative of the short story. Based on these parallels, one could say that perhaps Bartleby himself appears as a literal object, or more accurately, stages a kind of theatrical relationship with his beholder—the lawyer—in a manner analogous to the silent and looming object's relation to the critic. An outline of the most overt similarities between the literal object and Bartleby (as representative of the still figure in potentiality) should prove my point while explicating Fried's case.

The literal object stands as an ideal form (a shape, a figure) made concrete, a single whole form or gestalt. The artists Donald Judd, Tony Smith, and Robert Morris that Fried references as exemplary literalists create sculptures immediately recognizable as cubes (Judd and Smith) or columns and angles (Morris): basic geometric forms and shapes. When the narrator in Melville's story describes how, "like the last column of some ruined temple, [Bartleby] remained standing mute and solitary in the middle of the otherwise deserted room" (22), he could just as easily be describing a literalist sculpture in the middle of the otherwise deserted white cube of the gallery. For example, Morris's first minimal objects in 1961, fittingly called *Columns*, presented two large gray rectangular boxes, roughly human-size, one lying on its side and the other standing upright.

Here, in referring to a singular, isolated form, the definition of the "literal" breaks from sculptural work more broadly termed "minimal" by art historians and critics. As but one of many divergent examples, the almost hysterically iterative systems of Sol LeWitt with their many variations on a single possible form claim that, in the artist's words, "even a simple idea taken to its logical end can become chaos."[34] Even though these multiplicitous structures depart from Fried's description of the literal as a primary object, and do not receive the brunt of his attack, they are nonetheless included in his damnation of the tendency. In regards to Judd's structures segmented into equal parts or Carl Andre's lines of bricks and tiled floor—work that "carries the implication that the units in question could be multiplied ad infinitum"—Fried sees a depiction of order belonging to "nature" with its accumulation of "one thing after another" rather than a causal relation between parts prized in modern painting and sculpture.[35] Even in this tangential manner Bartleby approaches the literal/minimal. He repeats his formula of "I would prefer not to" as one thing after another,

Fig. 3. Robert Morris, *Columns*, 1961–1973. Painted aluminum. Two columns, each 8 × 2 × 2 feet. Photo Courtesy Leo Castelli Gallery, New York.

until it becomes a kind of ready-made form applicable to any situation. The statement clearly breaks with causal relations in that it acts as a common response to countless requests and demands. Bartleby's utterance maintains a monolithic identity, but as a form in constantly variable contexts, perhaps already pointing toward the appearance of difference within repetition inherent to much "postminimalist" art such as Eva Hesse's, and Andy Warhol's series of iconographic reproductions.[36]

Qualities seem to slip off the stillness of Bartleby, off the uniform surface of his space (devoid of detail) and his time (devoid of motion or change).[37] We see this in the neutrality of his appearance and complexion. He is repeatedly referred to as "pale" and unchanging in cast, which, in tandem with his gray eyes, approximates the nondescript gray that sculptor Morris would claim as default color in his early minimalist work.[38] The uniform surface also implies a negation or avoidance of the past common to both the potential figure and the literal object. In response to the trace of the artist's hand or brush that characterized much of the preceding generation of abstract expressionist painting, the literalists turned to industrial materials and methods, applying an even application of paint to produce work ostensibly unmarked by its maker's touch. The earlier painterly work, described as "action painting" by Harold Rosenberg, depicted on the canvas the consequences of an artist's past performance, so the span of a Pollock drip indexed the reach of his arm.[39] Painting became the record of a dramatic conflict between actor and materials. Seen as the consummation of an event, the painting was, like the Diderotian tableau, a proof of causality. But, here, in the literalist moment, the intent was to stage a surface in the present, an object without history.[40] Bartleby, too, does not have a determinate past (apart from his purported time in the office of dead letters, a stint already situating him in a suspended state between intention and reception), but merely arrives on the scene. One day the gallery opens and the object appears, waiting. This seeming reversal of expectation that the Friedian beholder experiences when confronted with the literal object ("reversal" in that it seems as if the object has been awaiting the beholder's arrival) mirrors that which the narrator experiences when confronted with the always already present Bartleby: "As yet I had never of my personal knowledge known him to be outside of my office. He was a perpetual sentry in the corner" (12). Bartleby waits like an eternal sentinel, as if only coming into being in the presence of the other, of the subject-lawyer. The narcissistic narrator asks: what is the sentry waiting for other than my arrival?

In the sense in which it always seems to be "waiting" for the arrival of a viewing subject, the literalist object stages a completely different kind of temporality than that of the modernist artwork. The modernist painting or sculpture presents itself as the culmination of an acting body, the consummation of a world order in an instant.[41] This is, of course, the presentness that Fried intends to draw our attention to in his epigraph by Jonathan Edwards. Facing the modernist artwork, Fried can imagine a perfectly transcendent moment of complete survey, a moment of grace in which his own subjecthood is sublimely erased before the presentness of a whole contained world. This notion of a lasting presentness stands at odds with the duration of the literalist object whose presence inspires the beholder to pursue the sense of the object beyond its immediate surface quality, to circle the object endlessly in quest of "something more," some point of entry into that obscured significance, a peek behind the curtain. It is this endless quest that prompts Fried to claim that the literal object opens up art to a durational rather than instantaneous encounter.[42] He writes, disapprovingly, that the literalist "is always of further interest; one never feels that one has come to the end of it; it is inexhaustible. It is inexhaustible, however, not because of any fullness—*that* is the inexhaustibility of art—but because there is nothing there to exhaust."[43] It is significant that such endless (lack of) interest derives not from the object itself, but from the beholder's experience of it, that "one never feels that one has come to the end of it." Bartleby, too, inspires a kind of constantly perambulating interrogation from his narrator (and from this author). The lawyer pursues various actions and ploys to reveal a chink in the scrivener's armor, to expose the secret of the presence before him. He, too, circles the obtuse one endlessly, seeking out entry.[44]

Two Anthropomorphisms: More-Than and Not-Quite Human

In distinguishing between the two temporalities instituted by the divergent modes of art, Fried also describes *two opposing kinds of anthropomorphism*: one that he sees as the goal of modern art and the other that he sees as a threat to it. While Fried does not make this distinction, I would like to suggest that both anthropomorphisms only *approach* the human, with the first exceeding the human in its quasi-divine perfection of its possibility as meaning-maker, and the second mimicking the intensity of a life that is not quite human. In discussing the first case, Fried recounts an understanding of anthropomorphism that one of his adversaries, Donald Judd, sees at work in modernist sculpture:

> It is worth remarking that the "part-by-part" and "relational" character of most sculpture is associated by Judd with what he calls *anthropomorphism*: "A beam thrusts; a piece of iron follows a gesture; together they form a naturalistic and anthropomorphic image."[45]

Judd derides such anthropomorphism, yet Fried celebrates it as the goal of the contemporary sculptor. He sees this gestural quality at work in the sculpture of Anthony Caro, for example, who presents a composition of separate parts that relate to one another as the grammatical components of

a larger statement or narrative held synchronously and self-sufficiently before our eyes. Or, in his own words, he claims that these pieces express "not
gestures exactly, but the *efficacy* of gesture. . . . It is as though Caro's sculptures essentialize meaningfulness *as such*—as though the possibility of
meaning what we say and do *alone* makes his sculpture possible."[46] Clearly
this notion of the stilled gesture—posed, as it were—depicts a discrete
world of possible actions rather than the gestural potentiality discussed in
the previous chapter. In other words, the syntactical sculptures of Caro and
other modernists do not present gesture as a pure means divorced from
ends, which would necessitate a kind of suspension without arrival, but
instead offer a pure ends without means: the arrival at a decisive constative
statement perfecting signification. They present the *efficacy* of gesture as an
effect of meaning; the perfect translation of the means into meaningful
ends has already taken place.

But Fried sees an entirely different kind of anthropomorphism at work
in the literal object. This second sense of anthropomorphism is based not
on the possibility of meaning that the syntactical/gestural composition expresses, but on the seeming presence of a (not-quite-human) life. This other
anthropomorphism derives from the impression of an "apparent hollowness of most literalist work—the quality of having an *inside*—[which] is almost blatantly anthropomorphic."[47] The literalist's inaccessible interiority
implies a life circulating within its "secret" confines. We looked at another
hollow sculpture occupying the stage in Didier Théron's version of *Bartleby*, a large balloon in a rabbit-like shape towering over the dancer. The
held breath implied by the hollowness of that object, its almost palpable
anticipation of release, conjures a sense of the living in the manner that the
art critic suggests.

Morris's 1961 sculpture, *Box with the Sound of Its Own Making*, also
sought to imply a life within the object by audibly investing it with its history of production. Inside a nine-inch cube the artist enclosed a tape recorder with an audio recording that played out the sounds that were produced during the three-hour construction of the form. The subsequent
postminimalist work of Bruce Nauman pointedly capitalizes on this aural
capture of the secret life of the literal. His 1968 *Concrete Tape Recorder Piece*
mimics Morris by encasing a tape recorder in a uniform block of concrete,
recalling the other's gray cubes and columns, but where the earlier *Box*
looked back on the past story of the object's construction, this piece directs
the recording into a different temporality. Nauman's sculpture copies the
present for a future auditor, but one who paradoxically would need to destroy the object in order to hear its telling. Encased in its concrete interior-

ity, the tape recorder can only be imagined within; we presume that its "record" button remains depressed (after all, what other purpose does the instrument serve except to record or to replay, and it does not do the latter). Bartleby moves from Morris's copyist of the past in the beginning of the story, to Nauman's copyist for the future, his story only "played" by the narrator after his destruction. I will return to the question of the literal as a witness below, but for now let me merely note that, if the syntactical sculpture of Caro presents a pure surface of signification without substance that Fried calls "weightless" (and thus timeless), in the boxes of Morris and Nauman, there is a vast and concealed interiority that seems to swallow up experience in its inaccessible hollow.

A more direct lineage connects the unarticulated literal object with the human body. Morris's early performance works, created while he was constructing his first minimal objects, blatantly engage with the anthropomorphic "secret" withheld by these forms. Married to Simone Forti (then Simone Morris), he had joined the pioneering choreographer in workshops with Anna Halprin in California and then, after moving to New York, began producing his own dances with the Judson Church group during the first years of their work. In 1961, the minimalist composer La Monte Young curated a program of seven-minute pieces with the Living Theatre. In Morris's offering for the evening, the curtain opened on a gray-painted rectangular box standing center on an otherwise empty stage. Roughly human-sized, it remained erect, stationary, and waiting as time passed and nothing seemed to happen. Three and a half minutes into the performance—exactly halfway through the allotted time—the column tipped over and then remained lying on its side for the next three and a half minutes. A string pulled taut caused the object to fall, but originally Morris intended to secret himself inside the box throughout, in order to push over the box from within (a minor concussion sustained during the rehearsal for the piece prevented his onstage participation). The set/costume/actor was identical to the *Column* that the artist had produced the year before and which he would exhibit in its two primary positions—upright and prone. "Clearly a 'performer,'" writes Kimberly Paice, "the column concentrated into two positions . . . the multitude of possible dance gestures, just as it literalized the way dance is meant to fill otherwise empty time. That the column was understood as a surrogate of the dancer's body was reinforced by Morris's intention that, although stripped of all 'expression,' the object should seem to move of its own accord."[48] A prime geometric form with even gray surface, moving in the tectonic terms of the vertical and horizontal, the column exemplifies the neutral expression discussed above. The photograph of *Box*

Fig. 4. Robert Morris, *Untitled (Box for Standing)*, 1961. Fir, 74 × 25 × 10½ inches. Photo Courtesy Leo Castelli Gallery, New York.

for Standing (1961) suggests the intended effect of Morris's column—that the geometric form could contain a body, could stand in place of one and pass its neutrality to the living. It shows Morris engaged in a performance with his object, standing inside a column as if it were a frame, in a single gesture displaying resistance to gravity as a lasting act, upright until a final breath brings it low.

It is this submerged anthropomorphic presence that disturbs both Fried and the narrator of Melville's story. To say that Bartleby is a literal object is to say that his stillness is not the stillness of the statue, with its implications of human contours and figuration, but something of a quite different order. At one point in the story the narrator compares Bartleby to a statue in explicit terms: "Had there been any thing ordinarily human about him, doubtless I should have violently dismissed him from the premises. But as it was, I should have as soon thought of turning my pale plaster-of-paris bust of Cicero out of doors" (10). In the previous chapter, I showed how the copyist's stillness resists qualification as a "pose," because it stages a kind of potential for/of gesture rather than the pose's expressive enactment that takes/makes account of its context. While the bust at least maintains a reference to the historical person Cicero—the Roman orator renowned for his treatises on the arts of rhetoric, on the styling of meaningful speech—there is nothing "ordinarily human" about Bartleby. He may seem a human figure when outside his "cube-icle," but masked behind the screens, he loses all access to the realm of gesture and action.

Quite literally, Bartleby appears as an unreachable interiority within the confines of a uniform structure. Sequestered behind his smooth surfaces of screen and wall, the copyist, too, disappears within the "primary structure" of a cube or rectangle. Moreover, the sense of isolation and distance that the literal impresses upon the beholder approximates the sense in which the narrator paradoxically feels most alone while in the presence of the scrivener: "Yes, Bartleby, stay there behind your screen, thought I; I shall persecute you no more; you are harmless and noiseless as any of these old chairs; in short, *I never feel so private as when I know you are here*" (26, my emphasis). As Herbert Blau has observed, a sense of aloneness is peculiar to the affect of what we call "stage presence," but in a reversal that holds significance for my reading of the encounter with potentiality, the narrator feels as if *he* were the one enclosed in a chamber of solitude.[49] Bartleby's final resting place in the walled courtyard of the prison, "the heart of the eternal pyramids" (33), only redoubles his habitation of the interior of a box.

Not quite human, but still living in an inexplicable manner beneath a uniform surface, it is the "surrogate person" of the literal object that provokes the art critic's greatest expressions of outrage and discomfort.[50] Threading together these various passages reveals what I see as the *unacknowledgeable* performance at the center of the encounter with the potential/literal other.

> Being distanced by such objects is not, I suggest, entirely unlike being distanced, or crowded, by the silent presence of another *person*; the experience of coming upon literalist objects unexpectedly—for example, in somewhat darkened rooms—can be strongly, if momentarily, disquieting in just this way.[51]

Setting a scene dramatically infused with not-so-subtle inflexions of the gothic or suspense novel (unexpected presences in "somewhat darkened rooms"), Fried describes the experience of being distanced and isolated by these objects as instituting a marked change in the viewer. Broken up by comas and dashes, his writing carries an almost breathless quality.

> Someone has merely to enter the room in which a literalist work has been placed to become that beholder, that audience of one—almost as though the work in question has been waiting for him. And inasmuch as literalist work depends on the beholder, is incomplete without him, it *has* been waiting for him. And once he is in the room the work refuses, obstinately, to let him alone—which is to say, it refuses to stop confronting him, distancing him, isolating him.[52]

Faced with this impassive surface, one acquires an awareness of oneself as the species of subject that Fried terms "the beholder." Here Fried invests the object with a kind of will of its own, but a will totally inaccessible to a theory of assumptions. The object "obstinately" demands a response from the beholder and "refuses . . . to let him alone." But who or what is doing the beholding becomes a somewhat uncertain matter. In what is surely an unintentional ambiguity embedded in the above quotation, by excising the first part of the sentence (the intended subject), one could also say that the "literalist work has been placed to become that beholder, that audience of one—almost as though the work has been waiting for him." In other words, it is the literal object that becomes an audience of one. Upon entering the room, the subject inescapably turns into the main attraction, just as a subject crossing a stage inescapably becomes an actor. He or she is being watched by a presence that demands an act:

> It is a function not just of the obtrusiveness and, often, even aggressiveness of literalist work, but of *the special complicity that that work extorts from the beholder*. Something is said to have presence when it demands that the beholder take it into account, that he takes it seriously—and when the fulfillment of that demand consists simply in being aware of the work and, so to speak, *in acting accordingly*.[53]

Continuing to read Fried's text slightly askance, I contend that this "special complicity" between the literal and the beholder is the compact shared between the audience and the performer, but, counter to expectation, it is the beholder that is asked to stage an action. The beholder must be "aware of the work," meaning the object, as a presence that observes him or her from afar, but perhaps also as his or her "work," meaning the task that he or she must undertake. If the viewing subject insists upon discovering the consummation of a possible world, then the literal object turns that demand back upon him or her, telling the beholder to "act accordingly," give a command performance.

But "according" to what? Edwards's rules of common assumption are no longer in effect. Looking back at the quotes above, we see that Fried occupies an "indeterminate, open-ended," and "unexacting" position in regards to the object: his future is undetermined, open to untrammeled potentiality. He feels himself attending the object, not as a part of a community of spectators, but as a singularity possessing an "aloneness" akin to the stage presence he disparages. Even Fried's nomination of the word "beholder" suggests such a reading: in addition to the meanings that immediately jump to mind (look, regard, observe, etc.), the *Oxford English Dictionary* tells us that "to behold" is "to hold by" or "to keep." Is it too much to suggest, then, that the beholder confronts his or her capacity to suspend, to hold or keep, a look or action—in other words, his or her potentiality?

Fried never says outright that the "theatrical" in question refers to the beholder's own performance, but in a few instances throughout his oeuvre he nearly states as much.[54] For example, while reviewing the argument from "Art and Objecthood" in his "Introduction to My Art Criticism" (1998), he writes: "My critique of the literalist address to the viewer's body was not that bodiliness as such had no place in art but rather that literalism theatricalized the body, put it endlessly on stage, made it uncanny or opaque to itself, hollowed it out, deadened its expressiveness, denied its finitude and in a sense its humanness, and so on."[55] The sentence is decidedly ambivalent, on the surface presumably referring to the affect displayed by the art object itself, but at the same time exhibiting a distinct slippage between the "viewer's body" and the "bodiliness" "put endlessly on stage." Whose uncanny, hollowed, inexpressive, and inhuman body is this: the beholder's or the object's?[56]

Later artists would consider the interpersonal ambivalence of such potentiality in a direct fashion. For example, after several years working as a minimal and conceptual artist in the late 1960s, Adrian Piper recognized an analogous relationship between her own presence and that of the literalist object. Departing from the object-based work she produced in her early twenties, which had been inspired in part by her friendship with Sol LeWitt, she began staging performative interventions in public spaces. For her *Untitled Performance for Max's Kansas City* (1970)—set in the bar that served as an epicenter of the New York art, music, and fashion world—Piper deprived herself of all sensory input by donning a blindfold, earplugs, gloves, and noseplugs. "I presented myself as a silent, secret, passive object, seemingly ready to be absorbed into [the beholder's] consciousness as an object. But I learned that complete absorption was impossible, because my voluntary objectlike passivity implied aggressive activity and choice, an independent presence confronting the Art-Conscious environment with its autonomy. My objecthood became my subjecthood."[57] Mimicking the terms that Fried uses to characterize the literal ("silent," "secret," and a slightly different sense of "absorption"), Piper's statement recalls the critic's strangely imbricated notion of objecthood and subjecthood. For the beholder, her passivity appeared an active choice to retain power, an "aggressive" affect that Piper would come to realize could not be disconnected from her identity as an African-American woman in a landscape dominated by white male artists and critics. As during her subsequent time pursuing a doctorate in philosophy at Harvard, where she was the only woman and only person of color in the department (albeit one who often unintentionally passed for white), Piper found herself objectified and stereotyped by the homogenous social surround. The artist took hold of her subjecthood by claiming possession of a literalist potential to do.[58]

In his excellent book, *In the Break: The Aesthetics of the Black Radical Tradition*, poet-theorist Fred Moten explains how the artist's work refigures Fried's fantasy of instantaneous beholding into a situation in which the object hails the beholder into an eventful performance: "For Piper, to be for the beholder is to be able to mess up or mess with the beholder. It is the potential of being catalytic. Beholding is always the entrance into a scene, into the context of the other, of the object."[59] Such literal potentiality is the "potential of being catalytic"; it is "to be able to" catalyze an excessive "mess" of reactions from the beholder, to force him or her to enter the scene and perform with melodramatic flair.

These ideas were present, if submerged, in the work that surrounded Fried in the late 1960s. Apart from Robert Smithson's letter quoted at the beginning of this chapter, which seems particularly aware of the art critic's role-playing in the gallery, it is in the work of Robert Morris that we see these issues most explicitly displayed. The mirrored cubes and flats that Smithson and Morris produced during this period, reflecting back the world of the beholder or camera, only literalize the object's attention to its interlocutor, but I would like to end this section with a glance at another of

Morris's performances, created in collaboration with the artist Carolee Schneemann. In *Site* (1964), a large rectangular box sits center stage, recalling the column from the 1961 Living Theatre performance. Morris, dressed in neutral white clothes and a mask, enters the space and begins to dismantle the literal object with workmanlike economy of movement. A reclining nude—Schneemann in the pose of Manet's infamous Olympia—is revealed underneath the uniform surfaces, looking out at the audience with an inscrutable gaze. Here one sees another ideal representation of the literal as potential: that the figure possessing her stillness is an artist herself profoundly concerned with the fullest panoply of embodiment and enactment (as apparent in *Meat Joy*, *Fuses*, and many of Schneemann's other performances and films) only further confers a "potentiality to do" in this particular suspension.

Like its nineteenth-century painted precursor, *Site* is concerned with the relationship between the beholder and art object. In *Manet's Modernism*, Fried focuses on the question of "facingness" that he sees as crucial to the project of the painter of *Olympia*. He writes:

> As Meyer Schapiro has noted in his pioneering essay on the semiotics of the image, a basic characteristic of the frontal view is that it is felt to address the viewer, to "interpellate" the latter in an I-you relationship with the facing element itself. At the same time, as I have remarked more than once, the terms of that relationship in Manet's art have been left undefined. More precisely, the notorious blankness or inexpressiveness of the outward gaze in such paintings as the *Old Musician*, *Dejeuner sur l'herbe*, and *Olympia* distanced and alienated the beholder even as it was felt to solicit his presence.[60]

The blank expression of Manet's Olympia as reperformed by the impassive Schneemann finds its counterpart in the stilled expression of Morris's performance of the masked worker, and reaches a limit case in the complete occlusion of the reclining figure within the rectangular form.

The title *Site*, then, functions in at least three registers. (1) It playfully *cites* a previous articulation of a problem common to the literalist sensibility. (2) It refers to the excavation (*site*) where a figure dwells within the potential form, an archaeological operation that unearths its early modernist predecessor. Michelangelo, and Aristotle before him, spoke of the unmarked block of stone withholding the potentiality to form a particular sculpture within. (3) But the title also refers to the potential placement or "siting" of *sight*. The literal object is always facing the viewer; it is all front—

six sides of blank canvas comprise the box—but, unlike the canvas of the painting, it is a front that radically refuses to interpellate the beholder in a definite or possible relationship; it stages a lack of acknowledgment. It is a face that refuses the promise of a face-to-face encounter.

THE MELODRAMA OF THE UNACKNOWLEDGED BEHOLDER

The reassuring eyes of Louise Bourgeois's *Nature Study, Velvet Eyes* (1984) are nestled deep within cavities gouged out from the unarticulated surface of an otherwise ordinary mass of rock. Encountering this stare, performance theorist Peggy Phelan recognizes the reciprocal nature of the spectator's gaze, which asks that the thing seen see us as well:

> Bourgeois' sculpture looks like a rather large and ordinary rock. Surprised by its apparent ordinariness, the viewer saunters over to it to get a better look and peering down, s/he sees nestled within the cavity of the rock a pair of all too human eyes staring back up. Startled by the hidden eyes, one sees how thoroughly blind one is to the eyes of images. But the feeling of shock soon fades and one feels oddly reassured. By giving the potential gaze (back) to the art object, Bourgeois makes visible the symmetrical *drive* of spectatorship: the desire to see always touches the desire to be seen. It is necessary then to speak of both the object of the gaze and the gaze of the object.[61]

Lacan's famous sardine can floating in the ocean returns his look as if to confirm a shared presence between object and subject: we see each other, so we both exist.[62] The *Velvet Eyes* with their stony stare literalize and localize this effect, a gaze that places one here and now in a kind of performative exchange with its beholder. But what if the sculpture did not reveal its eyes? What if they were hidden and isolated below the surface, everywhere and nowhere at once? One could imagine the viewer circling the sculpture indefinitely, seeking out some point of access below the object's surface, some meaningful conviction that acknowledges his or her presence. Without its pair of eyes, returned to its rocklike nature, the rock would mimic the inscrutability of the literal object, its presence demanding attention without the promise of a reassuring acknowledgment in return. I would like to suggest that it is this lack of acknowledgment—the object's refusal to behold the subject as willful subject—that forces the beholder to perform more and more excessively to get the attention of the other, to prove his or her intentionality, as it were. Encountering the literalist object's potentiality to do or show, its suspension of a capacity to engage, the subject feels that he or she must perform, must take up a possible part to compensate for that which does not perform. One must act in order to reclaim the validity of a world of possibilities.[63]

As a visual art, the anxiety surrounding the question of theatricality in painting finds its most direct representation in images of blindness. Fried's notion of *absorption* explored in the art historical writings (which, he claims represents the prominent strategy that painters in mid-eighteenth-century France employed in order to defeat theatricality) implies a kind of blindness toward the beholder. The eyes of the figures within the paintings of Chardin or Greuze are always for someone or something else; the children gathering around their dying father look to him solely, the boy building a castle of cards considers the card before him with infinite care, while the girl reading her book seems to scan the page intently, unaware of the world that surrounds, unaware of the beholder looking on.

In the final chapter of *Absorption and Theatricality* Fried examines work that more explicitly depicts this "blindness" of absorption. Here the art critic addresses paintings that face this avoidance of the gaze head-on by depicting scenes that show the great Roman general Belisarius now blinded in old age and begging for alms. Each of the paintings discussed by Fried display the retired general encountering a group of people who respond variously to his entreaties. In each canvas, one of the crowd is always a soldier who had previously served under the great general, shown at the moment when this subordinate acknowledges the state of his ruined commander. A look of great pity hangs over the soldier's brow, or he raises his hands up in shock, his mouth falls open in horror. According to Fried, such an affected figure represents the beholder's inclusion within the painting, his or her reaction to the acknowledgment of the images that face out, unseen by the painting itself. The soldier models acceptable possibilities of response for us. More than the girl with her book, who may turn to see us watching, the blind Belisarius does not, cannot, see the other characters in "his world" let alone the beholder standing outside of it.

There is a significant difference between the blindness of Belisarius and the lack of acknowledgment characteristic of the literal object (and of the figure of potentiality more broadly conceived). Both the absorbed and the blind figure direct their gaze and intention elsewhere, to a goal either within the painted world or within their implied interiority. However impossible their return of the gaze, the many blind Belisariuses are oriented toward other characters and safely pursuing an end—in other words, they perform actions—while completely unaware of the gaze of the beholder. Thus, the blind figures exemplify the absorbed's ignorance of being beheld, dismantling theatricality, while still maintaining the *efficacy* or significance of a gesture. Belisarius's extended hand, asking for charity, becomes analogous to Caro's syntactical structures with their beams thrusting out into space. These later high modernist sculptures also have no "eyes" for the beholder, but still hold out a possible end to survey; by presenting a posed statement they still acknowledge the beholder as a fellow meaning-maker.

But in what way does the literal refuse to acknowledge the beholder, if so much of Fried's outrage stems from the fact that such work "includes" or "belongs" to the beholder?[64]

One path toward the beginnings of an answer becomes apparent if we look back at Melville's story. In a last glance at *Bartleby*, we recognize that blindness and hiddenness also serve a significant purpose in Melville's story. Apart from Bartleby's unwillingness to engage verbally in the practices of social exchange, the copyist further dislocates himself from rational access in his progressive self-obscuration. The copyist's grayed eyes and unnerving blank stare (his "dead wall reverie") reflect the blank walls that enclose his inscribed chamber with its view of white wall, black wall, and the green screen that the lawyer inserts as barrier between Bartleby and the everyday. The blindness that progressively enrobes Bartleby ("I looked steadfastly at him, and perceived that his eyes looked dull and glazed. Instantly it occurred to me, that his unexampled diligence in copying by his dim window for the first few weeks of his stay with me might have temporarily impaired his vision" [21]), as well as his genuine lack of shame when the lawyer interrupts his sleep in the after hours of the office, leads Branka Arsić to infer he is a figure without self-awareness. He thus "erases the economy between seeing and being seen, the very economy of witnessing."[65] Bartleby refuses to recognize the copresence of the narrator, refuses to allow that they share a common presence. When Fried says that the literal has a "presence," it is a presence opposed to, and separate or distant from, that of the beholder. They do not recognize each other, are blind to one another.

This system of exchanges that Bartleby refuses is the bond between the subject and the object at work in Bourgeois's *Velvet Eyes*: I see you and you see me, therefore we both exist as such, have a presence and common presentness. We witness each other's existence as present and moving into a future. But as Giorgio Agamben has posed in his exploration of the question of the witness, the *complete witness* is absolutely submerged in the experience of the event and unable to translate a happening into common parlance, in a sense, unable to respond, "I see you, too." Alone, the pure witness cannot take part in the "economy of witnessing," but requires a surrogate to take up the subject-position that the complete witness, bound up in singularity, cannot claim. The two together form a joint position that Agamben refers to as "testimony."[66] Agamben's theory of the witness derives from Primo Levi's recognition that it was impossible to witness the complete extent of the atrocities of the concentration camps of World War II, the fact that those who experienced the full horror of the camp—of the death chamber—could not survive to tell of it.[67] So, too, the unknown child that could only say the incomprehensible "Hurbinak" over and over till his death required Levi's recollection to enter the realm of sense. Without an "I" from which to speak, the complete witness is rendered "subjectless" and silent by the burden of experience. Like Deleuze's "original," the complete witness possesses a truth that would cease to hold were he or she the one expressing it.

One might be tempted to say that, in a rather unsatisfactory manner, the narrator's project of telling the story of Bartleby takes up this mantle of bearing witness for the copyist who cannot—after all, as legal professional, he should be familiar with the necessities of witnessing before the law— but it seems that the lofty intent toward which the narrator endlessly struggles falls victim to his own histrionic performance. He does not produce a performance on behalf of the one that withholds its potentiality to perform. Instead, the narrator seems more concerned with playing out his own spectacle of tribulation. After all, the narrator's active avoidance of the pure witness in his office, culminating in his departure from the scene, ultimately instigates the imprisonment and eventual death of Bartleby.

I am more interested here in how the pure witness is a silent and obdurate presence, displaying its potential for an articulation withheld. Think again of Nauman's *Concrete Tape Recorder*, the pure witness in a box recording all, that to all intents and purposes is a nonwitness until another subject comes along to make the sculpture speak (by breaking open the box and finally pressing "Play"; in other words, by destroying the sculpture). Or think of the more quotidian relative of Nauman's piece, the black box that records an airplane's flight plan, but only "tells its story" after undergoing its destruction. All of which is to say that the figure maintaining its potentiality is not a blind presence, but merely one who completely holds its potential to witness.[68]

I would like to suggest that what draws Bartleby and the literal object closest to one another, what produces such a profound need to perform on the part of the beholder, is the fact of this silent observation of the complete witness. Here we see one mode of response to an encounter with the potential: an almost uncontrollable need to perform. As suggested above, such a response results from the potential's refusal to acknowledge the beholder, but the nature of this (lack of) acknowledgment deserves further inquiry. In order to do so we must take a brief detour through the writings of another thinker closely associated with Fried, one for whom the question of acknowledgment figures most prominently.

Implicit within Fried's writing is a notion of acknowledgment that benefits greatly from his contemporary and confidante, the ordinary-language philosopher Stanley Cavell. The two met in 1962 at Harvard, where Fried was a graduate student and Cavell had been appointed to a chair in the philosophy department (incidentally, Piper would complete her PhD from this same department a decade later). Soon thereafter they began an intellectual exchange in private conversation and in each other's classrooms and seminars that would profoundly influence their respective writings.[69] Fried attended Cavell's seminars on Wittgenstein, Heidegger, and others; Cavell attended Fried's lectures on modern art. Of particular interest to our investigation, Cavell's theoretical argument in "The Avoidance of Love: A Reading of *King Lear*"—published two years after "Art and Objecthood" as part of Cavell's first collection of essays, *Must We Mean What We Say?*—outlines some of the foundations of the concept of "theatricality" shared by both the philosopher and the art critic.[70]

It is important to note that, unlike Fried, Cavell states outright that his essay does not propose an all-encompassing theory of the theater or tragedy.[71] In Cavell's conception of the theater, the audience and the stage do not share a unified space but, instead, stake out opposing sides of a divide that one can never cross without interrupting and thus collapsing the theatrical apparatus itself. "The Avoidance of Love" offers us an imagined scenario in which a backwoods "yokel" attends a performance of *Othello* and, having never seen a play before, interprets the events depicted as "real" events. He rushes onstage to interrupt Othello at the moment when the noble moor is about to strangle Desdemona for her supposed adultery. The yokel believes that he shares a common space and time with the actors onstage, but as soon as he interrupts the action, the play ceases, its world collapses. Theatrical convention, however, teaches otherwise:

A character is not, and cannot become, aware of us. . . . I will say: We are not in their presence. . . . They are in our presence. This means, again, not simply that we are seeing and hearing them, but that we are acknowledging them (or specifically failing to).[72]

This last line draws our attention to one of the central concerns in Cavell's understanding of the theatrical: acknowledgment operates differently in the theater than in actual everyday life. In another essay from the same collection, Cavell writes that in everyday life "acknowledgment goes beyond knowledge. (Goes beyond not, so to speak, in the order of knowledge, but in its requirement that I *do* something or reveal something on the basis of that knowledge)."[73] In order to complete acknowledgment, one must *perform* a recognizable action in turn, whether in terms of an utterance ("I acknowledge that you are in pain") or in a physical response (a gesture or look of sympathy, perhaps). Acknowledgment requires not only recognition of the other, but also a performative revelation of the self.[74] This exchange of acknowledgment—which, incidentally, resonates with the exchange of witnessing above—constitutes the basis for ethical responsibility to the other.

In the theater, on the other hand, acknowledgment operates differently (or, rather, it fails to operate). Again, in everyday life we express acknowledgment

> by revealing ourselves, by allowing ourselves to be seen. When we do not, when we keep ourselves in the dark, the consequence is that we convert the other into a character and make the world a stage for him. . . . The conditions of theater *literalize* the conditions we exact for existence outside—hiddenness, silence, isolation—hence make that existence plain. Theater does not expect us to simply stop theatricalizing; it knows we can theatricalize its conditions as we can theatricalize any others. But in giving us a place within which our hiddenness and silence and separation are accounted for, *it gives us a chance to stop.*[75]

As the example of the yokel makes apparent, the conventions of the theater do not allow us to reveal ourselves to the onstage other. The theater, then, offers one a respite from the everyday burden of acknowledgment, because it lets one inhabit a site where the acknowledgment of the onstage world is impossible; in fact, like the literal object, it "literalizes" such hiddenness and distance. We are not responsible to those onstage because there is no way for us to be responsible to them. It is impossible according to the rules of the game. As Cavell reads *King Lear*, the play is a tragedy because it shows us characters distanced from others in their world, but stranded in that solitude without the excuse of theatrical cover. Lear, for example, refuses to reveal himself and so cannot acknowledge the other characters; he does not reveal his love for Cordelia and acknowledge her love of him. Blindness is at the heart of *Lear* as Gloucester's punishment makes painfully evident, and it is also at the heart of tragedy as a form, fathered as it is by blind Oedipus and foretold by blind Tiresias. Meanwhile, situated on the other side of the proscenium divide, we in the audience rest assured in our condoned inability to acknowledge: there is no other way. The theater "gives [its beholders] a chance to stop" acknowledging. For Cavell, this situation forces us to recognize the failure of acknowledgment within an acceptable place, so that we can go out into the actual world aware of the everyday tragedy of the unacknowledged.[76]

If a play like *King Lear* can offer a positive perspective on the problem of acknowledgment, why is the theatricality of the literal object so unacceptable? In the footnote referencing Fried, Cavell agrees with the art critic in claiming that the object's hold on us is theatrical. But I would suggest that based on the philosopher's more pointed engagement with the theatrical in the theater (albeit one that is still a problematically ahistorical entity), this characterization is cast in a slightly different register or direction.[77] Rather than the literal presenting "theatricality" as simply the awareness of the beholder's presence before the work of art, Cavell implies that *these objects watch us from the darkened theater without revealing themselves to us*. They reverse the gaze of the beholder in the theater, take up his or her hidden, isolated, and silent position, and thereby "convert the [beholder] into a character and make the world a stage for him." In *King Lear* we are the ones who are not acknowledging the onstage characters, but in the company of the literal it is "they" that do not acknowledge us.

Let me repeat this argument once more to ensure clarity: in Cavell's theater we, the beholders, are separate from the onstage characters and thus cannot acknowledge them. This impossibility of acknowledgment, based on the conventions of the theater as such, relieves us of the ethical responsibility to acknowledge another, a responsibility incumbent upon us in everyday life (and a responsibility upon which we often fail to deliver).[78] When Fried says that the literal operates theatrically, it is not to say that the object performs the role of the onstage character separate from us or to say that we can rest assured in our inability to acknowledge the object. Rather, and crucially, the object relates to us as if we were actors onstage, as if *its* inability to acknowledge *us* were condoned. The literal operates theatrically only insofar as it reverses its claim upon us. We enter the stage of the gallery and perform before a complete—and therefore silent—witness that will not communicate its sense of our event. It "experiences" our present and all our future presents; it holds those potentialities at bay. Literality "gives [the object] a chance to stop" acknowledging us, but also a chance to stop and hold still, to suspend its actions and meanings. The literal object is unacceptably theatrical because it makes the beholder a performer.[79]

One of the most frightening things about the literalist object for Fried, it seems, is that it places us in a position where we are seen, but denies us the ability to acknowledge the object that "sees" us. The object may be waiting to see us perform, but its hermetic remove and refusal to give up a response, to give the acknowledgment that will stop or resolve our blundering tragedy, recalls the separated anonymity of theater's audience sequestered in its black hole, eyes unseen. It stands there like an enclosed abyss, a black hole of attention, with countless eyes in secret below its surface. Suddenly beholden to its survey, one's experience is not so distant from the actor thrust upon a stage before the silent mass of an audience beyond. In Stanislavsky's *An Actor Prepares*, the author's actor-analogue Kostya recounts his anxiety when faced for the first time with the gaping black hole of the audience beyond the raised curtain. The moment serves as the foundational moment in Nicholas Ridout's consideration of stage fright, which he recognizes as a decidedly modern symptom of the meeting of the private and the public.[80] Ridout glosses Kostya's experience to suggest that it is not the darkness itself, the unending abyss, that stokes the actor's erratic passions, but rather the unseen and unreachable sense of an audience watching from within and behind the dark, demanding that he perform in an interesting manner. The abyss of the audience demands a performance from the panic-stricken actor, and he complies in exaggerated, almost comical, fashion. In order to cure stage fright one must recognize a human gaze returning to find or acknowledge the actor, a promise that the literal cannot offer. And, instead of an instantaneous spectatorship in which our everyday work is *"wholly manifest,"* it offers up an unending and unconsummated interest, an "endlessness, being able to go on and on, even having to go on and on, [that] is central both to the concept of interest and to that of objecthood."[81] This Beckettian weight of "having to go on and on" doing something interesting falls squarely on the shoulders of the beholder. As Robert Smithson recognized in his response to "Art and Objecthood": "What Fried fears most is the consciousness of what he is doing—namely, being himself theatrical. He dreads 'distance' because that would force him to become aware of the role he is playing."[82] Fried is the starring actor in the drama of the literalist object, for all the beholder can do in the presence of the literalist object is "simply be aware of the work," as the actor is aware of the darkness of the audience beyond the lip of the stage, and *"act accordingly"* (as Fried writes) to some as yet unwritten script.

Writing from the position of the obscured audience looking up at the actors performing, Cavell states:

> Their fate, up there, out there, is that they must act, they are in the arena in which action is ineluctable. My freedom is that I am not now in the arena. Everything which can be done is being done. The present in which action is alone possible is fully occupied. It is not that my space is different from theirs but that I have no space within which I can move.[83]

We can spell out this reversal phrase by phrase. Sequestered inside Smith's "human-sized" cube, in Morris's standing column, or lying horizontal in *Site*, there is no space for the interior life of the literal object to move or to act. It discovers its freedom by withholding potential, knowing that "everything which can be done is being done." Meanwhile we, exiled to the arena of the possible "in which action is ineluctable," do everything we can do to fully occupy "the present in which action is alone possible." We encounter the object, we move around it, then leave it, while it waits patiently for our return. We are put onstage, not the object, and it is our experience of living in a present in which, in Fried's words, "the situation itself *belongs to* the beholder"—to the potential—that constitutes the uncomfortable (non)revelation of the literalist object.

Based on the claims of Cavell and Fried, one might be led to believe that this just reproduces the situation of everyday isolation from an other, the incomplete acknowledgment that characterizes our lived actuality. After all, Fried ends his essay by proclaiming "the utter pervasiveness" of theatricality, that "we are all literalists most or all of our lives. Presentness is grace."[84] But I think that saying that we are perpetually literal is to familiarize the encounter with potentiality as one more possibility in our everyday exchanges of solitude and loneliness. Fried keeps trying to see Smith's obdurate cube sitting across the gallery floor as if it were another body on the subway, but its secrecy extends beyond the silence of an individual consumed with his or her own possibilities (coming home from work and wondering whether to cook up some spaghetti or reheat leftovers or order out, etc.), possibilities that, while hidden, are presumed intelligible. This quotidian silence of the fellow passenger presumably partakes of the common assumptions upon which Edwards would ground his theory of will. Literal objects, on the other hand, are lifelike, but frightfully uninterested in our interventions, our ordinary language. So, yes, the literal is everywhere and everyone, but only in the moment where this surround, that object or body, remains in the abyss of potentiality.

Which leads me to the question: is Fried's performance a tragedy like Lear or Othello or is it rather a domestic melodrama? Diderot's attempts at playwriting were resounding failures, but the techniques outlined in the essays that Fried references as well as his call for a new theater found their way onto the stage in the early nineteenth century as the new genre of everyday drama: the melodrama.[85] In *The Melodramatic Imagination*, Peter Brooks contends that the melodrama is a peculiarly modern form, developing after the French Revolution in the wake of the decline of the sacred and its chief institutions (the church and the crown). Staged in an everyday social context deprived of traditional absolutes, melodrama must reestablish the moral and ethical at every moment in the starkest black and white, good and evil, with no possibility of synthesis or reconciliation.[86] As a genre, it aims at the clearest articulation of the terms of its moral entanglement, feeds off of spectacular catastrophes that, even in the suspense of a cliffhanger, promise resolution. In the chapter of this book on possibility, we saw how tragedy seeks to tame potentiality by bridling its chaotic productions to defined possible ends. Melodrama works at this problem overtime, at every moment constraining its futures to the possible. According to Brooks, we encounter this in the speech of characters, particularly when they are given an opportunity to speak their private thoughts out loud. The tragic soliloquy serves as a site for the speaker to negotiate a crisis, while in melodrama the soliloquy operates as "pure self-expression, outburst, the saying of self and self destiny."[87] Its characters must name their actions before, during, and after enactment to ensure they do not misfire.

In this attempt to access unmediated signification, melodrama goes so far as to circumvent language itself. Brooks suggests that if tragedy orbits around the problem of blindness, then melodrama takes muteness as its central figure. He outlines a long list of melodramas that rely on a silent character as the witness whose inability to reveal the truth of crime or heritage stokes the engine through which plot progresses. These silences may result from physical inability (Brooks mentions a play in which a dog acts as the linchpin for dramatic revelation), or from a vow of silence or the like. Muteness marks the performative vocabulary of the genre, as well. On the individual body, the genre's roots in the pantomime meant that actors relied on codified gestural vocabulary for expression as much as spoken text. On a more compositional scale, the silent tableau that

Diderot championed froze a culminating moment into a readily transmissible text that simultaneously unveiled all its characters in legible visual relationships with each other and the event. In both cases, melodramatic productions employed syntactical gestures that, as meaningful as a pose, expressed "an effort to recover on the stage something like the mythical primal language, a language of presence, purity, immediacy."[88] These gestures sought the kind of primal transmission that Fried sees in the compositions of Anthony Caro, the epiphany of "the efficacy of gesture" outside of time, unshackled from mundane contingencies, weightless. Thus, melodrama perfects the soliloquy's intent of self-exposure by abandoning the mediation of language altogether and arriving at immediate (timeless and unmediated) communication.

If we look at Fried's essay as a piece of performative writing—a text that does what it says—can we not see it as just such a crusade to label in Manichaean terms an art world whose ideology of modernist purity no longer held purchase? Can we not see this as a sermon to exorcise the demonic literal from the stage, or rather the darkened house from which it watches? As implied by his use of Edwards as a framing device, Fried, like Bartleby's narrator, wants to believe in the lasting pertinence of an absolute divine. His emphasis on "conviction" and the sentence that introduces his final sally suggest as much: "At this point I want to make a claim that I cannot hope to prove or substantiate but that I believe nevertheless to be true: theater and theatricality are at war today" (163). These are the terms of faith above all else. Intentionally or not, he ends up performing melodramatically to try to reestablish some moral/ethical grounds for "acting accordingly" in a situation in which the preordained paths of possibility have been dismantled.

Fried would like his sculpture to be as blind to him as Belisarius, still begging for his attention. Instead he encounters a demonic life that chooses to maintain its potential to see (him) and speak (to him), not from inability or an oath of silence, but through preference alone. The appearance of potentiality is not a blindness or muteness or any such deprivation of faculty, but rather a replete attention, a living presence ready to do whatever. Looking into the abyss of potentiality Fried encounters his own open-ended potentiality, which he covers over with a melodramatic soliloquy playing out an extended performance of the possible. For perhaps (and here I, too, succumb to the melodramatic mode), as much as fearing what this Pandora's box will unleash, Fried is afraid of what he will do to seek acknowledgment when put onstage, afraid to discover where his possibilities will end.

LOVING POTENTIALITY

It should be apparent that these ways of beholding potentiality may also reflect the performance scholar's relation to the live event and its futures. Each of the texts discussed in this chapter represents a decidedly linguistic production developed in response to the provocation of potentiality. Lest we limit our understanding of the beholder's performance to the melodramatic avowals of a crusading art critic, or a tragically deposed king raging against the storm, let me suggest a final way of thinking through this relation to the potential's possession of what it can do. Is not love also an engagement with radical aliveness in all its unknown unknowns? The lover lives for a future consummation, not as an end or static relation but in the hopes of a lasting and infinitely multiplicitous exchange; the lover waits anxiously for acknowledgment, knowing that all forthcoming moments are fraught with potential encounters and overdetermined with significance. He or she thinks that the beloved is always witnessing and, yet, far too often ignoring his or her appearance. In the meantime, the lover portrays many guises and makes plays in many language games, signaling wildly for the attention of the obdurate one. I can think of no better example of such a beholder's dance of possibility than Roland Barthes's book *A Lover's Discourse*. In these final lines, then, I merely wish to sketch the faintest outlines of another textual performance opposite potentiality: that of the amorous subject beholding the beloved.

Unlike the other writings we have looked at in this chapter, *A Lover's Discourse* is an explicitly performative text: the first page declares itself a solo performance that intends "to stage an utterance, not an analysis."[89] In the series of eighty short fragments that follow, arranged alphabetically so as to prevent a logic or hierarchy from imposing itself, Barthes describes a compendium of roles that the lover may enact to affirm an attachment to the beloved. With reference to the gymnast's pose, he terms this collection a repertoire of "figures," calling forth previously articulated possibilities that individual lovers may play within, like predetermined parts (4). In other words, they are already known forms of engagement, ways of relating to the object, or coded languages of longing. A partial listing of these possible figures could as easily describe those taken up by Fried before his literal object or by the narrator of Bartleby's story: *anxiety, atopos* (without place), *catastrophe, to hide, to circumscribe, declaration, drama, exile, embarrassment, identification, unknowable, monstrous, silence, objects, encounter, alone,* and finally *will-to-possess*. They could also describe my own many roles in this book.

Yet to say that these are poses is not to say that they are frozen attitudes. They are frantic and fast-moving expenditures: "I perform, discreetly, lunatic chores; I am the sole witness of my lunacy. What love lays bare in me is *energy*" (23). The lover expends the potential energy of his or her love in an exhaustively kinetic manner, laboring to relieve a cathexis that will not deplete its store. Love works the lover like a machine of perpetual (e)motion, for his or her performance is a constantly renewed reserve, an endless pursuit or production. The lover profusely articulates the possibilities opened up by a single figure or shifts rapidly from one figure to another. Outcomes are imagined and scenarios rehearsed. These many figures keep sprouting up from a chaotic roil of attachment, without logical progression from one to the other, but as a momentary efflorescence.

The lover performs a solo that projects forward in time without interruption or respite, toward a future that seems to offer no end:

> I cannot keep from thinking, from speaking; no director is there to interrupt the interior movie I keep making of myself, someone to shout *Cut!* Volubility is a kind of specifically human misery: I am language-mad: no one listens to me, no one looks at me . . . I take a role: I am *the one who is going to cry*; and I play this role for myself, and *it makes me cry*: I am my own theater. (161)

"I am my own theater" because there is not a director to intercede and tell me what to do or how to, as Fried put it, "act accordingly." How foolishly excessive the lover acts—making a show by storming off or pouting in the corner, serenading in cracked tones or pronouncing doggerel—because the loved one does not respond sufficiently in the private language of a desire that speaks only to the lover. This frantic mugging is a melodramatic practice, for certain ("I am *the one who is going to cry*"), and in this regard is closely related to the theatricality that Fried declaims and in which he indulges.[90] As Barthes puts it, the lover's discourse is a drama in the classical—or perhaps more precisely, neoclassical—sense, a production of great declamations surrounding an event that is always relegated to the offstage (the moment of falling in love that has already happened). Think of Racine's version of Phaedra, already swept up in her illicit passion when the play begins and eloquently reeling through possibilities before a world that seems to watch her every move. She regards her own monstrous performance with a kind of horror and shame, wishing for nothing so much as a possible exit. All of this overproduction of affect and yet she is essentially unable to take meaningful action onstage.[91] Think of Hippolytus standing there like an unpitying and unmovable plinth, whitewashed over with the same uniform response: "I would prefer not to."

If the literal object is an inverted theater that brings the offstage space onstage, so, too, the loved object makes its surroundings a stage for the lover's passionate expressions. A great distance interposes itself between the lover and the beloved, as far apart as that between stage and darkened auditorium. Or so it feels for the lover; the loved one's response is always insufficient to the vastness of what he or she could potentially be doing right now or in the immediate future. This vastness is the source of both fascination and anxiety: like the literal object, the loved one is always of further interest, and yet the impassiveness of the potential inspires an ever more fervid desire for acknowledgment. One proclaims loudly—even writes whole books—in an attempt to make sense of the potentiality of, and for, the other.

The lover wants to put all of language in the service of the beloved, but ultimately craves nothing so much as a gesture toward his or her own potentiality to say or do, a gag in the order of the sayable. Says Barthes: "My language will always fumble, stammer in order to attempt to express it, but I can never produce anything but a blank word, an empty vocable, which is the zero degree of all the sites where my very special desire for this particular other (and for no other) will form" (19). The lover calls the beloved that tautological word "adorable"—one is adored because he or she is able to be adored—or says, "I love you" again and again, as a promise to continue feeling an affection into, and for, the future.[92] That formula announcing a preference ("I love you"), so mundane, so transferrable, and so indistinct, stands as witness to the most singular of abysses that cannot speak itself. When I stop performing all these ridiculous possibilities and simply say, "I love you," the other will become my capacity for speech, my potentiality for affection. I will fall back on the blank word and blank page, the potential on which my language stumbles and gags. I will deliver a love letter that remains unopened.

FIVE | Actualizing Potentiality

Chaos is the ultimate depth of being; more, it is the
bottomless depth of being; it is the abyss behind everything
that exists. And it is precisely through the creation of forms,
qua determination, that chaos is always present also as
cosmos, that is, as an organized world in the broadest sense
of the term, as order.
        —Cornelias Castoriades[1]

Genesis scares me more than the apocalypse: the terror of
endless possibility, the open sea of potential.
        —Romeo Castellucci[2]

I have looked extensively at work that suspends potentiality as a deferred
promise for future becomings, and I have caught myself in the act of looking.
As an absolute calm that any difference would disturb, these conceptions of
potentiality veer precariously close to passivity or, as that which can only be
retained by *not* actualizing a thing, threaten to become a form of negation.
The question remains: can an event affirmatively actualize difference without setting up an opposition with what could have been but is not? Can an
actualization sustain its potential energy even while expressing kinetic forces
like some machine of perpetual motion or endless production?

Live events present a passage in time facing two directions, toward the
ephemeral as it passes into the past (Phelan's ontology of performance as
that which "becomes itself through disappearance") and toward an original future as it appears and makes itself felt.[3] Can we not occupy that trembling threshold of potentiality between destructive ephemerality and creative origination, by continually creating and destroying all our surrounds
at once? Returning to our point of departure—to the theater—I would like
to offer here an alternative epistemology of the vibrant and active stage,
one that is dependent not on drama's possible futures or pasts, but on the
potentiality seething beneath its boards and behind its curtains.

One of the first attempts to explicitly isolate this active potentiality of performance comes to us in a fragmentary theatrical proposition by the modernist stage designer, director, and theater theorist Edward Gordon Craig (1872–1966). Here we find a potentiality that does not wait in the wings, suspending itself prior to the *beginnings* of possible action, as is the case with the character of Bartleby staged by Melville's narrator. Instead, we find a potentiality that expresses itself as a *conception* of many worlds or an *origin* without movement toward an end. Echoing Edward Said, we might say that "a beginning must *be thought* possible, it must *be taken to be possible*, before it can be one."[4] In other words, the form that will follow is presupposed from the beginning and participates in a set of transitive relations, always implying an orientation to an answering end. Origins, on the other hand, fold endlessly back upon themselves in constant differentiations to open up a plethora of intransitive relations fanning out in a flow of becoming and unbecoming. The calm of the blank canvas or empty page finds it opposite in a chaos of motions constantly embarking for the future. Our project here is to discover how a live event, however thickly encrusted with the age-old architecture of Western theatrical tradition, may stage such an origin out of chaos, what me might call *apocalyptic potentiality*.

THE LIVES AND AFTERLIVES OF
EDWARD GORDON CRAIG'S *SCENE*

You now will reveal by means of movement the invisible
things, those seen through the eye and not with the eye, by
the wonderful and divine power of Movement.
— Edward Gordon Craig[5]

In addition to authoring important essays such as "The Actor and the Über-Marionette," editing *Mask* and its subsidiary publications (the first periodicals to look at performance across cultures), and collaborating with Stanislavsky and the Moscow Art Theatre on an important production of *Hamlet* in 1911, the visionary Edward Gordon Craig is perhaps most remembered for his designs and writings on theatrical space and scenography. Alongside his contemporary Adolphe Appia, Craig's work represents the first modernist foray into a visual theater. My interest in the artist hinges on a proposition from early in his oeuvre that has generally been subsumed into the narrative of his subsequent career and overlooked as a singular incident. I want to take the proposition seriously, even if it troubles accepted readings of the artist's body of work as a whole. In 1907, before all the other accomplishments mentioned above, writing in words that recalled the Old Testament's staging of the origin of the world, Craig described his vision of a performance that displayed the genesis of a living world from out of the void. Such a move from an empty theater to an emergent form of life captures what I see as a fundamental aspect of all performance events, how they open the present into futures rife with unarticulated worlds. Craig's fantasy, imagined more than one hundred years ago, was never realized onstage. But it provides the theoretical basis for more recent modes of performance that stage the origin of a world in all its potentiality without arriving at form, figure, or possibility.

Edward Gordon Craig had been carrying a copy of Sebastiano Serlio's *Five Books of Architecture* with him since 1903, inspired by the Renaissance architect's images of street scenes and isometric studies in perspective to first propose his theory of manually movable screens. If Serlio's layers of horizontal planes receding toward a single point perspective were literally materialized in the theatrical "flats" of theatrical illusionism, then Craig abstracted these planes into pure colored surfaces, albeit surfaces bounded by frames and the limitations of hinged junctures. But in February 1907, after hearing of the Asphaleia hydraulic systems then appearing in theaters throughout Europe—systems that made possible the simultaneous independent movement of sections of the stage floor—Craig looked beyond the fixedly framed surfaces of his theater of folding screens to imagine a theater of continuous creation and variation.[6] Scrawling hurriedly in the back pages of his personal copy of Serlio's book, Craig relayed the following vision of a theater of the future:

> The place is without form . . . the floor seems to be an absence—the roof a void. *Nothing*—is before us—
> And from that nothing shall come life—Even as we watch, in the very centre of that void a single atom seems to stir—to rise—it ascends like the awakening of a thought in a dream—
> . . . there to the right—something seems to unfold—something to fold—what has unfolded? Slowly quickening, without haste, fold after fold loosens itself and clasps another, till that which was void has become palpable—some spirit seems to work there in the space, as in a gentle—A wind which blows open the void and calls it to life.

Craig's ideal theater would exist in concept alone, truly a *utopic* event in the etymological sense as a "nonplace." The 1907 vision haunted the artist for

Fig. 5. Sebastiano Serlio (1475–1554), *Set Design for a Tragic Scene*, 1545. Engraving. Bibliotheque de L'Arsenal, Paris, France. Giraudon / Bridgeman Images.

the remainder of his life, but technological limitations coupled with an increasing paranoia regarding the idea's exposure prevented a staged realization.[7] Craig's excessive suspicion of others taking credit for his innovations undermined many of his ideas, but he guarded none as closely as the event he would come to call *Scene*. His son, Edward Craig, recounts how, many years later, he secretly built a wooden scale model of *Scene* for his father's use. After revealing the model as a present, the designer's initial delight with the working model turned to outrage when he was told that Edward had consulted a friend regarding the technical feasibility of such a construction in a life-size theater. Fearful that too much had already been revealed, Craig set the model aside and never used it again.[8] For these reasons, aside from this hastily written description, most of the other textual reformulations that Craig fashioned of his *Scene* are intentionally shrouded in obscure language and suggestion.

The divorce between conceptual theory and material enactment was

Fig. 6. Edward Gordon Craig, *Scene*, 1907. Engraving. Publication with the consent of The Edward Gordon Craig Estate.

characteristic of Craig's relationship with the theater. As depicted in his models and engravings, the dimensions of the folding screens, for example, were far too large, heavy, and unwieldy for practical use when translated into an actual stage design. Similarly, his famous essay "The Actor and the Über-Marionette" simultaneously celebrated the grace of the puppet over the human performer and derided conventional wire attachments as producing "jerky" overly mechanistic movement, all the while neglecting to explain how to achieve the "rhythmical" manner of his ideal puppet.[9]

This is not to say that Craig did not attempt to find a means toward realizing his vision in the theater. In practical terms, Craig's initial plan for a theatrical enactment differs somewhat from the described experience. He proposes a model that divides the stage floor into a gridwork of movable sections with a ceiling segmented into an identically delineated arrangement—a kind of literalization of the coordinate grid of single vanishing point perspective. Such a model allows for fluid shifts between walls and chasms, columns and platforms. Craig acknowledges that this construction would limit the play of possibilities to strictly rectilinear configurations— the architecture of cellular building blocks in his many prints from this period. He writes: "We have, therefore, a room or place moveable at all parts, and all ways, *within certain laws and restriction*—That is to say we have the square and the right angle and the straight line . . . So far, then *we have produced a place possible of all kinds of movement: straight—square or angular.*"[10] Here clear edges and lines of action would presuppose a finite set of *possible* stage arrangements, "within certain laws and restriction": the angular. However, Craig's original description of the event quoted above, particularly the material-like folds "clasping" one another, surely signals a less geometrically organized intent. This original folding does not evoke the interplay of various fixed forms passing along predetermined paths, but a kind of fluid, even chaotic, stirring of the primordial soup.[11] In other words, there is a distinct difference between the vision and its proposed implementation. At least as imagined event, Craig wants to stage the genesis of the world anew, before shape and contour define place and use.

But what kind of life might this void manifest? Craig himself did not conceive of the event as an anthropomorphized representation of nature's motions. He exhibited several of the etchings of *Scene* in 1908 and wrote in the accompanying catalog: "The Imitation of Nature has no part in this art. The mood and thought of the artist passing through this Instrument shall raise by it one mutable form after another, living only a moment; ceaselessly, if imperceptibly, changing; arriving at last at its final and definite state—only to fade—to re-form itself once again, and again—an infinite progression."[12] Even its "final and definite state" does not fixate in an entity as such, but offers an invitation to further ceaseless movement. The initial vision does not describe a conclusion to his *Scene*, closing instead with the following phrase: "And may my love beginning, have no end." This endless production stages an inhuman labor without goal, a potentiality to do without defining a possible object as the resolution of its movement. The engraving provided Craig with a particularly appropriate medium for the depiction of emergence. Progressively working a single block of wood would result in a number of prints that revealed different stages or states within the process of a singular appearance.[13] Each print pulls out different scales of light and dark, changing as the artist works over the same material form. A single block of wood provides for any number of appearances, like an onion peeling back countless translucent skins. In a sense, one can imagine *Scene* as the endless production of such an engraving, a slow revelation of the appearance contained within the wood that keeps showing itself anew. Of course it is a fantastical promise, this ceaseless carving of the block of wood (and here one must recall Aristotle and Michelangelo with their imagined sculpture contained in the untouched matter), but perhaps this is what Craig's lifelong permutations on *Scene* sought to accomplish: "an infinite progression."

In other words, perhaps the original vision of *Scene* acquires its significant capacity to express such potentiality precisely because it never had to authorize a defined object. As semioticians of the theater would remind us, as soon as something appears on the stage it begins to mean something. Craig appears to understand this difficulty even in the transcription of his original vision, as evinced by the vague reference to "*something* that unfolds" and the many "seems" throughout the text (four uses of the word in as many sentences). It is as if he were reluctant to place the event in certain terms. Craig's refusal to characterize a staged content extends beyond the privileging of form over content common to modernist tendencies and passes into a willed effacement of qualitative possibilities. He leaves his question "What has unfolded?" unanswered, as if to say it is not so much a *thing* acting as an unfolding as such—the movement of unfolding. The entities depicted here do not claim a set identity, beholden to the authority of a hierarchical eye, but rather together form a single living whole or multitude.[14] They take the stage as a community in evolution, proclaiming a radical force that attempts to escape anthropomorphic prescriptions. It is as if the world of representation itself were in the process of generation, so that names and actions seem to slip off the sensation. Rather than an instance of Genesis that posits order atop the indistinct chaos of the void and seeks to name the indeterminate, as in the Old Testament's many divisions of light from dark, earth from water, this is a kind of Lucretian procession of falling atoms in constant variation.

This is to say that Craig's vision of a theater to come departs from the dramatic theater's delineated characters or objects pursuing conflicting plots through teleological action and instead attends to an uncharacterizable motion. This is confirmed by the director-designer's well-known aversion to the stage as site of textual representation. Initially Craig referred to the imagined event as *Motions* and then simply as *Scene*, suggesting that movement and scenic image are synonymous, but also that his utopic performance approaches the ontological roots of the theatrical event at large, an essence that he anchors in movement.[15] *Scene* manifests a theater where to move is to appear and to appear is to move, to change.

Nearly one hundred years after Craig first penned *Scene*, the Italian experimental theater company Socìetas Raffaello Sanzio staged a short site-specific performance, *Crescita XII*, at the 2005 Avignon Festival in southern France. In many respects, the piece recalled the intent of Craig's original spectacle of potentiality and its depiction of an undelineated living process becoming in constant variation before an audience. However, instead of attending to Craig's appearance of an atom center stage, the Socìetas Raffaello Sanzio performance brings those mysterious invisible unfoldings out from the wings of a kind of ur-theater to brush unseen against the spectator, a "wind that rushes over the void and calls it open to life." And instead of proposing its beginning from an empty void, *Crescita XII* presents a theater that must first destroy the world of representation in order to create anew. It must join creation with destruction, find genesis in the apocalypse.

At their assigned time, an audience of twenty gathers inside the Cloitre Saint-Louis, a sixteenth-century Jesuit seminary recently converted into a hotel and now headquarters for the monthlong international theater festival held every July in Avignon. Led up a set of stairs and along a stone corridor drenched in sun, the group walks past conference rooms where the press interviews artists and public officials, while amplified voices echo up from a public lecture in the courtyard below. Arriving at the corridor's end, they face a door like any other they had passed. Then stepping inside, parting thick velvet masking, they find a hermetically sealed black box theater nestled within the heart of the hotel. It is as if they have stepped from the world of recognizable and placeable reality, authorized by history's uses, into a pit of anywhere and anytime.[16] Three rows of seats in this most

Fig. 7. Romeo Castellucci / Soc̀ietas Raffaello Sanzio, *Tragedia Endogo-nidia, Crescita XII*, 2005. Photo by Emile Zeizig.

minimal of theater auditoriums all face a box set that has similarly been reduced to become the proverbial white cube, all even industrial surface with no maker's mark to mar the gleam. There are no entrances or exits, only the invisible "fourth wall" allowing passage—a brilliant hard edge of incandescent white against black velvet surround.

Some way back in the box is a small boy, maybe ten or eleven years old, sitting on a basketball and facing upstage. He is the only difference in a field of white. Slowly he raises his head to look at the blank wall opposite the audience. A moment. Eventually, he rises to his feet and walks a few steps to face the wall again, then picks up the ball and begins to bounce it calmly in an even rhythm. He is passing time with an object, but soon his attention turns more forcefully toward the ball, involving himself in the play with more intention, performing impressive maneuvers and manipulations. Not much happening, but utterly compelling to observe the boy's commitment to the playing, his almost virtuosic absorption in the object at hand. And yet, a nagging sense of expectation gathers. The white room sits inside the theater's playing space and it, too, is a character acting something out. Something has to happen.

The boy stops to regain his breath. He tosses the ball at the wall, catches it. Waits. Then a voice whispers from beyond the walls: "Sebastiano." He stops, clutching the ball and waiting. Then "Sebastiano" and a third time "Sebastiano."

Suddenly the theater is doused in complete and utter blackness and a great deafening roar pours out from the stage onto the audience. This is not the theatrical darkness of dim glow tape and exit signs to anchor vision, but a thick and viscous absence of light, forbidden by the strictures of commercial safety and sense.[17] Even more peculiar within this sudden void is the cool wind that batters from every angle, submerging the beholder in a chaos of motions. The roar runs through all registers of sound, overtones and undertows in all one's cavities, until one's voice seems to join in with screams and laughs of its own—no speech heard or made, but sound as sensation. Time stands still and surrounds the beholder, so that it feels like hours underwater or perhaps mere seconds. The remove of visual distance is not possible—one is in the midst of the event.

In any case, the material void does end eventually, the roar and its wind receding back into the stage and seeming to circle within the abstract white cube now lit once more. It is as pristinely bright as before, though now the child is nowhere in sight. His ball remains, a trace wedged in the corner of the room, but he is gone. Something else is wrong here: the white room now sits slightly tilted on one end, though it is initially unclear whether it has shifted or we have shifted—as if the entire world were thrown off its tectonic axis. It is like an earthquake that changes the laws of nature or proves them false. Craig's coordinate plane of columns and corners sits askance; the whole axis and orientation of escape thrown off, fleeing itself.

The door into the outside world stands open, and when the audience leaves the theater to descend into sunlight and the city beyond, the space remains behind, the sounds and winds still circling within the emptied cube. One has the sense that the white cube in its black box remains there still, hidden within that arbitrary room at the end of a hallway, or even that similar spaces of potentiality lurk behind other doors, maybe every door.

What world had called the boy out remains uncertain, though it would be hard to call it human. The sounds heard and the sensations evoked extend beyond any system of repetition or imitation, projecting rather as the voice or breath of a void. While we may have returned from the world of conception, he has not, instead remaining suspended in its midst. Perhaps this is the most appropriate solution to the conundrum of an endless staging—the fact that the performance must end at some time. By taking the child into the realm of the infinite as a sacrificial substitute, the performance allows us beholders to return to our everyday world of productive objects and produced subjects.[18] He, however, remains suspended in that other time of labor, sent backward from birth—the instance that splits one into the double of representation, as Artaud would have it—to the (endless) moment of conception, when and where stuff is forming, becoming, but taking action becomes impossible.

It follows that *Crescita XII* stages at least two different ways of thinking about potentiality. On the one hand it presents the "appearance" of utter darkness as a kind of revelation of one's sense of sight as a medium. In a passage from *De Anima* ("On the Soul") devoted to the notion of the potentiality of the senses, Aristotle writes of how the faculty of sight makes itself known through the experience of absolute darkness, an absence of color or light that nonetheless presents itself as a positive presence, the sense seen in its complete lack of content. Opening our eyes in the pitch dark, our capacity for sight is made apparent without confining its vast expanse to a focal point or object. This does not imply a lack of sensation or a blindness—one feels sight's liveness and preparedness for appearance—only that there is no object at which to look, on which to focus. The potentiality of vision appears in making present the lack of an actual object; in seeing that one could (is able to) not have a look, one sees the sense of sight. Such a notion of revealing potentiality through impotentiality aligns with the kind of suspension/possession that Agamben explores in his revision of Aristotle: "What is essential is that potentiality is not simply non-Being, simple privation, but rather *the existence of non-Being*, the presence of an absence; this is what we call 'faculty' or 'power.' 'To have a faculty' means *to have* a privation."[19]

But more significant to the version of potentiality I want to discuss here is the manner in which the void's positive presence actualizes the sensible body of the spectator as a chaos of difference in motion. For, apart from disclosing the faculty of vision as a potentiality for sight, the event creates a nearly synaesthetic experience as sound and touch imply a "vision" of movement outside the spectrum of visible light. The remove of optical distance is not possible, nor is it possible to visually define or delineate an object within the abyss. Utterly alone in perception, where the question of possession falls away, I can no longer determine whether an event belongs to my experience or I belong to its enactment. The limits of my body are no longer determinate and I cannot discern a possible end to my actions or the event's motions. The "actors" in question do not have names or forms. In other words, the entire discipline of possibility splits asunder.

Here potentiality expresses itself by absolutely exhausting the present moment's capacity to produce difference, a difference without reference. Each sensation thrusts itself up, singular and unrelatable in the midst of a chaos without compare. As Deleuze and Guattari write:

> Chaos is defined not so much by its disorder as by the infinite speed with which every form taking shape in it vanishes. It is a void that is not a nothingness but a *virtual*, containing all possible particles and drawing out all possible forms, which spring up only to disappear immediately, without consistency or reference, without conse-quence. Chaos is an infinite speed of birth and disappearance.[20]

This void is not an absence, then. Instead of retaining and holding back the capacity to form a world or motion, as in the case of the still body or Bartle-by's preference, such a chaos constantly exhausts and rejuvenates the full capacity of an event to be different from itself. Apocalyptic potentiality— destroy a world in order to affirm a radically different one.

As I will explain below, such a performance of constant variation need not exclude the visual. Rather, I would suggest that it was Craig's attempts at beginning with "nothing" that represented the deepest difficulty for any live engagement with such a performance of chaotic conception. For per-formance always takes place in an already constituted world comprised of audiences of quite distinct individuals, in architectures that inherit social and geographic relations—the story of a street corner, a building, and neighborhood. Even if that world is merely the ground opened up by an empty theater, the figure must emerge from something and somewhere. Nestled away in the architecture of a hotel with its own ingrained history of centuries past, next door to media representatives gathering to write the more immediate history of the day-to-day arts festival, *Crescita XII* pre-sented the minimal movement of a potentiality lurking in every crevice or corner of the quotidian, a ceaseless life still seeming to throb even here in the simplest of rooms.

We had stepped into the most minimal of theaters, some approximation of the essence of the medium: there was a space and an actor; he did things; an event waited in the wings.[21] If this is an event, it is one that is almost entirely illegible, and if it defines a protagonist, it is only in his sudden ab-sence from the aftermath. And when the possible world returns, as it inevitably must for those of us wanting to reclaim ourselves and act once more, we expect a difference marked in the system or a change in our location. But the world to come appears no different than that which came before, except for the disappearance of the sacrificial substitute, a literal shift in perspective and our accompanying awareness that this reality, too, may at any moment open up to another world. Walter Benjamin wrote about the Jewish Messianic tradition's view of the apocalyptic:

> The Hasidim have a saying about the world to come. Everything there will be arranged just as it is with us. The room we have now will be just the same in the world to come; where our child lies sleeping, it will sleep in the world to come. The clothes we are wearing we shall also wear in the next world. Everything will be the same as here—only a little bit different. Thus it is with imagination. It merely draws a veil over the distance. Everything remains just as it is, but the veil flutters and everything changes imperceptibly beneath it.[22]

Is this not an image of the theater par excellence, a world that is quite like our own, yet somehow distinctly altered or altering in the time that is always to come, a time bordered by the fluttering appearance of a veil or curtain? Can we not see the curtain as a kind of eyelid blinking closed on this scene and open on another; closing off our access to this present as it becomes past and revealing this imperceptibly different present as it becomes future? As it reveals a new world full of its own distinct potentiality?[23]

Such messianic thought would claim that, in order to create or conceive the world to come, one must first destroy the world as it is. In *Crescita XII,* this marriage of the end of a world and the beginning of another is writ large in the passage from the first white cube to the second, slightly different variation of the chamber. We may legitimately wonder whether that torrent of sound and darkness had been interposed as a cover for the laborious removal of one white cube and its replacement with another nearly identical twin. After all, isn't this what happens in the blackout between scene changes when incidental music covers heavy footsteps of stage hands, the creaking of a turntable or movable wall?[24] In *Crescita XII,* such a destructive genesis also appears more immediately in the shifting sensorium of the void itself, where one *repeatedly* experiences *different* sensations over and over again. Here potentiality expresses itself by absolutely exhausting the present moment's capacity to produce difference, a difference without reference.

All of which is to suggest that staging the genesis of a world from scratch as Craig had imagined it may, at this other end of the twentieth century, require a parallel *destruction* of preexisting possibilities. "Apocalypse" derives from the Greek word for "unveiling." Craig's *Scene* had imagined an accumulation of foldings and unfoldings as the movement of variation, an "unveiling" that did not reveal a nameable character, but only the *movement* of disclosure as such. Romeo Castellucci, director of the Socìetas Raffaello Sanzio, has spoken of the curtain as an "actor" concerned with an ambivalent task fundamental to the theater: "It closes, or it opens. What is the real function of the curtain? To close or to open?"[25] Closed, curtained, or veiled, the theater maintains its capacity to stage many worlds; the curtain holds them in abeyance just as the surface of the blank page contains infinite inscriptions. Castellucci refers to the task of the curtain in active terms: "to close" or "to open," but it is clearly both at once. Veiling is a motion that has not arrived in the stable state of the veiled, just as an unveiling moves toward the open without arrival. The curtain folds and curls upon itself in undulations, unveiling with one swell and veiling elsewhere, otherwise.

These affirmative voids live on even after they have been veiled again, after whatever god or director says: "Let there be light." Existing alongside our present moment, as it trembles under our many expectations, their messianic announcements open out into alternate worlds, strange and darkening, that live on without us. This is not necessarily a benign or positive proposition. Writing at the beginning of the twentieth century, Craig could imagine genesis in an abstract theater as a quasi-religious, transcendental potentiality called to life, to love, to hope. At this turn of the millennium, the messianic event's opening into the abyss of potentiality and its ending of this world's possibilities is also always coupled with an acute sense of Terror. Any room or road may suddenly break with our expectations, the sense of firm footing give way into free fall.[26] An improvised explosion, an atomic explosion, the sudden reduction to the formal movement of matter with Lucretius's atoms in fall(out) once more. A world will end and another will begin without us. To turn back to Donald Rumsfeld's own veiled unveiling with which we began this book: in the permanent state of emergency ruling the contemporary global landscape, the "known unknowns" of the possible no longer hold purchase upon our greatest fears, no longer offer a resolution to the catastrophic. Instead, we face the Terror of "unknown unknowns," the chaotic potentiality of a sudden end and sudden beginning from out of this moment. In staging apocalyptic potentiality—endings as beginnings—the live event forces its audience to encounter such potentiality as something that does not belong to us, but rather as something that takes us up. It allows us to set its fuse and practice abandoning ourselves to its cruel becomings.

SOCÌETAS RAFFAELLO SANZIO AND THE APOCALYPTIC FIGURE

The theater is, by its very nature, an apocalyptic art. Every night worlds flare into life and out of life within its crucible. It is an art that preoccupies itself with the disguise and the reveal, the curtain parting to unveil the bloody remains of the most recent catastrophe. Or, contrarily: Monty Hall takes the stage before a live studio audience and promises some prize or other behind curtain number 2.[27] The radical ambivalence of performance's apocalyptic potentiality is perhaps nowhere as apparent in contemporary theater as in the work of Romeo Castellucci and Socìetas Raffaello Sanzio. For more than thirty years, the company has pursued a profound engagement with the ontology of the stage and the problematics of representation, directly confronting the traditions of Western theater and the futures that lie before it. One of the most striking aspects of their work is the fact that it unleashes the full effects of potentiality to disturb not only the discipline of authoritarian possibilities but also the temptation to view such resistance as an inherently hopeful and progressive enterprise. This is a theater of the apocalyptic in all its ecstatic and terrifying glory.

Socìetas Raffaello Sanzio (henceforth SRS) was founded in 1981 by Claudia Castellucci (b. 1958), Romeo Castellucci (b. 1960), and Chiara Guidi (b. 1960) in their hometown of Cesena, a small city in northeastern Italy. Having received degrees from the University of Bologna and the Academy of Fine Arts in painting, painting and scenography, and art history, respectively, from the start the company's founders created work at the intersection of the visual arts and the theater. Theirs is an oeuvre that includes laboratory experimentation, theoretical symposia, gallery installations, works for video, musical concerts, and theatrical performances. Generally speaking, Romeo Castellucci directs the mise-en-scène, Chiara Guidi directs the acting and vocal work, and Claudia Castellucci constructs the dramaturgical structure of the pieces and the movement, though this changed somewhat in the work following the completion of the *Tragedia Endogonidia* cycle (2002–2004). While occasionally collaborating with Romeo in the subsequent years, Claudia Castellucci and Chiara Guidi have since pursued their own research projects and performances, convening laboratories and conferences on the voice in song and speech, on modes of dramaturgy, and philosophy's intersection with the performing body. During this latter period, Silvia Costa has often worked as Romeo's assistant director and Piersandra Di Matteo has operated as a frequent dramaturgical interlocutor. Beginning with the 1999 production *Genesi: From the Museum of Sleep*, which I will discuss below, and in all performances to follow, the company has collaborated with the Chicago-based sound artist/composer Scott Gibbons, who works with digitally manipulated found sound objects.

The first performance pieces of SRS were staged in Rome as part of the generation following the Italian avant-garde theatrical work of the 1960s and 1970s that critic Giuseppe Bartolucci would term the "post-avant-garde."[28] A variety of directors in the Italian avant-garde had responded to the French "absurdism" of the 1950s not by staging translations of foreign plays or by writing their own, but instead by deconstructing texts from the Italian canon. As Mario Prosperi characterized the movement in a special issue of *TDR* from 1978 devoted to Italian theater, "[The avant-gardes] interpreted these [canonical] works on a metalinguistic level, the performance being reduced to an essay, a demystification, an analysis and commentary *about* the original play and its sociological and political implications."[29] The political critique expressed in these "essays" did not follow the rational dialectic of a Brechtian epic analysis so much as a baroque mockery through grotesquerie and pastiche, replacing distant analysis with an intimate and multiplicitous disruption of the sensible. One could characterize much of the work by SRS from the 1980s and into the 1990s as a "metalinguistic" dissection of language, an excavation of rhetoric. Such is the claim that Gabriella Giannachi and Nick Kaye make about the company in their survey of that period in Italian experimental theater. For example, for the production *Kaputt Necropolis* in 1984 the company sought to construct a private language (*Generalissima*) consisting of eight hundred words and which featured "a privileging of speech . . . [according to which it was] only possible to understand each sentence of *Generalissima* from its pronunciation."[30] In other words, here language cleaved to an absolute performativity, acquiring its significance solely in the context of its momentary articulation.

While a strand of the company's work exemplified by Chiara Guidi's research workshops and concerts continues this investigation of the voice through the history of profane and sacred performance, it is the material world broadly conceived that takes precedence in many of the company's productions. Based on the belief that the encounter between an image and its embodiment is one of the (if not the) most prominent conflicts in the theater, the performances mine their textual sources for figures and icons that are then translated into concrete realities. This materiality plays out as a concern with literal, elemental, or ritual substances, such as dirt, milk, or gold, but also through an exhaustive focus on the embodiment of the actor. Animals share the stage with children and other traditionally "unrepresentable" bodies (those whose disability or extreme appearance exclude them from normative visibility). The physical object or sensible force exists on the same plane as the human performer, so that the performances stage a kind of material combat across forms and figures. Light, sound, space, and object are invested with an animistic liveliness and expressivity. The entire theatrical apparatus becomes a potential actor, an assemblage of activity, or series of sensory organs extending outward from the individual spectator's body. A liveness common to an event's many intersecting players emerges. Writing of such an ecological perspective that includes human and nonhuman actors, Jane Bennett claims that "each member and proto-member of the assemblage has a certain vital force, but there is also an effectivity proper to the grouping as such: an agency *of* the assemblage."[31] For Bennett, this requires a reconfiguration of the ethical relation away from individuals (such as that between performer and beholder) and toward the recognition of our involvement with the assemblages in which we participate. The audience is responsible to the event that they witness and that lives within.

These human and nonhuman actors are not ahistorical, essentialized presences. The remains of Western culture litter the stage in many of these pieces, reflecting the collapse of present and past that suffuses the landscape of a contemporary Italy where motorways circle the ruins of ancient Rome. In the 1990s the company began creating work that radically reconfigured the texts of the Western theatrical canon, including productions of *Hamlet, Julius Caesar,* and the *Oresteia,* among others. *Guilio Cesare* (1997), for example, staged Shakespeare's tragedy as an investigation of rhetoric, embodying the materiality of this most rarefied speech in the corporeality of the performers themselves.[32] A massively obese man played Cicero, proclaiming his treatises on rhetoric, thus literalizing the gravitational pull of oratory at the center of the play. At the other extreme, two anorexic women portrayed Brutus and Cassius, while an elderly man with a laryngectomy represented Mark Antony, only speaking with the assistance of a throat microphone.[33] The company's concern with canonicity extended to the foundational texts of Occidental literature and culture, including the epic of *Gilgamesh* (1990) and the book of Genesis in *Genesi: From the Museum of Sleep* (1999).

It is a body of work that would far exceed the bounds of a single book. Indeed, working in collaboration with Romeo, Chiara, and Claudia, performance theorists Nicholas Ridout and Joe Kelleher's impressive monograph *The Theatre of Società Raffaello Sanzio* (2007), speaks of the impossibility of encompassing the company's life in terms that I can only humbly echo. The first and only full-length study of the company in English at the time of writing, it limits itself to the discussion of SRS's most ambitious project to date, the vast eleven-part *Tragedia Endogonidia* cycle (2002–2004), and acknowledges the fact that the spectator/writer cannot detach him- or herself from the production of the event. My writing also stays close to my subjective experience of these performances, re-creating or restaging these undocumentable events as one would recount a memory, distortions and all. I focus exclusively on work from the new millennium in this chapter— *Genesi: From the Museum of Sleep* (1999), the *Tragedia Endogonidia* (2002–2004), the three-part *Divina Commedia* (2008), and *The Four Seasons Restaurant* (2012)—since I only began following the company in 2000. This decision also descends from my conviction that this period of performance work collectively considers the question of potentiality in its many guises.[34] I am aware of the fact that in constructing such a partial history of the company I am no better than Melville's lawyer, condemning this life to literature and narrative.

A note of qualification regarding the strategies that the company employs should be stated outright. Many of the images that SRS stage are archetypal and recall a vast and, at times, loaded history of Western representation. Men appear onstage as surrogates for patriarchal force, however compromised, and women appear as embodiments of a mythic maternity. One may recognize, for example, a tendency toward presenting the child as the embodiment of innocence and purity, as the vessel of futurity, in the piece discussed in the previous section of this chapter and increasingly so in the company's work to follow. As Lee Edelman has argued, within heteronormative culture the child stands as the symbol for the reproduction of the same, an unattainable transcendent figure for the future that justifies the continuation of this hegemonic culture at the expense of those excluded from its version of a reproductive system.[35] When it stages the infant as a privileged site of technique-less performance or as an innocent victim of the tragic system, SRS repeats such an investment in the archetype of "the Child" outside of history. It is my contention that such recollections of representational hegemony are vital to the functioning of the iconoclastic principle at the center of the company's aesthetic; my highly subjective retellings of these various events assume the validity and success of SRS's iconoclastic operations. But I also recognize that, like potentiality itself, the affects produced by these encounters are not politically or socially progressive by default.

Genesis and the Birth of the Actor

In 1999, at the end of the millennium and in the midst of what Frank Ker-mode called an apocalyptic "sense of ending" ruling the day, SRS returned to one of the beginnings of Western representation to stage the first book of the Bible.[36] But the world *beginning* here is the world of representation, de-fined and dictated by possibilities always already in relation to an end. *Genesi: From the Museum of Sleep* concerns itself with the darkest side of creation; it gives birth to a world that is always beginning to die, always beginning to kill.

The first of the three parts that constitute *Genesi* returns to the Garden of Eden as if to a long-buried archive, its faded and encrusted exhibitions lit by the faintest of lights, as if embedded in the low glow of amber. Every-thing is dusted with the patina of history, whitewashed with ash and age. However, in order to reclaim an original force of materiality from what are otherwise desiccated remains, *Genesi* stages its Adams and Eves, its Sera-phim, in an iconoclastic manner: the symbolic role is embodied in the base materiality of naked flesh or bone, but always with a supplemental differ-ence to redeem the life of the "dead" icon in an unexpected direction. A contortionist performs as Adam, folding himself into impossible arrange-ments within the confines of a narrow vitrine. Not a human being of clearly defined possibilities—an arm that bends only this way or reaches only this far—he explores a wildly inhuman articulation in the claustrophobic con-fines of Eden. His body "speaks" a concrete language, a semaphoric nam-ing of the animals outside of the socially (for what community can move in this manner, can repeat his physical phrasings?) and vocally representable. Elsewhere another such chamber slowly and inexorably crushes a sheep's head fresh from the butcher, while two stuffed sheep piston back and forth in endless mechanical copulation. These stand as perfect representations of the machinery of sacrifice and the prescribed nature of reproduction within God's watchful construction (for these are decidedly not animals, but fab-rications of a mad machinist dressed in perfectly taxidermied sheepskin). The second part, titled "Auschwitz," situates us in a white chamber arrayed with ominous machinery and devices, clearly echoing the "medical" labo-ratories of the death camps. A group of children (the six children of Chiara and Romeo) perform a variety of tasks and games amid and among all, a soporific haze clinging to the walls. One wears a bunny costume, another a small tuxedo with top hat as he rides a miniature train across the stage. Here, SRS stages the limits of ethical possibility, the ends of "evil," as the extreme consequence of the beginning initiated by Genesis. Finally, the third part presents an elegiac retelling of the Cain and Abel tale as a story

Fig. 8. Romeo Castellucci / Socìetas Raffaello Sanzio, Adam in *Genesi: From the Museum of Sleep*, 1999. Photo by Luca Del Pia.

of profound love between two men, where the murder, deprived of intentionality, is posed as an insistence from some director on high. Two German shepherd dogs wander the stage throughout.

I want to focus on a fragment of the first part of the self-contained trilogy and its manner of staging creation as the beginning of the possibility of death. The first book of Genesis opens, of course, with that initial conception of the world ex nihilo where the demiurge's speech creates that which it says, the performative speech act par excellence. But *Genesi: From the Museum of Sleep* does not begin with a staging of creation as such. Instead, the performance begins with the appearance of Lucifer in the laboratory of Marie Curie, the physicist who discovered "radioactivity," as he intones melodious Hebrew from a Bible that spills forth cold light. Radium is, according to Romeo Castellucci, "the only substance in the world that emits light. A light that gets into the bones. It's from radium (the discovery of which marks the beginning of modern physics) that you increasingly sink into the core of things until you break it."[37] It is as if the moment proclaimed: Let there be light, but let it be a radioactive light issuing from matter itself, a light that turns back on the substance of a previously created world and corrupts its composition in a beautiful and otherworldly fracturing of the image. Let it be the light that decays.[38] And so we do not witness the founding figuration of the icon in *Genesi*, but a space composed of preexisting imagery, touched by a light of attention that corrupts the icon from within. To be seen on this stage in this light is already to begin to die.

For SRS, Lucifer is the progenitor of the Judeo-Christian theater in that he is the first actor; he is the first to represent another by taking on the skin of the snake, but also by claiming, "It's true that god said," an utterance that irrevocably ties the performative to the determination of truth propositions. Lucifer creates what Romeo Castellucci calls "a relationship with the minimal, genital conditions of theater; genital in the sense of geniture . . . the minimal movement from which something is born."[39] This moment of birth is staged with elegant and frightful simplicity near the beginning of the piece. The tall and impossibly gaunt Franco Pistoni, playing the fallen angel and garbed in a heavy fur coat, approaches a pair of vertical bars, extending high into the rafters and out of sight with but a few inches separating them. The stage is pitch dark otherwise, inscrutable behind the thin scrim that, as in so much of SRS's work, skims a cataract over the eye between audience and action. Lucifer attempts to squeeze through this narrowest of gaps, but to no avail. Retreating once more, he strips off the coat that shrouds him, sloughing off his mammalian skin snakelike until he stands naked. A dwindled figure out of Giacometti, it is as if he somehow had stretched his own corporeality to its limits in mimicry of the twin bars, his bare body the long line of the snake filling the negative space between two lines. Spreading the metal lines apart only the smallest distance, he works his way through the opening.

Lucifer forces entry into Eden by parting the two lines that otherwise extend without meeting into timeless infinity, making the ur-actor the differentiator of the same, the identical, a figure taking up the space between the double stroke of the quotation mark.[40] To be born is to divide and be divided, to separate one's utterances from one's self and say, "I am not the one who speaks." To be born is to become an actor performing a role divided from that (mythic) unified self. If Lucifer captures the "genital conditions of theater," then, it is as the "birth" into a theater of representation, a birth that leads to that subsequent, ultimate possibility: death. Since SRS often works through the image and its disavowal, this is a birth that does not rely strictly on enunciation. Lucifer is, as his name proclaims, the "light-bearer," and, as mentioned above, to appear on this stage is to appear in the lethal radioactive light of representation.

This conception of the theatrical as an art locked in conflict between representation and creation derives at least in part from the work of Antonin Artaud. Indeed, Artaud's recorded radio performance *To Have Done with the Judgment of God* (1947), produced a few short months before his death, haunts the soundscape of the second part of *Genesi*. As explicated by Jacques Derrida in his influential essays on the artist, Artaud distinguishes between the theater of representation and a theater that expresses life as a unified force: the Theater of Cruelty. At the risk of restating a well-rehearsed reading (and simplifying Derrida's nuanced argument), let us say that the philosopher sees the inevitable iterability of the performative as the paradoxical contradiction at the heart of Artaud's Theater of Cruelty. Even more than Edward Gordon Craig with his fantasies of graceful puppet-actors and atomic churnings, Artaud's visionary conception of the theater remained for the most part a theoretical imagining during his lifetime.[41] Derrida claims that speech does not belong to the speaker, but to the system of representation through which it gathers meaning, that it is always already like a purloined letter, opened and deprived of address and addressee (this is the lesson that Bartleby learned so well during his apprenticeship at the Dead Letters office).[42] It is this separation of speech from the body—the letter from its writer—that was so terrifying for Artaud. The moment of utterance corresponds to the "birth" of the individual into language, a birth that inevitably produces twins: the human being and its representation. By being represented, one becomes a character employed in a set of tasks, and one is projected into a range of possible futures. To be born is to be born for something: the most definite end, death, but also any number of subsidiary ends along the way. In Derrida's understanding of Artaud, this scission marks the "judgment of God" and the making of the human in distinction from the divine: "[God] is the difference which insinuates itself between myself and myself as my death. That is why—such is the concept of true suicide according to Artaud—I must die away from my death in order to be reborn 'immortal' at the eve of my birth."[43]

Any theater organized around the principle of an absent/offstage logos—whether god, king, author, or language as such—against which the representation acquires significance is thereby a theological stage. Thus in SRS's *Genesi*, Lucifer not only gives birth to the subject-as-actor, but also, in a rather ironic turn, founds the theological stage. By instituting the separation of speech from being, a separation that repeats an absent God's original utterance ("It's true that god said") he marks "the minimal movement [through] which something is born." To stage a true instance of genesis is to trespass on the prerogatives of the creator, the moment when "God's breath hovered over the waters" of the void before representation began and God said "Let there be light" to differentiate dark from day.

The Theater of Baroque Iconoclasm

It is precisely in that moment of chaotic differentiation that potentiality might find expression, when an event becomes itself while at the same time becoming other than, more than, itself. In an essay on the performances of Carmelo Bene—an Italian director who belonged to the avant-garde generation immediately preceding SRS—Gilles Deleuze proposes a Theater of Cruelty that taps into the creative potential of the chaotic not by returning to an Edenic imaginary presymbolic time, but by unleashing the potential within representation itself. While the image of the theater appears elsewhere in Deleuze's oeuvre, the essay, "One Less Manifesto," is notably the only text in which he explicitly discusses a theatrical performance or the medium in an extended fashion. Bene first appeared onstage in a 1960 production of *Caligula* and until his death in 2002 staged and performed in a variety of deeply iconoclastic revisions of classics such as *Pinocchio*, *Othello*, and especially *Hamlet*, which he would mount in five different iterations. These deconstructions of the dramatic influenced SRS's subsequent approach to classical texts. Critics have often referred to Bene's engagement with the vocalization of texts in "surgical" terms: how he followed Artaud in dissecting language into screams and hisses, excising the organs of dramatic structure, image, and the cavities between, and then suturing the fragments into a new whole.[44] Pier Paolo Pasolini, for example, offers us the following memorable characterization: "There remains the exceptional case of Carmelo Bene whose Scream theater uses a language that desecrates and—to speak frankly—shits on itself."[45]

Deleuze also devotes much attention to Bene's vocal experimentation, yet it is Bene's irreverent interpretation of the theatrical canon (Shakespeare in particular) that to his mind releases "a new potentiality of theater, an always unbalanced, nonrepresentative force."[46] On Bene's stage, the King appears—often in the most theatrically authorized form under the auspices of the demiurge Shakespeare—but the performance develops as an accumulating series of "subtractions" from the fully constituted theological stage. Deleuze describes how Bene surgically removes the central representational role or power structure from a play, whether it be the character of Romeo from *Romeo and Juliet* or the royal system at large from *Richard III*. Without this keystone in place, the whole edifice of the performance collapses as its supporting figures and themes, previously relegated to the background or interior, evolve their own involute architecture. No longer subservient to Romeo's narrative, Mercutio takes center stage and begins a series of metamorphoses. This "constant variation" releases the subterranean forces contained within the role or system, sets them loose as expressions outside systemic representation, so that the destruction in question becomes an affirmation of difference.[47] The potentiality held in reserve or restraint by the representational order is thus expressed.

One could say that this process of destroying the stable form in order to free its creative potentiality—this process that Deleuze ascribes to Bene—applies more to the philosopher's thought than the stage director's actual work. Lorenzo Chiesa has argued that Deleuze's framing of Bene's theater as an *affirmative* decomposition contradicts the actual practice of the Italian director, which called for a subtraction toward *absolute negation* or *extinction*.[48] Without attaching too much importance to intentionality, especially when negotiating Bene's statements of overt provocation, it is worth considering that Deleuze's Bene is, like his Nietzsche, Spinoza, or Bergson, a "monstrous" perversion of the stage director's originating thought rather than an accurate portrayal.[49] This is to say that the promise that Deleuze sees in Bene's theater may be a selectively perverse revision of the director's project that proposes a utopic form of performance quite different from the subtractive mode, in a sense the philosopher's manifesto for a theater to come. In titling his essay "One Less Manifesto" (which plays off of Bene's production *One Hamlet Less*), perhaps Deleuze repeats the operation he describes at work in the director's performances upon that selfsame material—removing Bene himself from the manifesto.

It is this affirmative version of iconoclasm that SRS embraced as a founding mode of production. Claudia Castellucci writes:

> Our first preoccupation was to destroy that which exists, not merely because of the need for an empty space, but in order to rupture the representation of the world as it was already proposed. We needed to begin again at zero. In effect, even if iconoclasm addresses the diminution of images, the word is not at all negative, it is positive. . . . "iconoclasm" does not signify "[an icon]," nor "without-icon," but "I break the icon." That is to say that it needs to make something that remains visible. This is because *iconoclasm is always figurative*.[50]

A world of representation always precedes the event, and the only way to create anew is to break this representation open and actualize its potential to diverge otherwise. By presenting an icon and its negation, the work opens up a space between the binary of being and not-being where the spectator might assert his or her own interpretative presence. Iconoclasm releases an image from the stability of already known possibilities; it wages a "war against images *via* a fight conducted from the inside."[51] Or, to refer back to Nietzsche, SRS seeks to philosophize with a hammer, staging "idols, which are here touched with a hammer as with a tuning fork."[52]

The iconoclasm undertaken by SRS is not an attempt to convert the theatrical image into an insufficient, damaged, or defaced representation. Instead, it approaches images as if they were what W. J. T. Mitchell calls "hyper-icons," or "figures of figuration, pictures that reflect on the nature of images," images "in a double sense . . . in that they are themselves 'scenes' or sites of graphic image production."[53] Mitchell's examples of such hyper-icons include Plato's cave, Locke's dark room, Wittgenstein's duck-rabbit, Foucault's *Las Meninas*, Lessing's Laocoön, or—fittingly for our notion of potentiality—Aristotle's wax tablet. The theater of iconoclasm stages images that overtly concern the nature of figuration—images like the small toy robot that sits on the downstage edge of the proscenium in *Genesis: From the Museum of Sleep* and rises to clap (or not clap) at the end of the act, like some artificial skeletal remnant from the latter parts of the seventeenth century when audience members watched from the stage.

More radically, iconoclasm invests everything that appears onstage as a site of its own autonomous production. In what we might think of as an operation designed to free potentiality from the static, figures become means or grounds for further figuration. Minimalism reminds us that the rudimentary form without qualities is a ground for future productions: there may be Michelangelo's sculpture hunkering down in the unmarked cube, there may be distant echoes of construction, or there may be the breathing artist himself (Morris standing in his vertical column). Or perhaps even the artist has become otherwise (the reclining Schneemann occupying Morris's horizontal column). Even more forcefully, though, the theater of iconoclasm insists that there are potentialities without preconceived faculties in place. It teaches us that anything in its purview may become a medium, for as soon as something appears on the stage it begins to double itself over not only as a representation, but also as a force fanning out into a plethora of futures.

Here the company's namesake, the Renaissance painter Raphael (Raffaello Sanzio), serves as a lasting influence and means of thinking through a visible iconoclasm. In his prime, Raphael was known for paintings such as *The School of Athens* and *The Dispute* that demonstrate a masterful composition in strict perspectival stability. To follow a by-now conventional reading, these paintings are symmetrically balanced along vertical and horizontal axes exemplary of what art historian Heinrich Wölfflin termed the "tectonic" structure of classical art. In a sense, they show the image of a certain technology of representation perfected. But with his last paintings, especially *The Transfiguration*, which was left incomplete at his death in 1520 at the young age of thirty-seven, Raphael moves toward the involuted forms of the baroque.[54]

Critics have long struggled with the fact that *The Transfiguration* stages two separate biblical scenes in a single canvas. In the bottom half, a wild, possessed child stands at the center of a crowd (from Matthew 17:14–21), while the top half depicts the transfiguration of Christ before his disciples (from Mark 9:17–20). Both biblical events display a spirit escaping from a material body: in the lower half as exorcism, in the upper half as apotheosis. While the scenes concern the human form, such a rupture of the figure's bounds extends into the object world, as well. In the former episode, when asked by his disciples why they could not relieve the child of his demon, Christ replies: "If ye have faith as a grain of mustard seed, ye shall say unto this mountain, Remove hence to yonder place; and it shall remove; and nothing shall be impossible unto you" (Matthew 17:20). Christ teaches that faith can release the forces withheld by a material form, can perform impossible motions. As such, *The Transfiguration* describes through images an escape from the world of images.

This tension plays out in both the narrative content of the image (where the transcendent Christ rises above the unruly mob swarming the lower portion of the canvas) as well as in the technique employed to represent each component of the image as a whole. Gravity maintains the most tentative hold on the figures, each on the verge of scattering across the canvas. In spite of the prominence of the two central figures of child and Christ, one's gaze constantly gets caught up in the currents that seem to swirl about the other figures' skewed and frenzied gestures, their troubled garments. It is this tension between the fully constituted "perfect" representation that Raphael had so clearly mastered and its concomitant chaotic dispersion that interests SRS. As Claudia Castellucci writes in one of her theoretical essays: "The baroque image is tumor-ridden: . . . its degeneracy wears down the figure and its interior."[55] On the surface of Raphael's work one sees a stable figure, but the baroque image is hollowed out not with absence but a tumultuously positive abyss, the threat of a cancerous pressure pressing at the surface of the skin, as if the body presented were on the verge of fragmentation. Or, in Henri Focillon's description of the baroque tendency: "The skin is no longer merely an accurate mural envelope; it is quivering under the thrust of internal reliefs that seek to come up into

Fig. 9. Raphael (Raffaello Sanzio of Urbino) (1483–1520), *The Transfigu-ration,* ca. 1519–20. Oil on panel. Vatican Museums and Galleries, Vatican City. De Agostini Picture Library / Bridgeman Images.

space and revel in the light and that are the evidence of a mass convulsed to its very depths by hidden movements."[56]

This force pushing to escape its confines extends beyond the human figures to the scene itself. Without the anchor of classical perspective's vanishing point—without the figure of Socrates as the rational center of the world in *The School of Athens*, for example—nearly everything occupies the middle ground as the scene swells with a vertiginous swirl of fabrics, bulges of grassy earth, and a halo of clouds about the ascending Christ. The classical divides the image into discernible parts and individualized entities, all regularly bounded by linear limits—what we would call possibilities—that populate the space surrounding the counterpoint of the viewing subject, that gaping hole of the vanishing point. Serlio's schematic depictions of a city street bored through with a central vanishing point find a perfect correlate in Raphael's *School of Athens* or *The Dispute*. Meanwhile the baroque image brushes up against the spectator; its vanishing points scatter to surround us. All forms contain a black hole of attention at their core. Here, "Living beauty no longer resides in the limited, but in the limitless form."[57] The baroque does not descend into absolute flux; it attends to the moment when the form begins to escape from itself and joins others in a collective movement or force.[58]

Looking back at *The Transfiguration* once more we will see that the painting's proximity to the artist's death suggests a manner in which the baroque image stands at the crossroads between the actual body and the virtual force. Vasari's *Lives of the Artists* recounts how the painter died on the exact same day that he was born (April 6) and that upon the public viewing of the body, *The Transfiguration* was displayed in Raphael's studio alongside the artist's corpse. Apocryphal or not, one can only see this anecdote as proclaiming a strange marriage between the corporeal figure and canvas, birth and death, closely akin to the relationship portrayed in the painting itself, where forces transfigure the body into other registers. So Raphael (via *The Transfiguration*) occupies the threshold between two worlds, or rather—like Lucifer between his infinite lines—he divides the division between the two.

This, too, guides the project of SRS in its conviction that "theatre is the most carnal art and the closest to the experience of finitude in comparison with all the other arts. . . . There is nothing so flagrant, so close to life."[59] This flagrant proximity to life refers foremost to the theater's "privileged relationship to death" recognized in Herbert Blau's notion that the live performer is dying in front of the spectator's eyes. It is a claim that a host of artists and theoreticians over the latter half of the twentieth century have invoked to suggest that the live event is lost to its ever-present past. But, this "flagrant" proximity to life may also reference the generative capacity of the theater. Perhaps live performance makes itself known not so much through disappearance, which implies an irreparable loss, as through an escape toward other fields of potentiality?

Ultimately, the baroque provides a manner for thinking an iconoclasm that is not grounded in negation, as in Bene's "subtraction towards extinction," but in the affirmative production of difference. It stakes a resolutely material and cumulative claim on the field of the sensible. Deleuze writes: "There is a vast difference between destroying in order to conserve and perpetuate the established order of representations, models, and copies, and destroying the models and copies in order to institute the chaos which creates."[60] SRS employs the tactic of fully realizing a representation, but adding a divergence or contradiction to express a means of escaping that representation and, at least on a localized scale, "instituting the chaos which creates." Or, as Chiara Guidi wrote in a letter to sound designer Scott Gibbons, "The problem now is the same as it always was: the Figure must be set free from representation, which has something to do with the sort of feeling that gets into the flesh and the nerves. And this setting free happens through a fall. We must struggle, then, to bring about this fall."[61] This is a fall from the grace of a perfect image or language (with echoes of Fried and Edwards), from the promise of an unchanging future. Examples of such baroque iconoclasm can be found in *Genesi*, for example, where the image of Adam exceeds itself in literalizing his capacity to express a material "first" language. There are numerous other instances of such. There are the animals and children that appear in the other sections of the trilogy, each performing its task without any supplementary affect—they do not pretend to do anything other than what they do.[62] They wear their costumes too loosely, so that their materiality threatens to surge up and out through the seams.

In what may seem a meager example, I remember that the youngest of the children in *Genesi* had a rather nasty cough the night I first saw the piece. She fulfilled her actions with a remarkable grace, but that rasping sound kept asserting itself, like a branch scratching at the window, reminding me of the outside of representation. Something wanted out from the small and neat chamber of the part she played. No tumorous growth or plague, but something much more mundane, perfecting the living vulnerability of the child.

THE ENDLESS TRAGEDY AND COMEDY OF THE FUTURE:
THREE PERFORMANCES

The Tragedia Endogonidia Cycle

We are back with the boy. But instead of waiting in his white cube, filling time by playing with his ball, here he finds himself in a hyperrealistic box set, lying in a bed placed in one corner of the room with a door at the other. A comic book keeps him company. Faded white wallpaper and stained wood paneling suggest a domestic interior from our not-too-distant past, perhaps the 1930s or 1940s. His mother enters and puts the child to sleep, turning low the lights as a white curtain intercedes downstage. And now an onrush of wind seems to suck the lamplight and the architecture of realism out and away as the heavy churn of an engine coils about the pitch-black darkness that is suddenly upon us. It is the same roiling void encountered in *Crescita XII*, but appearing as it does here, in the final episode of SRS's *Tragedia Endogonidia* cycle (*Cesena—C.#11*), this tornado of motion has changed character. Writing of this version of the void-as-event, Nicholas Ridout associates the sensation with the thrill of piloting an airplane as it hurtles over land, an atomic bomb secreted away within and ready to let loose its absolute power:

> As the theatre vibrates around me, I feel that I have never flown so far or so fast. . . . As the lights come up, the white curtain is drawn to reveal the amazing new location to which the theatrical machine has transported me. The same room. Exactly the same. Except that the boy is gone from the bed, and a woman is now hoovering the carpet.[63]

The woman is, of course, cleaning the stage of the catastrophe, reordering chaos in a literal enactment of the catharsis ("purging") that plays out again and again in the tragic form. Here the catastrophe acts as a formal interruption in the narrative of a realistic representation—a system of representation at least superficially more concerned with content than form. The event shows the laborious force behind all theatrical production, especially that of realism, for the appearance of the woman cleaning the room is entirely possible within the genre depicted here in the *Cesena* episode. The *Crescita XII*, discussed in detail in the first section of this chapter, shows this same event in stripped-down form. In the language of the *Tragedia Endogonidia* cycle to which both pieces belong, we might say that the shorter piece staged the genetic code or Platonic ideal that this more domestic iteration has instantiated into a particular history. It took the boy and left us with the promise that it would touch down again in the future.

In the aftermath of *Genesi: From the Museum of Sleep*, the massive *Tragedia Endogonidia* cycle extended the iconoclastic beyond the decomposition of the single image to occasionally allow these sublimated forces free play over the full breadth of the theatrical scene. Potentiality was no longer limited to the individual figure. The cycle also exceeded the single event to realize a structural form that incorporated an evening's performance into a much larger plane of living, so that an event was never over but looked out to a series of other events one after or alongside another. As its title foregrounds, the *Tragedia Endogonidia* cycle conjoins the tragic drive toward death with a life-form that, possessing both gonads (or sexual organs), constantly replicates itself anew — the endogonidic, in biological terms. In performance terms, the cycle spawned eleven interconnected but discrete episodes in ten different European cities over three years (the first and last episode premiered in Cesena, Italy, the company's base of operations). Each episode stages a mutation on the original constellation of thought, sometimes in the reappearance of the same characters or concepts, sometimes in a related sound or rhythm, a structural element. When Romeo Castellucci speaks of the project as an "organism on the run," he refers to this genetic and geographic mutation, but also to a perpetual mode of escape, exemplifying the baroque tendency to use the figure to escape figuration. For, as Focillon writes, baroque figures "proliferate like some vegetable monstrosity. They break apart even as they grow; they tend to invade space in every direction, to perforate it, to become as one with all its possibilities."[64]

Running away from itself, the cycle also eludes documentation and discussion. In spite of a plethora of material traces, including a series of dramaturgical pamphlets printed alongside the cycle (*Idioma Clima Crono*), a six-hour "filmic memory" by the video artists Cristiano Carloni and Stefano Franceschetti, audio recordings of the sound score, and a volume of collected writings and conversations surrounding the piece, there is a profound sense that the thing itself has run for the hills, left our planetary orbit for some distant expanse. This mode of constant pursuit extended to the means of production, where the company would develop the individual episodes in short periods of residency at each theater, following the strand of a thought as it responded to a local landscape without ever surveying the whole of the project. Even more consciously operating in a rhizomatic fashion, the parallel series of *Crescita* ("tendril") expressed a select genetic "trait" of the larger organism in short site-specific pieces, new organic outgrowths of the larger whole.[65]

The "organism" of the tragic form replicates itself endlessly in each episode and *Crescita* not as a copy so much as a repetition with a difference, a constant departure. To speak of just one of many such differing repetitions: at the start of one episode (*Brussels — Br.#04*) we see a uniformed cleaning woman mopping a white marble floor that will later be covered in a pool of deep red stage blood. In another episode (*Avignon — A.#02*), a clown-like figure appears as her double. He, too, cleans the floor, but instead of wielding a mop, he uses a meat hook to maneuver a cow's liver across the stage — for, remember, the liver is the organ that cleanses the body of toxins and the like. In the manner of the mother vacuuming the floor in *C.#11* mentioned above, clown and cleaner literalize the tragic "catharsis" meant to purge the taint left by the tragic hero's disappearance. In a sense, everything becomes a substitute for something else in a system that cycles endlessly upon itself, a whirlpool that in swallowing down one figuration keeps spitting out new actualizations.[66]

In this regard, the cycle realizes one of the primary metaphors that Artaud relies upon for his conceptualization of cruelty — the plague. The plague is a potentiality lurking in the organic body, capable of taking it over and forcing impossible motions; it joins bodies in contagion, becoming packs of animals and humans alike. The plague exemplifies the body without organs, constituting a singular field of vitality across the discrete part-by-part nature of the organ and thereby retaining the body's "creative potential," its capacity to expand into unheard directions and provocations.[67] An instantiation of the plague will appear in the figure of the infected only as temporary articulation of a vitality that will move elsewhere, taking over a different host body. As explained by Deleuze in his subsequent writings, the body without organs may create ephemeral organs without creating an accompanying expectation that these explain the organization of the system. One provisional organ — the infected — follows another and another in an accumulation of differences. In "The Theatre and the Plague" Artaud writes: "Like the plague [the theater] reforges the chain between what is and what is not, between the *virtuality of the possible* and what already exists in materialized nature."[68]

This seemingly endless cycle of revision and division characterizes the formal structure of tragic substitution. Indeed, the *Tragedia Endogonidia* confronts the tragic as the architectural structure for both Western theatrical representation and Western sociopolitical order. As articulated by French philosopher René Girard in *Violence and the Sacred*, "The birth of the community is first and foremost an act of separation," a separation enacted via exclusion or destruction.[69] A chaotic mass of people suffused in undifferentiated violence reaches a crisis wherein a singular figure—the scapegoat—must be separated from the multitude in order to carry the burden of this collective negative energy. In the process the community forms itself in relation to the scapegoat who, by standing in as the surrogate object for all violence and submitting to exile or annihilation, allows the community to be reconstituted in harmony. The exclusion of the scapegoat posits a resolution to the catastrophe, a *possible* end to its eventhood. We saw this operating in *Crescita XII*, where the child's sacrificial disappearance from the scene allowed the audience to arrive at the end, back in that slightly changed white room, and escape the chaotic middle of the event. As the cure for the city's sickness, the scapegoat thus becomes the symbolic reparation for the city's evils, thereby explaining the dual definitions of the *pharmakon*, as both poison and antidote. Of course, such orderly existence remains in force only until violence's accumulating feedback plunges the common into a new crisis, at which point a new surrogate subject is once again invoked as consummately guilty and becomes the sacrificial victim. This subsequent pariah is a surrogate in two senses: first, as the stand-in for the guilt and violence of the mass, second, as the stand-in for the original surrogate. And so the ritual of sacrifice is repeated, the cure reclaimed.

Put in this light, tragedy marks the originating *birth* through which a community defines itself as distinct and possible from the faceless unknown unknowns of the future. Oedipus once again stands as the exemplary figure in this regard, in that his expulsion from the city marks the end of the plague and reconstitution of the state under a new king. He dons the mantle of the scapegoat by individuating himself from the crowd, by claiming the transgressively singular relationship as father of his siblings, husband to his mother.[70] In a paradoxical manner the progressive differentiation of the individual scapegoat reaches its culmination in the complete effacement of the figure, his/her expulsion from the terms of a comprehensible human entity.

We could say that the scapegoat actualizes the (violent) potentiality of the chaotic multitude into a singular difference. But this figure that has been separated from the undifferentiated chaos of potentiality at the same time contains within itself its own undifferentiated ground for all future figurations. Such potential ground contains the faces of all future surrogates and all its sacred uses from poison to cure, just as the iconographic role of Oedipus in Sophocles's play contains all future performances by all future actors. Even in its radical singularity this is precisely the danger and power of the scapegoat. Here, in spite of the problematic universality of

Girard's theory, we encounter a formal language for understanding the marriage of tragedy and the self-(re)producing life-form.[71] For the *Tragedia Endogonidia* does not restage tragedy as the possible way out of chaotic potentiality. Instead, the *Tragedia Endogonidia* folds the scapegoating machine over upon itself, and refuses the resolution of the ritual by focusing on the endless production and reproduction of the sacrificial subject. The scapegoat's separation from the mass, his or her manifestation as tragic protagonist, and the concomitant instantiation of the community/city/ state—all loop over and over again. The idea of the city, represented in the ten "host" sites, emerges from this crisis of differentiation.

Certain segments of the cycle isolate and condense this production of difference / exclusion to let the entire spectacle erupt in variation. Here potentiality expresses itself by absolutely exhausting the capacity to produce difference. One can think of this chaos as iconoclasm writ large, where the fully actualized image is destroyed by forces otherwise submerged in representation at the same time that it is realized in a radically different manner with its own distinctive halo of potentiality. No appearance ex nihilo, in order to stage a new world the theater must first kill off that which subsists on its creaky boards. If we return to Derrida's sense of Cruelty as *"the access to a life before birth and after death,"* we see that the theater of constant variation is not the utopic conception before the birth of representation, but the conception of a life *after* the death of representation. And isn't this the most appropriate ontological position for the future of a live event? If liveness is always at least in some way a dying gesture, an ephemeral departure from the shores of reproduction, then one must destroy a world to affirm a radically different one.

Let us look at one such staging of chaos in which potentiality is actualized through constant variation: the second part of the penultimate episode in the cycle, where, in a proscenium theater in the French port city of Marseille, SRS stages the origin of a world, or the origin of many worlds.

The woman that stands from the front row of the audience to appear in silhouette is our surrogate, of course, stepping forward to offer herself in our stead. She, too, is the sacrificial subject, the tragic protagonist, again, the ur-actor. We, the audience, see her as the lone figure in distinction from the uniform expanse of the lit field beyond, a surface of light that fills the entire proscenium frame in this old Italianate theater. But we can also imagine ourselves in her place, facing a tabula rasa that maintains its potentiality in suspension.

Suddenly the light evacuates the stage and a slow billowing rises from blackness. The volume heaves itself into sight like a great amorphous beast from the deep, in some color cognate of the cobalt blue of retinal afterimage spliced with a nearly organic green. Symmetrical, the emerging form evokes the mirrored halves of the face, the bisection of the animal body, or perhaps, more tellingly, some mutation of the Rorschach test—arguably the most recognizable "technology of the self" in the twentieth century. As Peter Galison asks in an essay on the test, "What are these cards? To answer (or even not to answer) is to present yourself. Just insofar as these cards are described, they describe the describer."[72] The ten official blots that comprise the Rorschach test were strictly guarded images, copied with the utmost attention to precise and stable reproduction—icons, if you will. In order to assure a consistent interpretation, the ten plates that the Swiss psychologist established as the official images of the test were beholden to the strictest criteria to ensure identical tone and hue across individual iterations.[73] Rorschach insisted on this consistency to approximate the repeatable test necessary for a claim to scientific objectivity, but also to prevent the incursion of any human intentionality or presence in the form presented.[74] In other words, one encounters contradictory impulses in the Rorschach blots: on the one hand, the images themselves seek to touch upon the inhuman potentiality of expression; on the other hand, the system of production, from its rigidly fixed means of reproduction to its quantified response, serve to restrain that potentiality to defined possibilities. In the test, the description of the subject "described" by the object sits within a carefully coordinated diagnostic apparatus that scores the response of the beholder according to a comprehensive quantification of psychological states. Each answer the subject offers to the blot's announcement of itself situates the speaking beholder in a particularly defined psychological cartography. In acknowledging the Rorschach blot in verbal terms, it acknowledges and determines your possibilities.[75]

The Rorschach test relies upon an exchange with the viewing subject, but as Nietzsche warned, "When you look long into an abyss, the abyss also looks into you." In *M.#10* our surrogate responds with a song of lamentation, raising her arms in an ambivalent gesture at once recognition, supplication, and invitation.[76] Here the darkness swells and folds over itself, the dust cloud from an eruption or detonation, settling into itself—a stirring of the primordial soup at the origin of a world and, at the same time, the aftermath of an apocalyptic nuclear fallout. It is both conception and end at once, for as soon as a form alights across the field it falls away to other forces, other faces. There are monstrosities, the curved smile of the abyss lingering like some Cheshire cat, many eyes dilating wide and then

Fig. 10. Romeo Castellucci / Socìetas Raffaello Sanzio, *Tragedia Endogo-nidia, M.#10—Marseille,* 2004. Photo by Luca Del Pia.

sealing shut. We see a momentous shifting of form where figure becomes ground, and ground becomes figure. Or as Deleuze describes the appearance of difference:

> Instead of something distinguished from something else, imagine something which distinguishes itself—and yet that from which it distinguishes itself does not distinguish itself from it. Lightning, for example, distinguishes itself from the black sky but must also trail it behind, as though it were distinguishing itself from that which does not distinguish itself from it. It is as if the ground rose to the surface, without ceasing to be ground. . . . This difference or determination *as such* is also cruelty.[77]

In the abyss of cruelty the figure escapes into a ground at the same time that it escapes into a figure, constantly carrying its potential to differentiate into its differentiation. The figure must become a ground for future figurations.

The screened image of the blot in motion stages this oscillation between figure and ground, falling back into its other, but the individualized woman still remains apart from this play of forms. The final moments of the Marseille episode, however, display the "rising of the ground to the surface" and the meeting of the two on a common plane. Here the woman stands alone again. As at the start of this segment, she is a silhouette against the field of light, the only difference. Slowly black curtains begin to close on either side of her, narrowing the luminous ground until only a thin column of light shines center stage between the encroaching dark. She pulls a black hood over her head, so that she, too, is draped in the darkness—a gesture that recalls the many other mourning women in the cycle (as in Kierkegaard's *Fear and Trembling*, these variations attempt to allow Sarah to mourn the loss of her son Isaac at the moment of his departure for Sinai or should the substitution of the ram not take place, come too late). She then reaches out to grab the edges of the curtain and pulls them around her, behind her, closing the seams and disappearing beneath.

The event almost exactly reverses the birthing of Lucifer from *Genesi*. Lucifer was born between identical lines, uttered himself as differentiator, the light-bringer. The woman joins the ground of the theater as a field of potentiality, withdraws into the depths of that undifferentiated blackness. Like a slow flash of lightning falling back into the night sky, she "distinguishes [her]self from the black sky but must also trail it behind" her. Remember, too, that the boy, the sole figure on the ground of the white cube, escapes to a darker offstage place. Where the narrator-lawyer of Melville's tale performed himself wildly to articulate a possible identity as if clambering for a solid stance at the edge of the abyss, the woman suspends her performance in joining the field of potentiality. I hesitate to say that this is an end since the darkened theater always remains waiting to become another world, its great maw opening to spit forth another figure.

The Divina Commedia

As the associated artist of the 2008 Avignon Festival, Romeo Castellucci presented a trilogy of new works based on Dante's *Divina Commedia*, continuing his investigation into the nature of creation and creativity, of the beginnings and ends of worlds that had inspired *Genesi* and the *Tragedia* cycle. As with the cycle that preceded it, this was a fugitive event that took up temporary residence in several local sites. It spanned the immense courtyard of the fourteenth-century Palais des Papes and the full verticality of its hundred-foot walls; a converted theater in a convention park on the outskirts of the city; and returned to the medieval city and into the hollowed structure of the Eglise des Celestins, altar-less and emptied of all the trappings of the fifteenth-century church. *Inferno* answered the graphic and excessive imagery of Dante's text in the most extreme of registers with a diverse cast of sixty locals, a dozen children, a pack of trained guard dogs, a white horse, a crashed car, and a piano set ablaze midstage over the course of some three hours. In this avowedly spectacular opening performance, Andy Warhol himself makes an appearance, playing Virgil, Lucifer, and Beatrice in one. For, if Dante's great poem presents the revolutionary depiction of a psychology of depth, then Warhol represents psychology as pure surface.

At the other end of the spectrum, the Avignon version of *Paradiso* invited a small group of spectators into a darkened antechamber for a five-minute glimpse into the radically transformed interior of the Eglise des Celestins.[78] Through a circular opening they saw the bare stone walls lit up with shimmering light, a glistening pool rippling across the entire floor of the nave, while a stream of water poured endlessly onto the burned out husk of the grand piano that would appear in each work from the trilogy (see the back cover of this book). The piano stood as the most human of instruments, a silenced potentiality like the open keyboard before David Tudor's hands, waiting for four and a half minutes into eternity. A large black piece of fabric—a veil or curtain—battered against the open eye of the portal through which the audience watched, interceding a blinking reminder of one's own temporal present and exclusion from this timeless paradise. Five minutes later (four minutes and thirty three seconds, perhaps?) and their time was up: the audience ushered out.

While the entire trilogy offers compelling instances that wrestle with apocalyptic potentiality, I would like to focus on the central piece, *Purgatorio*. This is because it is the part most concerned with the dramatic theater as such; because it stages the future as a conflict between what has been judged possible and the release of apocalyptic potentiality; and, finally, because it returns to the figure of the boy facing the end of the world.

The curtain rises on a hyperrealistic kitchen in 1970s high modernist decor, where a young mother prepares a meal for her son. The boy is not feeling well again, takes some pills, and goes back to bed, but before leaving the room asks if "He" will be coming tonight. The mother does not offer a response. All of this is presented in absolute realism: the tedious time it takes to complete each domestic task, the glare of lights in the refrigerator, running water over dishes in the sink, a knife cutting the loaf of bread. But there is a slight amplification of the audio in all these quotidian tasks, microphones holding each action's sound apart from the surroundings as if in quotation marks, as if pulling us into close-up or, again, swelling the perfected image from the inside. This artificiality behind the "realistic" is further accentuated when a large black disk descends from the rafters to conclude the surprisingly uneventful drawn-out scene. As a group of similarly amplified stagehands begin to move the furniture about and arrange a second room—the boy's bedroom—a series of projected texts recount the actions of the characters from the previous scene. This "script" with its stage directions troubles the notion of an intentionality assignable to the characters, unveils the theatrical's construction of the real and how it predetermines the possibilities of all its players. In the supertext's account of the scene everything is happening exactly the same "as always": it has already happened as it will happen. The characters are referred to as "stars," perhaps in reference to Dante's allegory where souls eventually become celestial bodies, but also in recognition of the highly cinematic quality of the piece (and recalling the Warholian frame that the preceding *Inferno* had established—everyone a star for fifteen minutes). These are not real people, merely representations playing out a ritual performance.

After the grand spectacle of *Inferno*, with its crowds, its horses, and the burning wreckage of cars, pianos, and television sets, Castellucci explains this disquieting shift into realism as follows: "Only the Purgatory is inscribed by Dante into the limits of a temporal duration, unlike the two other parts of the Comedy, because the Purgatory is the ultraworldly section that is more similar to the earthly existence: it is the double of the earth, it is the repetition of the human life that is known and lived in the daily and familiar tasks."[79] As mentioned at the beginning of this chapter, the last episode of the *Tragedia Endogonidia* cycle (*Cesena C.#11*) had represented a first foray into realistic illusionism for a company that had previously been more concerned with operating upon *material* reality. It had showed another boy preparing for bed in another bedroom moments before a void had taken over the theater. That other room had been arranged in almost exactly the same manner as the one now filling the stage (bed against the wall stage right, door on the same wall stage left), but where it had been firmly fixed in a historical period from the 1930s or 1940s, with its boy reading a pulp comic book, this one takes place in the 1970s and finds its boy occupying himself with its equivalent medium of escapism: the television. Another way to pass the time, to bounce the ball. Locating the scene in what seems an American domestic setting—confirmed by the ominous appearance of a cowboy hat in the scene that follows—the piece realizes theologian Richard K. Fenn's claim that

American society in particular has become a secular purgatory without hope of redemption from the pressures and illusions, the fictions and the constraints of time. Indeed one's lifetime becomes a theater in which the drama of the soul is played out and its substance or destiny both determined and revealed.[80]

This is a world without redemption, because its rehearsal of the past mimics the conventional historian's conception of the historical: a fixed form available for reuse in the present, a ritual to repeat without difference.

Tragedy, on the other hand, aestheticizes the sacrificial ritual's attempts to reclaim an already known cure for the future: the sacrifice worked once and it will work again. The tragic art—insofar as it echoes the ritualistic—thus performs possibility in an exemplary fashion, allowing a community to establish continuity from the past into the future. Written within this structure, both the *Tragedia*'s pre–World War II iteration of the bedroom scene and its repeated staging in the post–World War II *Purgatorio* give the sense that the scene has already happened, is already tragically decided. Yet the differences between the two events are informative: as in the earlier performance, the mother comes in to put the child to bed, but here the child has hidden himself inside his darkened wardrobe, has pretended himself into some other time and place, and here the void does not come onto the stage. At least not yet.

First we must venture into the living room, must watch as the father comes home again, too tired to eat the meal his wife has prepared. Earlier in *Purgatorio* the projected stage directions had followed each scene, reflecting backward, on the beginnings of the possible as the stagehands prepared the scenery for the acts to follow. Now the projected texts are cast onto the frame of the stage in medias res before the man can act, preceding his actions as scripted events. The dramatic stage directions closely determine the possibilities of its characters, and the man seems exhausted with the burden of such a demand. We must watch him ask for his hat—a cowboy hat—must watch his wife unexpectedly begin to cry and protest, as he finds his hat and calls for his son. We must watch as the supertitles' directions diverge from the onstage action to verbally tell the story of another possible world, a world where the family plays out a scene of domestic contentment, laughing and dancing together, "listening to the music." But here, materially present before us, the man is determined by other possibilities: he must take the boy up the long flight of stairs and into a room offstage. And as the projection's fantasy lingers on the words "the music," we hear a horrific event taking place out of sight, sounds of beatings, groans, and screams—the echoes of some unbearable sexual/physical abuse. In its strictest form, the one officiated by neoclassical dictums, the tragic theater forces the scandalous event offstage, into the ob-scene, as the unrepresentable catastrophe deemed impossible to digest. During this excruciatingly long moment, it is impossible not to project one's own interpretation of the unseen event, to stage one's own imagined version of the scene. In witnessing the performance we become coproducers of the shameful act. We have joined the unseen creator of this world—the director/God—who demanded that this be played out as such, who wrote the scene and its possible unfoldings. We, too, are responsible for making this happen and envisioning what might happen next.

Dante's *Purgatorio* creates a world in which the guilty are forced to repeat their crimes in an allegorical version of the sin, until they have been redeemed according to the judgment of a divine power. The concept of a heaven and hell had long been a feature of Christian faith, but the Italian poet essentially invented the imagined reality of Purgatory.[81] The reperformance of a past act is resolutely constrained by a retrospective moral judgment. Its ends have already been determined by the naming of the action as "sin"; even though the father figure here may desperately seek an escape into the potentiality of the event, to redeem his past by exposing other futures, he is constrained to reproduce his character as already written. *Purgatorio* posits this demand as the engine driving the apparatus of the dramatic theater—or more pointedly, the tragic theater—as if recognizing that—to echo another Italian writer, Luigi Pirandello—the life we see onstage is captured by the burden of a scripted character.

But that is only half of the story. *Purgatorio* also realizes the redemption of apocalyptic potentiality by tearing open the past to allow the alternative becomings of other worlds. I say "redemption" in recognition of the religious undercurrents in this particular theological stage and in reference to Walter Benjamin's offer of an alternative to the historian's version of a set past. Benjamin conceives of the historiographer as one who holds the past object or event up to the light of the present and unveils that previously defined body's potential to become undefined. In the light of this redemptive method, that which was interpreted as playing a specific part in a historical narrative is set loose to its alternative becomings. If, as the cliché has it, "History is written by the victors," then the redemption of the past serves to revive the vanquished, the excluded, the forgotten; it gives them breath and voice again. As described by Stéphane Mosès in his study of the redemptive philosophy of Benjamin, Gershom Scholem, and Franz Rosenzweig:

The inertia that perpetuated past injustices can be broken only by the eruption of something radically new, which could not be deduced from the sum of past events. It is this break of historical temporality, this appearance of the unpredictable, that Benjamin called Redemption. But this is not located anywhere at the end of time; on the contrary, it happens (or it can happen) at any moment, precisely as each moment of time—grasped as absolutely unique—brings a new state of the world into being. The qualitative difference of each of the fragments of time always bring a new possibility of an unforeseen change, a brand-new arrangement of the order of things. . . . In this sense, the Last Judgment takes place every day.[82]

This redemption recalls the world to come that is arranged just as this one, whose only difference lies in the fluttering of a veil, the veil of the apocalypse. The Jewish Messianic tradition believes that, by performing the rituals defined by divine law, the believer joins the quotidian present with the kingdom to come, so that the two progress simultaneously in parallel. Making coffee, cleaning the kitchen, the believer already lives in an apocalyptic present.

A black wall descends between the audience and the stage where the father has just returned from brutalizing the son. The only opening is an exaggerated scrollwork that magnifies the design on the wardrobe doors within which the boy had hidden in the earlier bedroom scene, and out of which he had peered as the lights had dimmed. We have cycled back in time once more, repeating the event again, this time from within. The perspective is reversed; now the boy is on the other side of the threshold—on our side, in the audience—looking into the stage along with us. Soon the scrollwork window is replaced by a circular opening, several feet in diameter—the inversion of the black disk that had descended between the preceding scenes (and another reversal of perspective). The lens-like window belongs to the photographic or filmic medium, or at least to the focus of gaze associated with telescopes and microscopes, machines for seeing further, deeper into a field.

At the end of that earlier bedroom scene the projected text had declared "The 2nd Star enters his atomic shelter" (in reference to his wardrobe) and that "holding his ray gun to his chest, the 2nd Star has fallen asleep in his shelter." Now, somewhere between a dream and make-believe, we see (with the boy) a vision of a world to come after the eradication of human representation. Safe within our bomb shelter, we see the end of one world in an atomic catastrophe and the beginning of the next.

There is a haze of white light behind the opening, fluttering and flickering, and clouds congeal in the distance as some storm reels by. Colors shift in and out of the strobe's glare. The boy presses his hands up against the screen or window to peer in or to steady himself, or perhaps even to keep this new world at bay (an ambivalence that recalls the woman's nearly identical gesture from the Marseille episode of the *Tragedia Endogonidia* and ties a common thread between these two apocalypses). A great and gorgeous flower looms on one side of the portal, saturated with lush color, as another crosses the stage from the opposite direction. They dwarf the child. A procession of the natural world struts before our eyes as the storm rages on. It is as if the boy (and we, by extension) were glimpsing into a world after the flood, a glorious return to the Edenic awe of a landscape without humans. Shreds of mist rake across the scene and now other flowers inch their way into view, more vast and expressive than the ones before, shuddering some as they brush against the opening, their leaves and stems catching each other in tangled embraces before lurching free. The world seems growing larger or ourselves smaller in a paradox of becoming analogous to Alice's change of size in Lewis Carroll's tale: one simultaneously becomes smaller than one was and larger than one becomes, so that, pulled in both directions at once, one manages to "elude the present."[83] The flowers continue to increase in size, growing monstrous and deformed, turning sinister, until a bloom of garish scarlet fills the hole. It is there in the photograph gracing the cover of this book: the blossom a bleeding pupil in the eye of the stage, looking back at the boy, looking back at us. Like some mutant radiated growth from a 1950s sci-fi flick, its painfully vibrant petals so thick and swollen seem to pulse in the fragile light. The atmosphere, too, is flashing reds and purples, and the screeches of feedback and distant screams somewhere between guitar and voice overwhelm the transcendent chants that had opened the scene. The event ends as a jungle of green stalks gather about to obscure our gaze, as if the flowers had grown too tall for us and we were trapped in the darkened underbrush beneath.

Certainly these are forms and figures against a ground, but their unruly production departs from an arboreal part-by-part understanding of the biological order of distinct genus and species to present instead the efflorescence of a single rhizomatic growth. These stalks of green are grass, too (Deleuze and Guattari's exemplar of the rhizomatic), and one imagines these endless flowerings as outbursts from the same teeming life-form, a common root structure spanning a field, a stage without wings, just on the other side of the shelter's hatch. After the bomb there is only a natural world alive without human interference or action. No anthropomorphic scale to declare a measured taxonomy, no ordering principle of the name ("rose by any other name"), this is the untamed wilderness of nature.[84] We have returned to the paradisiacal origin of the Garden of Eden where the baroque mass of a life-form without limits appears over and over. It draws to a close entangled in that root structure, the obscurity of a jungle of stems and stalks.

This chaos of appearance is answered in the final moments of *Purgatorio* in a chaotic unfurling of dis-appearance. Another scene is playing out in the living room of the house, though the walls are now whitewashed, the furniture gone. The glare cast by the headlights of the Father's car as he turned into the driveway swings endlessly back and forth across the blasted stage in a kind of pendulum of perpetual motion. The father is there in his hat, but he is not the same man. He is shrunken and bent over now, played by an actor with cerebral palsy whose body resists each gesture to curl in on itself. To see this as a manifestation of his moral disfigurement in the eyes of that distant Judge—as punishment for a past sin—is to recognize the inadequacy and unacceptable nature of such a charge. The boy enters the room, but he too has changed, become hugely tall and looming. The father will reach for the boy's hand as before, but will fall to the floor in seizure. The boy will lie atop his restless form, pin him down in some semblance of an embrace and crucifixion all at once. Who carries whose burden? And as the father slips from beneath the now transfixed boy, prostrate on the floor, as he slowly makes his way up the stairs to that room at the end of the corridor, the boy begins to dance a kind of formalized version of the seizure that has limb attacking limb, shuddering to shake off some other skin, to return to that undifferentiated state.

In front of all of this the disk descends once more, as it had between each prior scene: first to blind us via the stage direction's prescription of the possible; then, in the case of the apocalyptic vision of the natural world described above, to reveal that which had been potentially bound up within the real. It is transparent now, as when we had looked with the boy into that roiling garden. It is a great lens looking into the stage and out from the stage.

The disk begins to spin clockwise as a mechanism within somehow injects a stream of pitch-black ink into the core of the surface (perhaps there are two such windows pressed against each other and the ink fills the interior?). Long fingerlike curling lines stretch across the circle's span. The center remains transparent like some eye of a storm as beautiful arabesques of the black ink layer atop one another in an increasingly tangled mass, writing a text that we cannot make out, continuous lines that extend outward a web of variation striving to form an opaque blackness over all. The blackening disk keeps spinning, churning out productions and further obscuring the lens as the lights dim, another endless production trailing off into a blackout.[85]

One is reminded of the torturing machine described so memorably in Kafka's short story *In the Penal Colony*, a device of extensive, and seemingly inscrutable inscription upon the body of the judged. But the differences between the two machines are revealing. In Kafka's story the stylus writes an excruciatingly intricate sentence that none can read except the absent divinity of the machinic judge and the judged himself. It carves its victim's flesh until it reaches an end, an end concomitant with the victim's death. The machine leaves the body marked by a moral and juridical statement, the revelation of the victim's character to an intensely private analytical gaze, a message passed between absolute authority and absolute individuality. Yet in *Purgatorio* the inscription keeps curling further and further into the blackout as the disc spins on endlessly. As with the material void of *Crescita XII*, the formal injection lives on past the limits of the performance's end. Here the judgment shadows the whole spectacle, on the "body" of this eye that looks out and that looks in. In spite of this shared inscription, it is doubtful that any can read its writing, recognize the character described therein. What is revealed, instead, is the capacity of the visible to become other than itself. These looping curls of ink write the Aristotelian darkness that exposes the capacity for sight, the sense seen by striking out all content. Set against the moralizing frame of Dante and the similarly motivated analytic gaze of the dramatic, these snaking forms scrawl an active affirmation of difference without reference to the order of judgment. Or, rather, they express the potentiality for judgment with which the theater is always wrestling but without the actual consignment of a strictly fated possibility.

In the *Marseille* episode (*M.#10*), the veiling at the end of the piece allowed one to see that what had preceded it had functioned as a continuous "unveiling" of both the woman and the scenic field. But in donning her veil and pulling the curtains close, she had also escaped from the spectator's representational world in which she stood as a figure apart. She had escaped in order to join the ground, take it into herself and possess the capacity to differentiate.

Recall from our discussion above that apocalypse means "unveiling," but an unveiling that simultaneously describes the veiling of the same curtain. Could one not say that the mechanism at the end of *Purgatorio* is both a veiling and an unveiling at once? Certainly, the machine veils the stage through its progressive blinding of the eye/lens: it veils the actual image of the representational. At the same time, in the many tendrils of differentiation peeling outward one sees a form unveiling its potentiality. As with the

example of Alice becoming both larger and smaller than herself, the movement of apocalypse is at once a veiling and an unveiling pulling in both
directions simultaneously. Here, at the end of *Purgatorio*, is an action of
form without content and without end; it is an expression of a means or
motion in the process of actualization. A nonhuman conflict on the plane of
matter takes its course. These strands of actualization are reminiscent of the
infinitely unfurling spirals of the fractal, always doubling back on itself,
but while the geometrical construct of the fractal repeats the same shape in
smaller and smaller iterations ad infinitum, the curls of ink spurt forth an
organic difference-in-itself before symmetry. As Focillon describes the initiation of a life of formal ornamentation, "Even before it becomes formal
rhythm and combination, the simplest ornamental theme, such as a curve
or *rinceau* whose flexions betoken all manner of future symmetries, alter-
nating movements, divisions and returns, has already given accent to the
void in which it occurs and has conferred on it a new and original existence."[86] The ephemeral figures and organs of the saturated flower petals
and the darkened blooms of ink share a common fibrous root system: both
confer a new and original existence of the void before future symmetries
and returns.

The Four Seasons Restaurant

These performances expose an individual surrogate to the apocalyptic potentiality of the theater, but how does such exposure work on a community
like the one in which we sit in our darkened velvet seats, however temporary its measure? In closing, I turn to a last performance from Castellucci's
most recent cycle—a trilogy derived in response to Nathaniel Hawthorne's
1836 story "The Minister's Black Veil"—in order to wonder toward what
political ends these endless cycles of potentiality might be directed.[87]

Mark Rothko's extraordinary murals that were commissioned by the
Four Seasons restaurant in 1958 depict a series of fields in dark red or ma-
roon, nearly black, many inset with rectangles mimicking the canvas's
edge. Frames within frames, they recall, perhaps, the proscenium of some
theater or the rich red of a curtain on a stage abstracted of all content. They
inscribe afterimages on the eye, written in some dark blood-like coagulate
of time. The occasional pillars that stand on the canvases act as figures
briefly shadowing an empty stage. The theater appears to disappear.

The paintings never appeared at their intended site—Rothko refused to
have them exhibited at a restaurant so dedicated to the excessive consumption of capital—and they never appear in Castellucci's 2012 performance

The Four Seasons Restaurant. Instead, we are told to look at the thing that is not there, to see the artistic act as an event where creation couples with decreation, a decreation that Simone Weil described as seeking "to undo the creature in us."[88] Looking into this abyss, we will see the abyss in us. But what is gained in this preference not to show oneself or one's work? In Hawthorne's story "The Minister's Black Veil," the eponymous minister one day inexplicably dons a black veil that he refuses to have removed even after his death. His decision to retain possession of his appearance, his potential to express, produces excessive and manic responses in the eyes of his beholders. They imagine powers—divine and demonic—in his obscured visage, project onto that black curtain their own phantasmagoria of whatever expression might be hiding beneath. Just as Bartleby's formula produces tumultuous reactions from the lawyer, just as the blank face of the minimal or literal object inspires the many performances of Fried, this veil provokes its beholders. So, here, the act of disappearing becomes a profoundly creative gesture. Castellucci's staging of *The Minister's Black Veil* in 2011 was canceled after its initial run in Antwerp because the director was unsatisfied with the performance.[89] Intentionally or not, his renunciation recalled the action of the minister of the story.

The performance *The Four Seasons Restaurant* begins, as *Purgatorio* ends, with a machine for making the dark void present. Yet if the spinning window from the earlier performance makes the abyss visible, here is a machine for making the abyss audible. In the darkened theater a projected text tells the story of a satellite at the far reaches of imagined distance, recording the sound of a black hole discovered in the Perseus galaxy some 250 million light years away. Originally a document outside the range of human hearing, the noise has been transposed into an audible register, its hazy rough cackles and deep throbs cast huge and terrifying in a crescendo that seems to go on too long. The sublime depths of the universe speak a glossolalia that contains whole worlds of diversity. This is a record of the end of sight and matter, taking away the paintings and all else.

The darkness cuts out and lights rise on an empty gymnasium—a space for disciplining the body—all white as if in memory of the cube that began our inquiry. There is even a ball in the corner. The young woman that comes forward to the edge of the playing space and looks out at the audience is another kind of satellite around the black hole's open mouth. Costumed in an Amish dress of homespun cloth, a peculiarly timeless sort of uniform, she is an "actor" learning to translate this other abyss—the great open maw of the proscenium theater backing all staged voids—into a form that might be communicated. In one hand she carries a pair of scissors and in the other she takes her own tongue, holds it firm as the twin blades close decisively once, then twice, and it is done. The flesh falls to the floor. A whimper, a swelling—she is about to retch—a handkerchief to her mouth. And now there is another similarly dressed young woman beside her, having entered from the rear. She, too, holds gleaming shears and snips away, weeping the while. And another woman and another, they keep coming down to stand directly in front of the audience and do the deed. Each action is visceral and unbearable, each repetition the most definite of possible ends, a new forgetting of what pain felt like before. When they are finished a German shepherd dog comes onto the stage, almost sheepish with tail between its legs as it gobbles down the tongues in quick succession. Nature takes back its flesh; there is no return from this act, no end to the gag.

Artaud wrote with terror about the everyday act of speech not only because sound cannot stand still or it would cease to be, not only because it must always leave us, but also because in order to appear in speech, one's peculiar singularity must disappear behind the uniform word *I*.[90] Artaud would be proud of these uniformly dressed disciples. They have willed their separation from speech, forestalling the incision between speaker and spoken word with a cut of their own devising. One might say that they have refused the fruit of knowledge, refused even to sit at the restaurant, and have instead suspended themselves in a pre- (or post)lingual state of potentiality.

It seems a linguistic and social suicide, irrevocable, but however gut-wrenchingly realistic, it is a theatrical game. And so when they do the seemingly impossible and speak again, one can only be so surprised: the end of one world instantiates many others. The young women perform a version of *The Death of Empedocles*, the unfinished *trauerspiel* (mourning play) that the German poet Friedrich Hölderlin wrote between 1798 and 1799. Exiled from his city in Sicily because his influence threatened its politicians, the ancient philosopher Empedocles turned his back on society even as his people begged him to lead them. Like Rothko, like Hawthorne's minister, he decided to retain possession of himself *for* himself rather than for a public. Seeking to join his own infinite potentiality with the infinite sublimity of nature, the philosopher threw himself into Mount Etna, his suicide born of a desire to transcend his human form. Supposedly, his bronzed sandal was spit back out, either mocking his ambitions or proving his apotheosis to his disciples. Something always remains from a departure, an echo across the distance, a shadow on a canvas, a small bit of flesh.

As the Socrates depicted in Plato's *Phaedo* affirms his encroaching suicide as his transfiguration into the purity of an eternal idea, so Hölderlin's

Empedocles is a poet who repeatedly mourns his distance from a natural world that once felt his immediate extension. In three successive versions, Hölderlin never finished his play; he kept abandoning his writing short of that final leap into the void. The poet struggled to present the philosopher's suicidal decision to rejoin the infinite as an affirmative act, not to escape life, but on behalf of it.

The young women perform Hölderlin's play in a very presentational manner, all stylized gestures and occasional tableaus at the rear, as if it were a dance that they had been taught by others, or a ritual handed down for generations (Castellucci refers to the quality of the Noh theater in discussing this section).[91] Indeed, on the edges of the playing space those who are not in the scene right now take turns mimicking the gestures of the performers onstage. They rehearse the part for their eventual turn, understudies preparing for when they will be called up. At times, the young women switch roles, never entirely inside their part. And, as the play progresses, the women's voices also become divorced from their particular bodies, seeming to issue from the costume itself, as if the part spoke on their behalf (indeed, speakers are placed inside each dress). When this happens, they lip-synch along, awkwardly, displaced from their own articulations. So, too, the supertitles above the scene—a prominent component of the mise-en-scène no matter where the performance is staged—preempt or lag behind the spoken lines. The many disjunctions of script, of speech, of voice normally occluded in the dramatic theater come to the fore. As in the dislocated script of *Purgatorio*, the possibilities of these characters seem to sit above the performers, dictating their course in this disciplined world of games and exercises.

Castellucci's performance does not simply long for an untrammeled sublimity divorced from political consequence. The young women all wear Amish dresses; like anchorites of old, or Empedocles shunning the city for the mountains, they mark their separation from the contemporary world. But theirs is not a hermitage of isolated individuals so much as a mass joined together against the idea of the single subject. The communal gathering turns increasingly sinister as the reenactment progresses: they don red armbands out of some Nazi rally, unfurl Confederate flags to drape about the back, to tie on as kerchiefs, or to hang at the rear of the stage. The symbolic intrusion not only recalls the idea of a revolution from within society—a civil war and a lost war—but also carries with it the threat of an ugly violence that might be unleashed. Sure enough, guns are distributed and slung across the shoulders, a pistol carried about, then spray-painted gold to match the gilded wreath that is passed around to signify the role of Empedocles.

And now the young women huddle together in a mass of bodies on one side of the space, gathered about some unseen center of gravity or black hole. From the outside one of the young women stands alone and holds aloft the golden pistol—perhaps she is playing Empedocles right now. She aims into the tangle and fires a single shot. Throbbing and heaving like an organism alive, the mass squeezes one of its number out onto the floor. Birthed or born again (an event with clear religious associations), this one is then stripped bare as she lies in fetal position shivering on the ground. The others lift and embrace her, and then, newly born, she exits the space, holding her own naked body close. One by one, the women undergo the same ceremony, leaving the stage for the dark beyond. When it comes to the last of the group, her own hands enact this stripping, as if her actions belonged to another, predetermined by fate or destiny or whatever name tragedy goes by. The lights dim on the husks of clothing, but the voices continue speaking from the folds of cloth in the blackout. The bodies have been carried away into the eternal night offstage and outside where galaxies create and destroy life. All they leave behind is the garment of their speech, the age-old costume that preceded them and that another will put on.

If Artaud saw birth as the doubling of the self into being and its representation, and the simple act of speech as the regular recurrence of this same division, then am I witnessing the women's attempt to leave behind representation through a collective rebirth that cancels out the prior, social one? The cutting of the tongue didn't seem to work, so now they have cut themselves off again by disappearing from the theater entirely. All the same, they have as before accomplished this departure only through an iterative act, each as one in a series. Framed by all the fascistic insignia, there is the sense that these individuals head toward some darker purpose or sacrifice, cleansed and prepared for whoever or whatever waits outside. Such gatherings and ritual actions before the sublime may occasionally take place in theaters, in churches, and in political rallies—all sites that can turn malevolent, where armbands, flags, and guns may be held up in honor of whatever divine or demonic transcendence. The sublime potential at work in Castellucci's theater with its spectacular voids and ritualistic patterns is here acknowledged as a descendent of Wagner's proto-fascistic *Gesamtkunstwerk*, foreboding transcendence into a content-less political *mise en abyme*.[92] This theater is a dangerous place, perhaps most of all in those moments when it leaves one speechless, when it retains its potential to say or do many things at once.

What follows is more difficult to describe. No more human actors and less the work of actions than a series of formal motions of the theater as

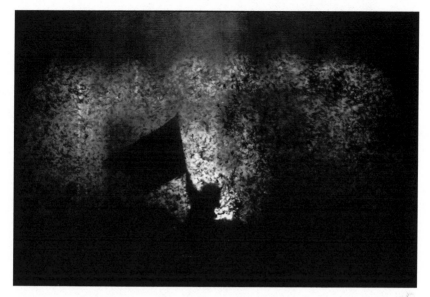

Fig. 11. Romeo Castellucci / Socìetas Raffaello Sanzio, *The Four Seasons Restaurant*, 2012. Photo by Christian Berthelot.

light, sound, and space.[93] But I want to tell you about one last instrument for apocalyptic potentiality. If the opening of *The Four Seasons Restaurant* played the sound of a black hole 250 million light-years away as it swallowed worlds whole, the closing moment answers by having the theater alight on its potential to hide many worlds within its own black hole.

The curtain ascends to reveal a chaos of motion: black ash or dust swirls ceaselessly occluding the entire view of the stage, showing and not-showing the heart of Etna, chips of sight sinking in the whirlpool of Perseus. The dark matter eddies and gusts like a galaxy's spiral of stars in negative while a passage from Wagner soars over an ocean of noise. It is as Edward Gordon Craig foretold it: "that which was void has become palpable—some spirit seems to work there in the space, as in a gentle—A wind which blows open the void and calls it to life." And somewhere behind the roar of sound and sight a not-quite-human figure shadows my attention. Creature-like, it dives in and under the heaps of black stuff, then childlike throws limbs high as if playing in black snow. At times the figure gets lost in the blossoming faces and shapes that my eyes imagine on the scene, the swarms gathering in temporary organs and apertures. But now it is there for certain, waving a black flag within the raging storm. The veil detached from the minister's face and held aloft, it is the same black fabric that had buffeted against the peephole into *Paradiso*, maybe even the same black fabric as the curtain itself.

What dark and otherworldly country does its wild gesture claim? Is it some unnamed territory of the lost and perpetually divided, the Confederacy triumphant after the bomb? Is it calling us close or warding us off? The figure and its flag are "signaling through the flames" as Artaud had it, or rather signaling through the ashes:

> When we speak the word "life," it must be understood that we are not referring to life as we know it from its surface of fact, but to that fragile, fluctuating center which forms never reach. And if there is still one hellish, truly accursed thing in our time, it is our artistic dallying with forms, instead of being like victims burnt at the stake, signaling through the flames.[94]

The flag claims that "fragile, fluctuating center which forms never reach," the live potential of a future becoming behind the scenes. This is the cruelty of constant variation, where ground and figure are one and the same. It is as if I am finally able to glimpse the boy moving in his great darkness (*Crescita XII*), finally able to follow the woman behind her curtain (*M.#10*), to trespass offstage however temporarily. Rothko's paintings suspend such a curtain in the process of unveiling, in the transition to blackout where one can only just see an image taking leave. The final moments of *The Four Seasons Restaurant* similarly suspend an oscillation between veiling and unveiling at once, without settling on a scene or sense. Worlds flicker past so fast that I think myself hallucinating alone in my particular corner of perception. Castellucci has said that the spectator is the subject of the theater of the future, meaning that the theater of the future concerns itself with what it means to be a spectator.[95] Just as the villagers in Hawthorne's story project all manner of spirits onto the veil of their minister, so I see my potential to see and to not see, to create and to destroy, for better and for worse.

Throughout the preceding conversation I have perhaps too easily been enthralled by the seductions of these performances of potentiality. These actualizations of potentiality propose a world to come without the human form and willingly court the tantalizing awe of the sublime as self-eradication. I see myself up there in these many boys who face the theater with a mixture of horror and wonder, see myself again staring into the darkened empty house after hours, or watching the closed curtains and waiting for something to emerge. I am often terrified by the prospect of what may come—human or otherwise—in the future that is always before me. And I am just guilty as Michael Fried for striking a melodramatic pose and indulging in a certain gothic style all the while. But I am not alone in my terror; recall once more Artaud, who presciently wrote in the middle of the last century, "We are not free. And the sky can still fall on our heads. And the theater has been created to teach us that first of all."[96]

There are, of course, other ways of seeing this work. One may, for example, focus more fully on how these techniques of alienation reveal the constructedness of such theatricality, how seduction in the theater is a matter of strings and wire.[97] Yet I believe it is vital that, alongside the temptation toward a more humanistic affirmation of the hopeful dimensions of the theater and the live, we recognize that potentiality swings both ways, and many ways in between. Yes, potentiality may hope for another world to come, a world that does not succumb to the disciplinary logic of possibility. Perhaps Bartleby embraces such a potentiality, but it is not for us to know through the language of the narrator—the language of the Law. It is my conviction that Romeo Castellucci and SRS do not come to us as messiahs of such a utopic "coming community," but as harbingers of some other darker apocalypse, that W. B. Yeats would say "slouches towards Bethlehem" not to be born as an individual, but to originate the end of individuality over and over again.[98] As in the terrifying floral procession of *Purgatorio*, the theater auditorium becomes a kind of bomb shelter, the proscenium a window into, and protection from, a chaotic development or black hole that excludes us. If we were to enter, we would cease to stand as a human figure, but evaporate into the field of potentiality.

SIX | Preferring Not to End

We are going to find out where the theater ends.

So say the two men to the one woman in the final moments of Let us think of these things always. Let us speak of them never. *by Matthew Goulish and Lin Hixson's performance company* Every house has a door.

"Selma," says Stephen, "I'm going to go out of the theater and shout your name. Then I'll come back, and you tell me whether you heard me or not. Then I'll do it again a little further away until you can't hear me anymore. That way, we'll establish where the theater ends. Ok?"[1]

His companion, Mislav, translates the words into Croatian and the woman, Selma, consents: "Ok."

The two men walk off into the wings and there is an indefinite pause as we and she listen together to the silence left behind before their voices call out: "Selma." She smiles, they return and ask: "Did you hear us?"

"Yes."

They leave again and now the stillness and our collective waiting lasts longer, as we imagine where they might be headed, through what doors and passageways, down what stairs, perhaps passing stagehands and managers, out into the city streets. A more distant chorus faintly calls out: "Selma." We all let out our held breath, smile, and again wait as they retrace that imagined pass. When they appear it is like we are greeting old friends. "Did you hear us?"

"Yes."

They are gone a long time and everyone's collective attention—audience and Selma—narrows on the absence that fills the space. We are all at the ready, awaiting their announcement. We are listening to the rustle of a body's adjustment, to the shifting patterns of the air, all the while thinking we might be hearing some definite edge in the calm of the space, some line of horizon where this world ends and the other begins. We are waiting, perhaps for four minutes and thirty-three seconds, perhaps longer still.

Selma will rise and she will leave the stage. The lights will dim to blue, and then rise on house and stage. There will not be a curtain call.

CURTAIN CALL

> At the end of the zero zero decade, for the first time in my
> life, I've been obliged to recognize that the actor is absent:
> you see actions, but you don't see an actor. Actions without
> an actor play out on the ground of social visibility, but they
> don't create any common ground in the space of
> consciousness and affectivity. Actions are performed in the
> theater of social production, but the agent of recombination
> is not there, in the theater, but backstage, and the
> consciousness of the process does not belong to the process
> itself.
> —Franco "Bifo" Berardi[2]

I would prefer not to end. I would prefer not to pretend that these means were somehow justified by a concluding resolve. While majoring in creative writing in college I found that whenever I would write a poem it would always try to describe the poem I had not written, the book full of blank pages. For my thesis I prepared a collection of poems titled *An album of photographs taken in the dark without a flash*. And of all the stories that I wrote as a child, not one could find an end. They kept circling through other rooms and doors and days. New names kept appearing. So when I was eight years old and spent weeks and weeks filling a marble composition book with the tale of a wandering knight, the story quickly devolved into an increasingly convoluted description of choices between one path and another, a constantly bifurcating departure from what could have been. Had I already begun flipping through those *Choose Your Own Adventure* books, starting in some middle and falling back and forth from one choice into another? I never revealed where my errant surrogate was going or why he had left. Rest assured, I told my hypothetical reader, we would get to that part later, in the future.

In the book there is the epilogue, promising a continuation after the plot has ended; in the theater there is the curtain call. We stand there, clapping and hollering uproariously, witnessing our extended farewell while refusing to let the actors leave the stage as they bow on and on. As Bert O. States observes, "The curtain call is a seam in social nature: actually, a beginning *and* an ending, a return and a farewell."[3] It begins the possible world of the everyday again and returns us to social and bodily obligations; it enacts the ending to this temporary world that has been. It also returns the potential of the ground to its static state, awaiting another performance. The curtain call marks the human actors as being capable of a life beyond the possibilities of the evening's entertainment, so that the role played is here revealed as some part of a larger potentiality that they now contain. Olivier now includes the fictional world of Hamlet as a supplement to his own more mundane world. The theater, too, is revealed in similar terms; it shows itself an actor that could do much more.

Sometimes, when the actors have finished their individual bows, they will turn to the wings and gesture offstage or, facing out front, raise their hands toward the back of the house. To whom or what are these actors gesturing, as if to say that the performance could not have been played without this final, most central performer? If, as the epigraph to this chapter proposes, the "agent of recombination" (the actor) is no longer onstage, then what is it that lingers backstage as the impetus behind an event we can not process in dramatic terms? Some stagehands may emerge, but they are only a surrogate for a much larger uncharacterizable mass of dark matter swelling in the offstage space.[4] Indeed, oftentimes the performers offer nothing apart from the gesture toward the house, like a door in their world swinging open, saying, *Every house has a door*.

We clap and the actors stand there, their hands extended outward to the wings and to the flies above, but no one comes. It is not quite, or only, us that they hail; rather, it is the theater itself that this last ritual of the curtain call acknowledges. The gesture indexes nothing less than our entire surroundings, it expresses a means it cannot take in hand. Like the place at the table left waiting for Elijah, the glass of wine full and the moment pregnant, this lack of response—or at least a perceptible one—confirms a sacred task. As I asked above: "Who can say what Bartleby does on the other side of the office screen? Who can say how bright his halo glows?"

The gesture prefers not to find its end. It affirms "out there," directs our attention elsewhere. And, like the gesture offered by the woman in the *Marseille* episode of the *Tragedia Endogonidia* cycle, this raised hand is both a greeting and a farewell.[5] The hand signals an ambivalent movement: come or go, but do not stay. It signals a transition between this world and whatever comes afterward. Even when the theater seems to end, it goes on.

THEATER AT THE LAST FRONTIER

The two young lovers stare out wide-eyed before the endless expanse of the New World, a grandeur that only they can see. Among the first settlers of colonial America, they have traveled long and far, leaving all behind

them to arrive here and now. Terrified, she doubles over with nausea. He
calls out to her over the music's soaring chords:

JORIS: Catalina. Look at me. look at me. This is happening.
CATALINA: It is.
JORIS: You are here.
CATALINA: I'm here. (*Looking out*) It's beautiful.
JORIS: It's unbelievable. Catalina this is unbelievable.

It is a scene that recurs again and again in *Mission Drift*, the contemporary
musical by the Brooklyn-based ensemble theater company the TEAM
(shorthand for the Theatre of the Emerging American Moment) that premiered in New York as part of the 2012 COIL festival at PS122. At several
moments in the performance, the actors look out over the lip of the downstage edge, over the heads of the audience. Transfixed in the here and now,
they are repeatedly dwarfed by a sublimity at once charged with entrepre-
neurial promise and a concomitant awe of massive destruction. Before
them stand virgin forests primed for clear-cutting, untrammeled mountains ripe for strip-mining, and the prospect of the desert blooming in the
fallout from an atomic bomb test. If, as Tim Flannery would have it in his
The Eternal Frontier: An Ecological History of North America and Its People,
"The over-exploitation of the frontier was akin to going out in a blaze of
glory," this is the performance of America at its most glorious, a big show
going on just beyond our view.[6]

I began this book with the words of Donald Rumsfeld and his performance of a deeply conservative and authoritarian potentiality. Preferring
not to engage in dialogue with the public, the secretary of defense held his
own against the potentiality of a Terror of unknown unknown proportions.
Subsequently, the character of Bartleby and his many still companions
have shown how a seemingly passive potentiality to do or make might actively dismantle the certain futures—narrative, dramatic, visual, and
otherwise—that authorities impose upon an individual or an event. These
final pages return to the contemporary American scene in order to show
potentiality's affirmative and negative casts at once.

Set in both contemporary Las Vegas and against the expansive backdrop of four hundred years of American history, *Mission Drift* tells the
story of the nation's doomed love affair with an idea of freedom inextricably linked to the freedom of capital, a love affair sustained by the repeated
promise of another frontier. The play follows an immortal Dutch couple,

Catalina and Joris, perpetually fourteen and suspended on the cusp of ado-
lescence, as they traverse American history while moving westward.
Mythic personifications of neoliberal individuality, they exhaust one mon-
eymaking enterprise after another from the New Amsterdam colony in
1624 (New York) to the westernmost reaches of California's Gold Rush—
even beyond, since Catalina shares her name with a small island off the
coast of Los Angeles.[7] At land's end, they double back to the deserts of
contemporary Las Vegas, where the American dream of another jackpot
has finally run dry. Here, the couple raises skyward the most fantastical of
casinos—Pyramids and Castles and even a replica of Noah's Ark—before
razing them to the ground to make room for newer and more grotesque
versions of the American Dream. We see the consummation of the capitalist
cycle where production requires a parallel destruction or even, in Naomi
Klein's notion of late twentieth-century Disaster Capitalism, destruction
becomes the ground for possible growth.[8] Where the waxing and waning
of an industry like mining or lumber would take place over the span of
decades, here the cycle recurs in ever smaller and smaller circles and wilder
and wilder dance numbers. Here, the cycle of "regeneration through violence" that Richard Slotkin associates with the idea of the American West is
contracted and tightly choreographed in flashy spectacles.[9]

  As personifications of a national obsession with the new and youthful,
the timeless teenage love affair between Catalina and Joris at first reflects a
romantic attachment to the unknowability of the frontier: every time they
level a wall or building vast panoramas of the future open out. The couple
realizes the dream of endless American western expansion as one that is
inextricably intertwined with white heterosexual reproduction. Looking
out over the land they have cleared of the "messy" tangle of indigenous
communities, histories, and ecological complexity, they embrace a return
to a particularly homogenous version of potentiality's blank slate. Jane
Tompkins describes the imperialistic drive behind this version of tabula
rasa as follows: "[The] blankness of the plain implies—without ever
stating—that this is a field where a certain kind of mastery is possible,
where a person (of a certain kind) can remain alone and complete and in
control of himself, while controlling the external world through physical
strength and force of will."[10] While Tompkins writes of the lone male cowboy, here we have the power couple, striding off hand in hand into the
terra nullius of neoliberal promise.

  What better place to stage this collision course between the past and the
future, reveling in the creative potential of destruction, than Las Vegas, the
birthplace of the postmodern? As the architect and theorist Robert Venturi

first proclaimed in his groundbreaking study *Learning from Las Vegas* (1977), the city is all sign, all front; it faces an audience of consumers and gamblers. It is also a deeply theatrical city that asks one to perform a part: the bohemian in Paris, Paris; the centurion in Caesar's Palace; a knight at Excalibur; or, more generically, the decadent and well-heeled at places like The Wynn or The Venetian. It is not just that history collapses into itself, presenting a scene where Eiffel towers rise above the courtyards of ancient Rome. But the city also performs a remarkable contradiction in felt temporality. On one hand, time distends into a limitless expanse where windowless halls filled with twinkling lights still the rhythm of night and day. Caught in perpetual dusk or sunrise, here is the city that truly never sleeps (a miniaturized version of the Manhattan skyline serves as the backdrop for a roller coaster ride at the casino New York, New York so that the original sleepless city is nested within the larger palimpsest that is the Strip). On the other hand, history lurches with cataclysmic violence as one day's icon leaves no lasting impression. Venturi writes: "The most unique, most monumental parts of the Strip, the signs and casino facades, are also the most changeable."[11] During a monthlong residency in Las Vegas developing *Mission Drift*, the TEAM visited the Neon Boneyard, a repository for all the signs from casinos long gone. Here sun-bleached and sand-scarred shapes pile high, the sole monuments to whatever ostentatious metallic dinosaurs once stood tall above the desert.

This may recall echoes of Sam Shepard's post–World War II excavations of the myth of the West, where cowboys and other icons of Americana stalk a frontier at the end of modernity and the beginning of postmodernity. The geographic frontier exhausted, Shepard's scenes border a desert composed not so much of unknown landscapes, as of unknown events. These plays, especially the early works from the 1960s and 1970s, are swollen with the threat of nuclear terror, the end of days; now—some fifty years later—this is but one of many terrors that may surround us. There is the scene at a barbecue in Shepard's 1965 play *Icarus's Mother*, for example, where a group of young middle-class men and women not too distant from Catalina and Joris stare skyward at a fireworks display on a typical American summer evening. Theater historian Christopher Bigsby describes the scene as follows: "Despite its apparent naturalistic setting, the play is concerned with potential, with a fear that lurks just below the surface of routine, so that when one of the characters describes the firework display his language simultaneously contains a reference to the apocalypse of which the display is itself merely an image."[12] If the display is "*merely an image*" and the language only a reference, it is because both systems of representation can only partially accommodate the apocalyptic, as such. As I have tried to show throughout this book, it is extremely difficult to stage a future full of what Bigsby calls the "potential" that "lurks beneath the surface of the routine," the *potential* that promises the unexpected.

The TEAM's *Mission Drift* does not attempt to represent this tension between production and destruction in a spectacular onstage event. Instead, the performance again and again projects the sublimely terrible out over the audience's heads. Like Shepard's crowd staring off in wonder at the scene we in the audience cannot truly see, it is the theater itself that performs its miracles behind closed curtains, beyond the wings, or over arched and craning necks. These performances redirect our attention instead to the community that witnesses the awe-inspiring, the awful. As in Eno's *Tragedy: a tragedy*, the stage is filled with messengers slack-jawed and shading their eyes before the abyss that does not acknowledge them. We behold others acting out as they behold potentiality. And so, whatever power the two protagonists seem to possess at the beginning of the performance is increasingly figured as a presence beyond their control, outside of their reach.

Indeed, the mythic rush through the western frontier that ties the characters in *Mission Drift* to the grand narrative of American exceptionalism dead-ends in the echo chamber of Vegas. In 1979 Jean-François Lyotard famously wrote of the postmodern condition as one in which the grand narratives of progress are no longer possible, heralding a continuous present in the endless, nonstop crises of the twenty-four-hour news cycle. More recently, in his 2011 book *After the Future* the Italian radical philosopher Franco "Bifo" Berardi has expanded this critique to specifically emphasize the faith in futurity that infused these now-defunct narrative structures. According to Bifo, the modernist promise of a better time to come that was inaugurated in the twentieth century with the Futurist manifesto in 1909, petered out again and again in increasingly desperate articulations toward the end of the millennium, until we now live in a temporality without direction, with no future. The financial crisis of the first decade of the new millennium, based on the anticipated performances of various "future stocks," represented the last gasp of this faith in the prospective.[13] This isn't to say that the temporal dimension of futurity is lost, rather that the *characterization* of such a time is no longer possible. Objectives and actions are not possible. As the TEAM's director Rachel Chavkin has put it: "In a profession in which we regularly imagine the unknown, I constantly encounter universes for which I do not possess the genetic code. I think characters in the TEAM's plays are always confronting this problem in large and small ways—dealing with worlds they do not recognize, levels of change they cannot fathom."[14] The characters in *Mission Drift* have lost the orientation of a cultural mission, drifting on the edge of a terrain that escapes from their objectives and reasoning. Their possible futures do not align with that of the world in which they find themselves. The actor on the raised stage who so recently performed legible actions and was engaged in productive dialogue stands stock-still and stares dumbfounded out at the event offstage.

What is happening out there? Two of the many awestruck stares toward the end of the TEAM's performance regard a kind of spectacle particular to Las Vegas. The city's first great population boom derived in large part from the many scientists and technicians that moved to the area in the 1940s to contribute to the atomic bomb testing one hundred miles north of the city at Area 51. From the city of simulacra they sallied forth to prop up meticulously realized replicas of small-town suburbia and submit these stage sets to the forces of the bomb in an effort to see what could happen. Residents in Vegas would host parties for the distant light show playing out across the horizon. Toward the end of the piece, *Mission Drift* re-creates such a party for beholding these rehearsals of the possible consequences of nuclear warfare and pairs it with a parallel event of creative destruction. Las Vegas may be the city that has produced fantastical monuments of surface, but it has also perfected the art of the implosion—where engineers carefully and precisely choreograph the detonation of a building in such a manner that the structure folds neatly in on itself. These are architectures in negative, designed to make room for the construction of a new casino. They also recall an intentional and scripted version of the spectacular improvised happening of 9/11. Perhaps *Mission Drift*'s recurring performance of collective witnessing marks a return to September 11, that traumatic event where the expectations of the everyday world suddenly split open to reveal the seemingly implausible, the unpredictable abyss behind any wall. Amid the many images from that most public of traumas, there is a remarkable photograph by Patrick Witty of a crowd of New Yorkers on the streets watching in shock as the south tower of the World Trade Center falls. We see ourselves in this image, but also the thing that we cannot acknowledge: the terrible potential of that live event that cannot be represented in a framed manner.

As the company's name self-consciously proclaims—the Theatre of the Emerging American Moment—this is theater that speaks (and sings) in the voice of a generation emerging from the end of America's place as the global superpower and moral compass on the world stage. Formed by a group of recent graduates of New York University in 2004, their subject matter is contemporary America, postmillennium and in the aftermath of 9/11. What distinguishes them from those characters frayed by anxiety and exhaustion in Shepard's postmodern worlds or the studied, ironic remove of some of their precedents in the New York experimental theater scene is a passionate, even willfully sentimental, commitment to the prospect of hope or change in the midst of catastrophe. They do not cower or dry out like some Beckettian remnant holed up against the unknown; they bare themselves with abandon, risking an affirmation however unformed. It seems appropriate to a generation that turned to the calls of "hope" and "change" that Barack Obama offered during his first presidential campaign as an embrace of potentiality and in response to the reactionary logic of the Bush era and Rumsfeldian refusal of the unknown unknown.

While this is not only an American question, it is very much a part of the nation's proclaimed identity. In *Mission Drift*, the TEAM reminds us that America is a place where, in the lasting words of Catalina, "it sort of feels— like there's every possibility." It is the end of the play and our heroine is staring into the audience one final time, looking out in wonder and mourn- ing over all that has come before: great new worlds begun and great worlds destroyed forever. Through an impossible leap of logic, she has returned to the East of four hundred years before the apocalypses of Vegas, back to her first steps in the brave New World. She has returned to the beginning of historical (European) time for the land that would become the United States of America. A fellow pioneer asks her what lies ahead westward and she stumbles over the prospect before her, that this American past can be redeemed: "It sort of feels—like there's every possibility."

By returning to the moment when the American frontier covered nearly the entire continent, before the cycles of regenerative violence had ravaged the land and its peoples, this would seem to be a movement that recovers the potential of a culture. If history seeks out what is possible according to the causes that have been written, then this redemptive historiography re- vives the potentiality of the forgotten or seemingly decided, makes present its capacity for change. This is what performance theorist Adrian Kear sug- gests when he writes that "because the past has been a future, to some ex- tent, it is the future itself that is disclosed in the representation of past events. Not the future as actuality, but the future as potentiality: the prom- ise of what has been returning as what is to come."[15] In their larger oeuvre, too, the TEAM see the theater as such a living playground of the aborted and abandoned. *Particularly in the Heartland* (2006) finds the ghost of Bobby Kennedy celebrating Christmas in Kansas with aliens from Mars, while *Ar- chitecting* (2008) sends Scarlett O'Hara wandering through the wreckage of post-Katrina New Orleans. In this theater the past is *not* closed, its future is not written; rather it is made available to alternative rearticulation in our present moment.

What is out there, out beyond the last ranch and road sign pointing back to Vegas? Catalina answers: "It sort of feels—like there's every possibility." I want to believe that she is speaking of the theater, too, offering us a glimpse at what may be the last and only frontier: that forever emerging moment "now." The lip of the stage over which the characters in *Mission Drift* repeatedly stare demarcates the frontier where the scene encounters the obscene, where one world butts up against another, and where *what is* looks out to *what could be*. It is the edge of every known unknown. But there is something deeply resigned in the way that performer Libby King delivers these lines, offering a final glance out at us before an unceremonious blackout ends this epic performance on the smallest of notes. I now think that the "every possibility" she foresees refers to the exhaustion of named futures available to this America of frontiers and growth. Yes, the return to America's past promises another beginning, the cycle restarted, but it prophesizes every variation of progress in this era of American hegemony and thus forecloses all its futures as projected and ended possibilities, not potentiality. It kills this world of capitalist accumulation, ends it in a blackout, so that another may begin offstage or behind the curtain. Not the world of every possibility, but the worlds of endless potentiality.

THE GREAT MEDIUM OF REDEMPTION

> The great Theater of Oklahoma is calling you! It is calling only today, only this once! Anyone who misses this opportunity shall miss it forever! Anyone who is thinking of his future belongs in our midst!
> —A poster in *Amerika*[16]

Like Catalina from *Mission Drift*, the protagonist of Franz Kafka's unfinished first novel, *Amerika: The Missing Person*, is an immigrant to the United States. But while the TEAM's ingénue jumps from success to success like the animus of American economic ingenuity, this young teenager, Karl Rossman, drifts from job to job, failing at all endeavors to make a place for himself in this strange new world. In Kafka's dark picaresque on the American Dream, Karl is abused, discarded, perhaps even raped, though he is largely innocent of wrongdoing.

In a last tantalizing episode disconnected from the main body of the narrative, Karl comes across a poster announcing that a mysterious enterprise, the Nature Theater of Oklahoma [*sic*], is seeking any and all applicants for membership in its ranks. Part recruiting function and part theatrical spectacle, the event will be open for one night only. Arriving at the advertised location, he discovers a scene of staggering proportions that would not be out of place in Vegas: rows and rows of women costumed as giant angels trumpet out a welcome in an attempt to recruit whoever may pass by. If seven angels with seven trumpets announce the apocalypse in the book of Revelation, here the instruments are scattered amid countless bodies, a mass of actors proclaiming the end of times and inviting salvation in their company.

Old and young, child and vagabond are welcomed into the collective, each finding a particular place according to a part played in his or her past: the profession-less Karl is eventually brought on board as a technician through the Office for Former European Middle School Students. The company thus allows all its members to return to the past in order to redeem its potentiality. For, like all the other recruits accepted into the nomadic theater, Karl is freed from the consequences of his errors: "Everything he had ever done was forgotten, no one would reproach him anymore."[17] The poster states: "Anyone who is thinking of his future belongs in our midst!" In other words, exchange your past for another chance at the future. In his essay on Kafka's aesthetic, Walter Benjamin explicitly connects the (American) theater with a redemptive calling: "For the members of the Oklahoma troupe [*sic*] the role is their earlier life; hence the 'nature' in this Nature Theater. Its actors have been redeemed."[18]

This personal redemption is also a national one, even if the America imagined by Kafka in early twentieth-century Prague belongs to a possible world set askance from our own. It is, we might say, a version of the nation after the apocalypse. As Adam Kirsch writes in a review of the book for the *New York Times*, "Amerika is not America; it is a cipher for Kafka's dream of a country he never visited."[19] Like the book's title, the intentionally distorted Oklahoma (Kafka consistently misspelled the name of the state in his manuscript) signals the divergence of this theatrical world from the actual.[20] Supposedly one of many such subsidiary troupes spread throughout the country and engaged in the recruitment of any and all, the Nature Theater is a kind of fantasy of the American frontier. It dreams of the untapped potential of the great middle of this country. At the Chicago's World Columbian Exposition in 1893, Frederick Jackson Turner had famously proclaimed the American frontier "closed" since westward expansion had reached its further shore. The Nature Theater loops back on the no-man's-land of the national past, revisiting the actual Oklahomas that were overlooked, overworked, and overrun in the constant expansion of this future-bound country. Among the chorus of angels, Karl encounters an old friend who assures him: "Though I've never seen it myself, some of my co-workers who've already been to Oklahama say it's almost limitless. . . . remember that we're taking on people in every city, that our recruiting troupe is always out traveling, and that there are many more such troupes."[21] The theater company occupies an ever-expanding universe of performance. And like SRS's *Tragedia Endogonidia*, the Nature Theater is an organism on the run, spreading its roots underground in every direction across the Great Plains.

It is fitting that this extended description of the theater's peculiar recruitment procedure is the penultimate fragment in Kafka's incomplete novel. As configured by translator Mark Harman in his recent version of the text, a last one-page scrap of writing closes the book by taking us on board an endless train ride with Karl as he makes his way toward Oklahoma or its theatrical double, Oklahoma. Everything he sees out his fast-moving window exceeds its frame. Looking out at mountains that rise to peaks beyond the view afforded by the window frame, at valleys that wind their way around bends out of sight, at waters rushing under bridges over which they clatter, "only then did Karl come to understand the vastness of America" (288). What is out there, out the window of the train speeding westward across the blank Great Plains? He does not arrive, because the potential of the book remains unwritten.

And yet, lest we think that this redemption is necessarily a positive recurrence or that potentiality's windows only look out on romantic vistas, a last note here. Kafka would write two more novels, also unfinished: *The Trial* (1915, published in 1925) and *The Castle* (published in 1926). As many have noted, the protagonists of these novels, named Josef K and simply K., respectively, are surely some analogue for the young Karl—and all three are likely a surrogate for Kafka himself. These strangely passive men are trapped in worlds riddled with anxiety, the workings of inexplicable bureaucracies and occurrences increasingly confining their quarters. They, too, travel through unnamed territories toward an endless future rife with potential, but the labyrinths of choice that they inhabit are always walled in by an inaccessible force that they cannot reach. The Law in evidence here does not disclose itself, but remains as sphinx-like as Rumsfeld. K, for example, cannot even enter the eponymous Castle, but remains on its outskirts trying to find a way in. All three keep traveling deeper into the unknown spiral of their solitude.

PURSUING POTENTIALITY

He is running toward the storm again. There, in the distance of this field where the dust kicks up around the soft pad of his every step, a new tornado is taking shape and beginning its way across the dry plains. And, loping forward now, he is gauging its expected path, and when he thinks he sees his chance, sprinting at full pace. Perhaps they miss each other, the column of wind turning aside faster than his feet can carry him or taking off again into the ether. Or perhaps they do find each other for a fleeting moment and he disappears in its shroud—he transubstantiates—before he is thrown back outside again. Catching his breath, dusting off the camera, he rises in order to run after another. He is always running toward the storm.

I am watching Francis Alÿs chase tornadoes in Mexico. For the past ten years, the Belgian-Mexican artist has recorded his attempts to enter the eye of these small, localized storms that annually congregate in the fields south of Mexico City during "Tornado Season." The thirty-nine-minute film that was the centerpiece for his retrospective at the Museum of Modern Art (New York) in 2011 collected these many hunts into a single document interspersed by the whiteout of a camera's failure or cuts between long shots of the artist moving across the field and the handheld camera with which he runs, through which we see the end of the visible world. The document is unfinished, the chase incomplete. The end is suspended into the future.

The piece exemplifies a certain mode of production that has consumed Alÿs for a number of years, across a variety of media and projects, both loosely and explicitly connected. His is an investigation of the art of pursuit, but a kind of pursuit reserved for the thing at which one can never arrive, either because the goal is always retreating or, as in Zeno's paradox, half the distance covered always remains uncovered. In Zeno's paradox the arrow somehow manages to find its mark, but it is what happens in the process of becoming this end that sets the mind off and running. In *A Story of Deception* (2003–2006), for example, Alÿs takes up the practice of the Tehuelche people of Peru who hunted the nandus bird, a kind of ostrich, by walking after them for weeks until the birds would die of exhaustion. While filming his own long walks reenacting these pursuits, the artist discovered that the distance where road met horizon would come alive in a shimmering mirage with his approach:

Without the movement of the viewer/observer, the mirage would be nothing more than an inert stain, merely an optical vibration in the

Fig. 12. Francis Alÿs, *Tornado*. Milpa Alta, 2000–2010. Video documentation of an action, 55 minutes. Courtesy David Zwirner, New York / London.

landscape. It is our advance that awakens it, our progression towards it that triggers its life.[22]

Consider how Alÿs chases and films an empty plastic bottle as the wind tosses it around the central square of Mexico City in *If you are a typical spectator, what you are really doing is waiting for the accident to happen* (1996). The lengthy title for this performance derives from the fact that, in the course of filming the bottle's journey, the artist wandered into the road whereupon he was struck by a passing truck. The title marks the spectator as one who is always anticipating a future end to define the spectacle, while rendering his remove a dangerous fiction. Or, in the animation *Song for Lupita* (1998), consider how he shows us a hand-drawn woman endlessly pouring water from one drinking glass to another, so that the water seems again and again a column momentarily held in the air. If there is an image that crystalizes these works, it is a form displayed in suspense: a plastic water bottle caught midair; a stream of water passing endlessly between two containers; the dispersed wind given a form and shape, a center around which to spin.

Tornado plays out like a parable of desire in the most simplified of forms.

It is a three-part narrative upholding the Aristotelian structure of beginning, middle, and end rehearsed over and over again. The artist sights the tornado, chases the tornado, and captures or misses the tornado. I imagine, then, that Alÿs is attempting repeatedly to find the calm at the eye of the storm, the perfect resolution of the narrative in the perfect resolution of a clear view held in that tight coil of wind and dust. For the tornado is like a shaft of lightning suspended midstroke, gracing this place for a long moment, a line tethering earth to sky, a fast-moving passage to transcendence. Nietzsche wrote how we cannot separate the lightning from its striking, cannot claim the bolt as a subject apart from its active appearance; doer and deed are shown as one. Perhaps here event and actor share a common potentiality?

But when the wind welcomes him inside and he finds himself suddenly in the midst of that hole in sight, where man and tornado become a single event, it does not follow that there is anything transcendent achieved, no end where all is disclosed—at least not for me as I look on from without. I cannot know the point where Zeno's paradoxical arrow of attention meets its target or if it spirals endlessly closer and closer into the heavens. Instead, the camera is streaked over with curtains of dust, the sound muffled and scratched away. There is the flicker and crackle of the instrument before it and he are thrown to the ground outside the circle of wind. So if Alÿs does undergo some epiphany in those sudden disappearances, it is lost to the rest of us watching behind that obscuring tumult of documentation. The means of showing take on a material presence; they fill the screen and block out the show.

To rehearse the thing that we know will not arrive, that we know will not end and that we know will not show itself, is to make the means into the event itself. Here is a performance of pure expenditure and absolute renewal, where the potentiality of a means is fully taken up and fully exhausted with every step. There is something immensely freeing in this frustrated or suspended end. We are relieved of the threat of a moment when we will finally be finished—no stage fright, no curtain call—there is always another tornado to chase in the future. So, too, do I *chase after* events not only in the spatial sense as one trying to capture fugitive figures in words and images, but also in a temporal sense as one who always comes after, belated. I never get inside the storm of a happening with any clarity, but keep switching angles from close-up to long shot, and keep thinking my writing a very pedestrian means of approach, uneven step by uneven step.

What better way to leave the work alive and living than to sight another storm on the horizon and to begin again, the same but differently?

Notes

CHAPTER 1

1. Eugène Ionesco, "Notes on Theatre," in Richard Drain, ed., *Twentieth-Century Theatre: A Sourcebook* (New York: Routledge, 1995), 54.

2. From Donald Rumsfeld's press conference of February 12, 2002, here set to verse by Hart Seely in his *Pieces of Intelligence: The Existential Poetry of Donald H. Rumsfeld* (New York: Free Press, 2003), 2, my emphasis.

3. Slavoj Žižek has referred to this quote in a number of essays surrounding the War on Terrorism. In various reiterations, Žižek suggests that the defense secretary tellingly ignores a fourth configuration for this binary arrangement of knowledge: the "unknown knowns." These are, according to Žižek, the text-book definition of what psychoanalysis would call "the unconscious" with its traumatic event that has been experienced, but has not yet been processed. The unknown known forecasts a future in which we are doomed to repeat the past, a possibility that is obscured to the subject but may be apparent to the analyst. See Slavoj Žižek, "What Rumsfeld Doesn't Know That He Knows about Abu Ghraib," "The Empty Wheelbarrow," and "Censorship Today: Violence, or Ecology as a New Opium for the Masses" online at http://www.lacan.com (last accessed December 12, 2012). See also Slavoj Žižek, *Iraq: The Borrowed Kettle* (New York: Verso, 2005), 9–10.

4. Henry David Thoreau, *Walden* (New York: Houghton Mifflin, 1906), 12.

5. See Baruch Spinoza, *The Ethics and Selected Letters*, trans. Samuel Shirley (Indianapolis: Hackett, 1982).

6. Giorgio Agamben, *Nudities*, trans. David Kishik and Stefan Pedatella (Stanford, CA: Stanford University Press, 2011), 113 and 114.

7. See, for example, Judith Butler, *Bodies That Matter: On the Discursive Limits of "Sex"* (New York: Routledge, 1993), Richard Schechner, *Between Theatre and Anthropology* (Philadelphia: University of Pennsylvania Press, 1985), Herbert Blau, *Take Up the Bodies: Theatre at the Vanishing Point* (Urbana: University of Illinois Press, 1982), and Peggy Phelan, *Unmarked: The Politics of Representation* (New York: Routledge, 1993).

8. George Steiner, *Grammars of Creation* (New Haven: Yale University Press, 2001), 7.

9. See the chapter "Imagination" in Konstantin Stanislavsky, *An Actor Prepares*, trans. Elizabeth Hapgood (New York: Theatre Arts Books, 1964), 59–78.

10. Schechner, *Between Theater and Anthropology*, 6.

11. As just one example of my terminological divergence from my philosophical interlocutors, consider the sense of potentiality introduced by Aristotle in his *Metaphysics*. He conceives of it as a predetermined essence, such that the acorn holds the potential oak tree in reserve. Following the discovery of evolutionary biology, however, there is no such stable essence to be actualized, no certain "possible" oak tree to project into the future. John Dewey writes that "potentiality [as conceived by Aristotle] never means, as in modern life, the possibility of novelty, of invention, of radical deviation, but only that principle in virtue of which the acorn becomes the oak." John Dewey, *Reconstruction in Philosophy* (New York: Beacon Press, 1948), 57.

12. Describing the etymology of the word, Victor Turner states that "it has nothing to do with 'form,' but derives from Old French *parfournir*, 'to complete' or 'carry out thoroughly.'" Victor Turner, *From Ritual to Theatre: The Human Seriousness of Play* (New York: PAJ Books, 2001), 13.

13. Schechner, *Between Theater and Anthropology*, 36.

14. J. L. Austin, *How to Do Things with Words* (Cambridge, MA: Harvard University Press, 2003). I return to speech act theory's place in a theory of potentiality in "Withholding Potentiality."

15. As Austin Quigley wrote in his investigation of the dramatic stage as a site for representing alternative conceptions of a world, "The drama helps us recognize the ways we rescue from the threat of a relativistic chaos domains of stability and continuity, domains in which we can establish firm but not final bases for growth, coherence and renewed commitment." Accordingly, drama stages domains that, however divergent, are parallel to our own everyday ways of thinking through time and space in that they always already adhere to logics of possibility. Austin E. Quigley, *The Modern Stage and Other Worlds* (New York: Routledge, 1985), 261.

16. Aristotle, *Poetics*, trans. Gerald Else (Ann Arbor: University of Michigan Press, 1967), 32–33.

17. Susanne K. Langer, *Feeling and Form* (New York: Scribner, 1953).

18. Ibid., 308.

19. Paul Virilio, *The Original Accident*, trans. Julie Rose (Cambridge: Polity Press, 2007).

20. "The theatre was the last human venue in as much as its objects were measured, not for their potential to act, but for their impotential to be realized. . . . The human animal was witnessed, unlike any other high-achieving, perfectly realized creature, to make play of this impotential. Other animals could not quite make affective theatre because they did not have the capacity to disappoint." Alan Read, *Theatre, Intimacy and Engagement: The Last Human Venue* (New York: Palgrave Macmillan, 2008), 4.

21. On the performativity of the promise see Jacques Derrida, *Limited Inc*, trans. Jeffrey Mehlman and Samuel Weber (Evanston, IL: Northwestern University Press, 1988) and Shoshana Felman, *The Literary Speech Act: Don Juan with J.L. Austin, or Seduction in Two Languages*, trans. Catherine Porter (Stanford, CA: Stanford University Press, 2003).

22. The exact phrase is that the performer "can die there in front of your eyes; is in fact doing so." Blau, *Take Up the Bodies*, 83. See also "Universals of

Performance: Amortizing Play," in Herbert Blau, *The Eye of Prey: Subversions of the Postmodern* (Bloomington: Indiana University Press, 1987).

23. "Performance's only life is in the present. . . . Performance's being, like the ontology of subjectivity proposed here, becomes itself through disappearance" (Phelan, *Unmarked*, 146). For more on liveness as disappearance, particularly in regards to the problematics of documentation, see Nick Kaye, "Live Art: Definition and Documentation," *Contemporary Theatre Review* 2:2 (1994), 1–7, and Matthew Reason, *Documentation, Disappearance and the Representation of Live Performance* (New York: Palgrave Macmillan, 2006).

24. Blau, *The Eye of Prey*, 181.

25. Phelan, *Unmarked*, 27, my emphasis.

26. See Peter Brook, *The Empty Space* (New York: Simon & Schuster, 1996). While he does not use these terms, Philip Auslander's attack on the ontological basis of liveness points to such deadliness in the theater as an argument against its proposition of nonreproducibility. Auslander speaks of franchised performances of musicals, staged with identical blocking in multiple cities simultaneously, as exceptions to the idea of a nonreproducible live event. Discounting variations in casting, audience, architecture, and any number of contingent variables, this kind of theater works hard to contain liveness understood both as loss and as a means toward futurity. See Philip Auslander, *Liveness: Performance in a Mediatized Culture* (New York: Routledge, 1999).

27. Auslander has recently advocated for a liveness of the record insofar as it is a coproduction of the spectator and the object: "Liveness is an interaction produced through our engagement with the object and our willingness to accept its claim." Philip Auslander, "Digital Liveness: A Historico-Philosophical Perspective," *PAJ: A Journal of Performance and Art* 34:3 (September 2012), 9. In a talk on Marina Abramović's *Seven Easy Pieces* at the Museum of Modern Art, Phelan offered a revised definition of the live: "At the core of this liveness is the possibility that both performers and spectators might be transformed by the event as it unfolds in the same time and space." Peggy Phelan, "Seven Not So Easy Pieces: Marina Abramović's Re-Do's," talk at the Guggenheim Museum, New York (April 7, 2005). This mutual transformation centers the question of liveness upon an ethical relation, but also, significantly, locates it in the capacity for a changed future. Erika Fischer-Lichte's turn to copresence as basic to performance is similarly invested in what her book calls *The Transformative Power of Performance* (New York: Routledge, 2008).

28. Rebecca Schneider, *Performing Remains: Art and War in the Times of Theatrical Reenactment* (New York: Routledge, 2011), 32–60.

29. Ibid., 90–99.

30. See Jill Dolan, *Utopia in Performance: Finding Hope at the Theater* (Ann Arbor: University of Michigan Press, 2005) and José Esteban Muñoz, *Cruising Utopia: The Then and There of Queer Futurity* (New York: NYU Press, 2009).

31. Muñoz refers to Adorno in order to define his sense of the utopic as "the determined negation of that which merely is" redirected "to what should be." See Ernst Bloch and Theodor W. Adorno, "Something's Missing: A Discussion between Ernst Bloch and Theodor Adorno on the Contradictions of Utopian Longing," in *The Utopian Function of Art and Literature: Selected Essays*, trans. Jack Zipes and Frank Mecklenburg (Cambridge, MA: MIT Press, 1988), 12.

Quoted in Muñoz, *Cruising Utopia*, 64. We might consider the subtitle and refrain throughout Muñoz's book, that the utopic promises to leave the "here and now" for the "then and there." This formulation is intentionally ambiguous, as the "then and there" refers to both a future alternative to the present and also a past formulation. This coordination of a place and a time projected as an end outside the present could be called a possibility arrived at through the revision of the present.

32. Karl Marx, *Das Kapital I* (Berlin: Dietz, 1947), 180. Quoted in Ernst Bloch, *The Principle of Hope*, vol. 1, trans. Neville Plaice, Stephen Plaice, and Paul Knight (Cambridge, MA: MIT Press, 1995), 76.

33. Kimberly Jannarone's excellent book *Artaud and His Doubles* (Ann Arbor: University of Michigan Press, 2010) describes the liberatory and reactionary sides of Artaud's cruelty.

34. Dennis Puleston, the naturalist who owned the barn with his wife Betty, recounts his circumnavigation of the globe by sailboat in the 1930s in his book *Blue Water Vagabond: Six Years' Adventure at Sea* (New York: Doubleday, Doran, 1939).

35. See Marvin Carlson, *The Haunted Stage: The Theater as Memory Machine* (Ann Arbor: University of Michigan Press, 2003).

36. See Muñoz, *Cruising Utopia*, 97–114.

37. In a plenary presentation at the 2014 American Society for Theatre Research conference with far-reaching implications, Rebecca Schneider voiced concern about "an a-historicality in the new materialist turn, a potential essentialism (an essentializing of potential), a universalizing and if not anthropomorphizing then a molecularizing (read biologizing?) that can rush in at the door of a generalized animacy." With reference to critics of new materialism like Alexander Galloway and Jordana Rosenberg, she asserts that "the living labor of the affect factory and the liveness of the new materialism must be thought together." While I hope that this book has not succumbed fully to such a generalized animacy, I am convinced that there is further work to be done in this direction. See Rebecca Schneider, "Lithic Liveness and Agential Theatricality" (presentation, Annual Conference of the American Society for Theatre Research, Baltimore, MD, November 22, 2014). Thanks to Rebecca Schneider for sharing this text with me.

38. Edward Said, *Beginnings: Intentions and Methods* (New York: Columbia University Press, 2004), 48, my emphasis.

39. Frank Kermode, *The Sense of an Ending: Studies in the Theory of Fiction* (New York: Oxford University Press, 2000). Bert O. States makes a related claim in his analysis of drama: "The beginning is nothing more than the origin and onset of the ending." Bert O. States, *The Pleasure of the Play* (Ithaca, NY: Cornell University Press, 1994), 9.

40. Phelan, *Unmarked*, 27.

CHAPTER 2

1. Henri Bergson, *Creative Evolution*, trans. Arthur Mitchell (New York: Dover, 1998), 96.

2. Tristan Bernard, *Contes, Répliques et Bon Mots* (Paris: Livre club de libraire, 1964). My translation.

3. The quote attributed to Valéry is actually a translation by François Jacob in the published version of his lectures, *The Possible and the Actual* (Seattle: University of Washington Press, 1982), 66. George Steiner in *Grammars of Creation*, among others, has raised a similar claim about the human as uniquely future-oriented. See introduction.

4. I recognize that a director could stage Nora's departure as a radical break from the realm of possibilities that the play text has made available to her (as in Lee Breuer's Mabou Mines production *Dollhouse* from 2003), but such a rupture would also necessitate a departure from the norms of dramatic possibility outlined below.

5. See Gertrude Stein's essay "Plays" in *Last Operas and Plays* (Baltimore: John Hopkins University Press, 1995), xxiv–lii, and "Composition as Explanation," in *Look at Me Now and Here I Am: Writings and Lectures, 1911–1945* (New York: Penguin, 1967), 23–30.

6. Peter Szondi, *Theory of Modern Drama*, trans. Michael Hays (Minneapolis: University of Minnesota Press, 1987), 5. It should be emphasized that alternative modes and traditions of performance operate in very different manners and may or may not exhibit similar concerns with the exposition of possibility described in this book.

7. See August Wilhelm von Schlegel, "Lectures on Dramatic Art and Literature," in Bernard F. Dukore, ed., *Dramatic Theory and Criticism: Greeks to Grotowski* (New York: Harcourt Brace Jovanovich, 1974), 496.

8. Szondi, *Theory of Modern Drama*, 9.

9. In the words of Szondi's English translator Michael Hays, the characters in these dramas "are locked inside their own subjectivity and their metaphysical helplessness." Michael Hays, "Drama and Dramatic Theory: Peter Szondi and the Modern Theater," *Boundary 2*, 11:3 (Spring 1983), 76.

10. Aristotle sees Euripides's tragedies, for example, as problematic divergences from his model of the plot, in part because they do not exhibit expected possibility. As J. Michael Walton puts it, "A central requirement for Euripidean drama, it would seem, is that it will reflect, rather than account for, the unpredictable in life." J. Michael Walton, *Euripides: Our Contemporary* (Berkeley: University of California Press, 2009), 17.

11. States, *Pleasure of the Play*, 60.

12. For an overview of these variations within the larger structure of the plot see Peter Burian, "Myth into *Mythos*: The Shaping of Tragic Plot," in P. E. Easterling, ed., *The Cambridge Companion to Greek Tragedy* (New York: Cambridge University Press, 1997), 178–208.

13. States, *Pleasure of the Play*, 58.

14. Andrew Sofer, *The Stage Life of Props* (Ann Arbor: University of Michigan Press, 2003), 169. Sofer devotes a chapter, fittingly titled "Killing Time," to the gun onstage.

15. Aristotle, *Poetics*, 32–33.

16. "Brecht advocates techniques that will make the audience react to his provisional theatrical worlds by recognizing its own world as similarly provisional, a possible, rather than a necessary, structure: 'if we play works dealing

with our own time as though they were historical, then perhaps the circumstances under which [the spectator] himself acts will strike him as equally odd; and this is where the critical attitude begins'" (Quigley, *The Modern Stage*, 31). The quoted text is from Bertolt Brecht, *Brecht on Theatre: The Development of an Aesthetic*, ed. and trans. John Willett (New York: Hill & Wang, 1964), 190.

17. "For the reason they take pleasure in seeing the images is that in the process of viewing they find themselves learning, that is, reckoning what kind a given thing belongs to: 'This individual is a So-and-so'" (Aristotle, *Poetics*, 20).

18. According to Jauss, the horizon particular to the text meets a second horizon in the reader, the two producing a dialectical exchange that together establishes a field of possibility. See Hans Robert Jauss, *Toward an Aesthetic of Reception*, trans. Timothy Bahti (Minneapolis: University of Minnesota Press, 1982). Performance complicates the matter as a multitude of horizons interweave through the "readings" of the various designers, actors, directors, and practical questions of architecture and context, creating a panoply of exchanges with the audience. See Fernando Toro, *Theatre Semiotics: Text and Staging in Modern Theatre*, trans. Mario Valdez (Toronto: University of Toronto Press, 1995), 102–105.

19. Jacques Roubaud, introduction to *The Oulipo Compendium*, ed. Harry Mathews and Alastair Brotchie (London: Atlas Press, 1998), 41. Daniel Levin Becker's account of the history of the Oulipo and its offshoots, *Many Subtle Channels: In Praise of Potential Literature* (Cambridge, MA: Harvard University Press, 2012), details the continuous pursuits of, and divergences from, a definition of potentiality at the heart of the group. As his book wittily displays, the protean writers of the Oulipo would make any of my attempts at pinning them down a fruitless and antithetical endeavor.

20. Oulipo's understanding of uncertainty is closer to John Cage's *chance* (a selection from a set of values) than to his *indeterminacy*. Cage writes: "A performance of a composition which is indeterminate of its performance is necessarily unique. It cannot be repeated. When performed for a second time, the outcome is other than it was." John Cage, "Composition as Process," in *Silence: Lectures and Writings by John Cage* (Middletown, CT: Wesleyan University Press, 1961), 39.

21. Jacques Bens's "Queneau Oulipian," in Warren F. Motte Jr., trans. and ed., *Oulipo: A Primer of Potential Literature* (Lincoln: University of Nebraska Press, 1986), 67, my emphasis.

22. Here Umberto Eco's semiotically inspired notion of an "open work" explicated in his 1960s collection of essays *The Open Work* deserves mention. The open work exceeds the hermeneutic capacity of the reader, engulfing him or her in an excess of information, while forcing him or her to select a single narrative of actualization from amid many possible actualizations. Only certain doors and windows are open in the open work. See Umberto Eco, *The Open Work*, trans. Ann Cancogni (Cambridge, MA: Harvard University Press, 1989). This informational overload may be an overabundance of signification, but it still represents a discrete system of signs, however vast.

23. Certain analytic philosophers have proposed a complementary notion in the theory of possible worlds, based on the hypothesis that multiple possible

worlds sit parallel to the actual one in which we exist. Such theories enable the explication of a range of questions surrounding modal logic, by proposing different worlds in which different truth-values are consistent. For each world a unique set of propositions holds true. This "Canonical Conception" of possible worlds theory indicates that possible worlds refer to the subjunctive past ("what *could* have been" —my emphasis) in constructing multiple presents. Futurity in a possible world plays out according to opinions of what is already feasible in our actuality; it configures the range of variable qualities only in accordance with facets of our own actuality that can be clearly phrased as true/false propositions. As Manuel De Landa has argued, belief in such alternate worlds or possible parallel universes always returns us to a form of anthropomorphic essentialism since, from these perspectives, "we commit ourselves to affirm that objects possess some of their properties necessarily while others only contingently." Manuel De Landa, *Intensive Science and Virtual Philosophy* (London: Bloomsbury Academic, 2005), 53. For a good overview of modal logic's various approaches to the theory of possible worlds, see Michael J. Loux, ed., *The Possible and the Actual: Readings in the Metaphysics of Modality* (Ithaca, NY: Cornell University Press, 1979). A longer discussion of the interplay between drama and possible worlds theory would be fruitful but lies beyond the scope of this manuscript.

24. This emphasis on the performance of reading a text extends to the precedents that the group claims as part of its genealogy of formal innovators (Oulipians before the group was officially founded, these writers are termed "anticipatory plagiarists"). In particular, they look to the Italian early modern theater form of commedia dell'arte as an ancestral "potential" form, where the terminology I have employed would see its array of scenarios rearranging fixed archetypal characters as a form of performance quintessentially concerned with the play of possibility (see Jacques Bens's "Queneau Oulipian," 72). After all, improvisational theater may produce a vast array of actions, but these always seek to stage a legible performance, a "solution" to the game or narrative world within which the event takes place. Commedia dell'arte and more recent forms of comedic improvisation such as those performed at the Second City theater in Chicago or on the 1980s-1990s television show *Whose Line Is It Anyway?* operate within determined systems of rules and behavior. The *lazzi* of the former and the "games" of the latter define the rules of engagement. A great deal of the humor and enjoyment attached to such work hinges on the recognition of a shift from one possible world to another or the playing out of a possibility at the furthest limits of a particular world.

25. Members of the group have produced other performance pieces and dramatic texts that operate in a quite different, even willfully paralogical, manner.

26. Churchill quoted in Ben Brantley's review of the production at the Brooklyn Academy of Music, "Finding Appalling Sense in a Giddy Anarchy," *New York Times*, February 1, 1999. *Blue Kettle* depicts a young man who for reasons that are less than clear approaches a series of older women under the pretense that he is the child that they had given up for adoption many years ago. As this story of mutually misplaced longing proceeds, the words "blue" and "kettle" begin to insinuate themselves into the dialogue as substitutions for other

words. This steady eclipse of linguistic communication increases until, in the final scene, the characters are almost completely reduced to verbalizing the disassociated letters in the two words as their only means of vocal expression. The remainder of the performance proceeds apace, with the characters performing actions and intentions occluded in the written script. Churchill does not provide her interpreters with the key to this lost event; there are no stage directions to illuminate the action and only the occasional words that remain intact hint at the content of the final scene's dialogue. Performed in a manner that does not compensate for this lost material, the intrusions of viral words open a rift in specific verbal actions to let a broader range of possibilities pour in. However, even in the last scene of *Blue Kettle*, when one character's line "T b k k k k l?" is answered by a final "B. K.," a range of expected meanings emerges from the operations of plot and character set up by the earlier intact scenes. As we recede from the scene we are invited to interpose our own imagined content to complete the scene, a content that is inevitably provided by the set of possibilities we expect to be available to the world of the play and its characters.

27. Caryl Churchill, *Blue Heart* (New York: TCG Publications, 1997), 5.

28. Ibid., 6.

29. Georg Büchner, *Complete Plays and Prose*, trans. Carl Richard Mueller (New York: Hill and Wang, 1963), 111. Roland Barthes recognized a similar function at work much earlier in Racine: "Between the Chamber [the silent and invisible source of power] and the Antechamber [the stage where one waits and speaks] stands a tragic object which menacingly expresses both contiguity and exchange, the tangency of hunter and prey: the Door." Here, the door leads into the indefinite and inexpressible heart of the throne room, the nexus of potentiality. See Roland Barthes, *On Racine*, trans. Richard Howard (New York: PAJ Publications, 1983), 4–5.

30. Churchill, *Blue Heart*, 32.

31. See the final section of the next chapter, "Withholding Potentiality," for a more replete discussion of the means without end.

32. Bergson, *Creative Evolution*, 5. See also page 46 of the same.

33. Bergson's writings were hailed by a range of contemporaneous thinkers and became an important precursor to the development of phenomenology and existentialism, while in the arts his thought influenced cubism and the vitalist art criticism of midcentury critics such as Herbert Read. Scientific evidence against the existence of a vitalist impulse and associated criticism relegated Bergson's work to the background by the late twentieth century. In recent years, at least partly inspired by Gilles Deleuze's reclamation of the thinker as central to his own theory of becoming, Bergson has received renewed attention by those interested in a broad range of disciplines including media studies, architecture, and film studies, to name a few. See Mark Hansen's work on new media art and the body, *New Philosophy for New Media* (Cambridge, MA: MIT Press, 2006), Elizabeth Grosz's intervention into architecture, *Architecture from the Outside: Essays on Virtual and Real Space* (Cambridge, MA: MIT Press, 2001), and Deleuze's writings on cinema, among others. Jane Bennett's *Vibrant Matter: A Political Ecology of Things* (Durham, NC: Duke University Press, 2010) revises Bergson's vitalism to reconsider an ethics that acknowledges the life of things.

34. In reference to Bergson's methodology, Garrett Barden writes: "To do philosophy guided by Bergson is not to read and believe but to repeat the experiment." Garrett Barden, "Method in Philosophy," in John Mullarkey, ed., *The New Bergson* (New York: Manchester University Press, 1999), 34.

35. De Landa is writing about Gilles Deleuze's use of the Bergsonian concept. De Landa, *Intensive Science*, 37, my emphasis.

36. Bergson, *Creative Evolution*, 12.

37. Intellectual analysis "reduces objects to elements already known, that is, to elements common both to it and other objects. To analyze, therefore is to express a thing as a function of something other than itself. All analysis is thus a translation." Henri Bergson, *Introduction to Metaphysics*, trans. T. E. Hulme (Indianapolis: Hackett, 1999), 24. John Mullarkey describes this relationship in the following manner: "[The self] does not make a choice between really preexisting alternatives, *it creates the image of these alternatives in the retrospective light of its accomplished action.* Representations of possibility are based on the assumption of the sameness of subjects and of situations." John Mullarkey, *Bergson and Philosophy* (Edinburgh: Edinburgh University Press, 1999), 25, my emphasis. The network of future choices available to the intellect is created in the present moment, but based on one's previous understanding of how entities function.

38. Henri Bergson, *Matter and Memory*, trans. N. M. Paul and W. S. Palmer (New York: Zone Books, 1990), 211.

39. Rancière's concept of the distribution of the sensible describes "the system of divisions and boundaries that define, among other things, what is visible and audible within a particular aesthetico-political regime." From Gabriel Rockhill's introduction to his translation of Jacques Rancière's *The Politics of Aesthetics* (New York: Continuum, 2004),1.

40. Bergson, *Matter and Memory*, 21, original emphasis. The articulation of an available use is vital to the construction of an intellectual concept. Bergson writes in his *Introduction to Metaphysics*: "To try and fit a concept on an object is simply to ask what we can do with the object, and what it can do for us. To label an object with a certain concept is to mark in precise terms the kind of action or attitude the object should suggest to us" (Bergson, *Introduction to Metaphysics*, 39).

41. Jacob, *Possible and Actual*, 56, my emphasis.

42. "[This book] contains what one might call the description of a walk into unknown worlds. These worlds are not only unknown; they are also invisible." Jakob von Uexküll, *A Foray in the World of Animals and Humans*, trans. Joseph D. O'Neill (Minneapolis: University of Minnesota Press, 2010), 41.

43. Duration divides up constantly, "but it does not divide up without changing in kind, it changes in kind in the process of dividing up; This is why it is a nonnumerical multiplicity, where we can speak of 'indivisibles' at each stage of the division." Gilles Deleuze, *Bergsonism*, trans. Hugh Tomlinson and Barbara Habberjam (New York: Zone Books, 1990), 42. Or, in another example that Bergson employs, we may say that an emotion seems a composite of several feelings, but if one were to isolate these component parts one would arrive at an entirely different emotion.

44. States, *Pleasure of Play*, 78.

45. Aristotle, *Poetics*, 29.

46. Walter Benjamin, "Oedipus, or Rational Myth," in Walter Benjamin, *Selected Writings*, vol. 2, *1927–1934*, ed. Michael Jennings (Cambridge, MA: Harvard University Press, 1999), 579. Later in this same essay, Benjamin broadens this notion to include all of classical tragedy, citing Franz Rosenzweig's claim that "the tragic hero has but one language that is wholly appropriate to him: silence."

47. As Joseph Roach suggests, Stanislavsky's *An Actor Prepares* is a paradigmatic text in that it was "sufficiently powerful to deflect a group of practitioners away from competing theories and methods of investigation [and] openended enough to create a whole new set of problems 'for the redefined group of practitioners to resolve.'" Joseph Roach, *The Player's Passion: Studies in the Science of Acting* (Ann Arbor: University of Michigan Press, 2007), 14. Sharon Marie Carnicke's *Stanislavsky in Focus: An Acting Master for the Twenty-First Century* (New York: Routledge, 1998) identifies and corrects the conventional reading of Stanislavsky's work. While acknowledging Carnicke's necessary work, my intention here is to explore the consequences of these misapprehensions in terms of the futurity that they have fostered in mainstream dramatic theater.

48. Stanislavsky, *An Actor Prepares*, 12–32.

49. Ibid., 53. This criticism recurs at various points throughout the text. For example, the Director later claims that "the mistake most actors make is that they think about the result instead of about the action that must prepare it. By avoiding action and aiming straight at the result you get a forced product which lead to nothing but ham acting" (ibid., 117).

50. Ibid., 40.

51. Ibid., 121, original emphasis.

52. Marina Caldarone and Maggie Lloyd-Williams, *Actions: The Actors' Thesaurus* (New York: Drama Publishers, 2004).

53. See Carnicke's *Stanislavsky in Focus* and Bella Merlin's *Beyond Stanislavsky: A Psycho-physical Approach to Actor Training* (New York: Routledge, 2001). Other Western approaches to actor training also rely on the projection of a possible end point into the future. Declan Donnellan's popular book *The Actor and the Target* (New York: TCG Publications, 2006), for example, describes how an imagined target orients the actions of the performer. Even if this target is constantly shifting its qualities and shape moment-to-moment, it is the anchor of expectation that fixes the present's futurity.

54. Melissa Bruder, Lee Michael Cohn, Madeleine Olnek, Nathaniel Pollack, Robert Previtio, Scott Zigler, and David Mamet, *A Practical Handbook for the Actor* (New York: Vintage, 1986), 13.

55. Ibid., 18.

56. Stanislavsky, *An Actor Prepares*, 124.

57. Bruder et al., *A Practical Handbook*, 35.

58. The translation quoted in *A Practical Handbook* comes from F. Storr's Loeb Library version of *Oedipus* (Cambridge, MA: Harvard University Press, 1912), lines 327–328.

59. Possibility's teleological action informs not only the textual object and its articulation, but also the means of theatrical production at large. For example,

the stage realism of the nineteenth century follows naturalism's interest in displaying the effects of a physical and social environment upon the bodies that inhabit that space. Christine's famous silent scene in the beginning of Strindberg's *Miss Julie*, for example, details a series of interactions with the set itself, the pots and pans at the root of kitchen sink realism, so that even once she has finished the prescribed actions, the audience presumably believes that she could do other appropriate things with those unused towels in the corner, wash that spoon, and so on. Naturalism and its aftereffects filled the mise-en-scène with a field of details that clearly define the parameters of its characters' possibilities.

60. *Oxford English Dictionary Online.* www.oed.com.

61. Szondi, *Theory of Modern Drama*, 10.

62. States, *Pleasure of the Play*, 61–62.

63. George Steiner's *The Death of Tragedy* (New York: Faber and Faber, 1996) is the most famous of many examples. Giorgio Agamben writes: "The Greek hero has left us forever; he can no longer bear witness for us in any way. After Auschwitz, it is not possible to use a tragic paradigm in ethics." Giorgio Agamben, *Remnants of Auschwitz: The Witness and the Archive*, trans. Daniel Heller-Roazen (New York: Zone Books, 2002), 99.

64. Will Eno, *Flu Season and Other Plays* (New York: TCG Publications, 2006), 81. All references to text in parentheses henceforth.

65. David Hume, *An Enquiry Concerning Human Understanding*, ed. L. A. Selby-Bigge (London: Oxford University Press, 1967), 24–25.

66. Perhaps the most notable exception to the supposed exclusion of violence from the stage is Sophocles's *Ajax*, with its mad protagonist slaughtering countless sheep onstage and eventually killing himself in full view of the audience.

67. Jean Genet, *The Blacks: A Clown Show*, trans. Bernard Frechtman (New York: Grove Press, 1984), 84.

68. See, for example, René Girard's *Violence and the Sacred*, trans. Patrick Gregory (Baltimore: Johns Hopkins University Press, 1979), discussed in more depth in "Actualizing Potentiality" below. As Michael the Legal Advisor puts it: "We are waiting for a disclosure of some sort from someone with, we hope, a clearer understanding of the night, and of the question of liability" (Eno, *Flu Season*, 81).

69. "As the bearer of the message, the messenger appears . . . but he must also disappear, or write himself out of the picture, in order that the recipient hears the words of the person who sent the message, not the messenger. When the messenger takes on too much importance, he ends up diverting the channel of transmission to his own ends." Michel Serres, *Angels: A Modern Myth*, trans. Francis Cowper (Paris: Flammarion, 1997), 99.

70. "The project [of the book] involves a reversal of the conventional Aristotelian idea that drama is the medium of action. Instead, I want to consider action itself as a medium with its own conflicting tendencies and to examine those conflicts and contradictions." Alice Rayner, *To Act, To Do, To Perform: Drama and the Phenomenology of Action* (Ann Arbor: University of Michigan Press, 1994), 3. In Rayner's book, drama becomes the tool for such a reexamination.

71. Burke's theory of "dramatism" fittingly exposes the workings of actions through the grammatical analysis of drama. As outlined in the *Grammar of Motives*, Burke considers action as a limited subset of a larger field of motion: "As for 'act,' any verb, no matter how specific or how general, that has connotations of consciousness or purpose falls under this category. If one happened to stumble over an obstruction, that would be not an act, but a mere motion. . . . 'Dramatistically,' the basic unit of action would be defined as 'the human body in conscious or purposive motion.'" Kenneth Burke, *A Grammar of Motives* (Berkeley: University of California Press, 1969), 14. In Burke's analysis, as in Bergson's, action is determined by a purpose, an intention to accomplish something that can be named in language, a verb. Encountering an obstruction diverts action from its intentional fulfillment and breaks with representational habits, opening up an "unconscious" field of motion, a literal/physical Freudian slip.

72. Rayner, *To Act*, 8.

73. Ibid., 60.

74. Ibid., 27–36. See also "The Third Meaning: Research Notes on Several Eisenstein Stills," in Roland Barthes, *The Responsibility of Forms: Critical Essays on Music, Art, and Representation*, trans. Richard Howard (Berkeley: University of California Press, 1985).

75. Friedrich Nietzsche, *On the Genealogy of Morals*, trans. Walter Kaufmann (New York: Vintage, 1969), 45.

76. Rayner, *To Act*, 61.

77. "[The witches] demonstrate the quality, the demonic aspect, of the deed: and deed *is* inhuman because it is without the doubt, delay, or hesitations of discourse. It has no outside or privileged view" (ibid., 69).

78. Ibid., 107.

79. Lucian, *The Works of Lucian*, trans. H. W. Fowler and F. G. Fowler (Oxford: Clarendon Press, 1905), 2:245. Quoted in Stephen Orgel, *The Jonsonian Masque* (Cambridge, MA: Harvard University Press, 1965), 10.

CHAPTER 3

1. Benjamin, *Selected Writings*, 2:686.

2. The Zhuangzi text is quoted in François Jullien, *In Praise of Blandness: Proceeding from Chinese Thought and Aesthetics*, trans. Paula M. Varsano (Stanford, CA: Stanford University Press, 2004), 73.

3. Ibid. See also François Jullien, *The Great Image Has No Form, or On the Nonobject through Painting*, trans. Jane Marie Todd (Chicago: University of Chicago Press, 2012); *Detour and Access: Strategies of Meaning in China and Greece*, trans. Sophie Hawkes (Cambridge, MA: Zone Books, 2000); and *The Propensity of Things: Toward a History of Efficacy in China*, trans. Janet Lloyd (Cambridge, MA: Zone Books, 1999).

4. The site's mission statement explains: "And so, Bartleby.com—after the humble character of its namesake scrivener, or copyist—publishes the classics of literature, nonfiction, and reference free of charge for the home, classroom, and desktop of each and every Internet participant." "Welcome to Bartleby.

com," http://www.bartleby.com/sv/welcome.html (accessed December 12, 2012).

5. Herman Melville, *"Bartleby" and "Benito Cereno"* (New York: Dover Publications, 1990), 3. All subsequent parenthetical citations from the text refer to this edition.

6. The only other names mentioned by the narrator (John Jacob Astor, Jonathan Edwards, and Joseph Priestley) actually exist as referents outside the fictional world of the story; they are not characters.

7. They were purloined letters, to borrow from Poe's story of that name published eight years before Melville penned his Bartleby. See Poe's "A Purloined Letter" as well as the responses in Jacques Derrida's "The Purveyor of Truth," trans. Willis Domingo, James Hulbert, and Moshe Ron, in *Yale French Studies* 52 (1975), 31–113; and Jacques Lacan's "Seminar on the Purloined Letter," in *Écrits: A Selection*, trans. Bruce Fink (New York: W.W. Norton, 2002).

8. "Had there been the least uneasiness, anger, impatience or impertinence in his manner; in other words, had there been anything ordinarily human about him, doubtless I should have violently dismissed him from the premises" (Melville, *Bartleby*, 10).

9. Michel Foucault, *Discipline and Punish: The Birth of the Prison*, trans. Alan Sheridan (New York: Vintage, 1995).

10. Michel Serres, *Genesis*, trans. Genevieve James and James Nielson (Ann Arbor: University of Michigan Press, 1997), 28.

11. James C. Scott, *Seeing Like a State: How Certain Schemes to Improve the Human Condition Have Failed* (New Haven: Yale University Press, 1999), 183.

12. Gilles Deleuze, *Essays Critical and Clinical*, trans. Daniel Smith and Michael Greco (Minneapolis: University of Minnesota Press, 1997), 74.

13. Herman Melville, *Moby Dick* (New York: W.W. Norton, 2002), 165.

14. Giorgio Agamben, *Potentialities*, trans. Daniel Heller-Roazen (Stanford, CA: Stanford University Press, 1999), 244.

15. Plato, *Plato: The Collected Dialogues*, ed. Edith Hamilton and Huntington Cairns (Princeton, NJ: Princeton University Press, 1961), 1177–1178.

16. Melville's interest in the body as inscribed surface is most memorably realized in *Moby Dick*, which recounts how the character Queequeg's tattoos supposedly describe the workings of the universe in unreadable symbols: "And this tattooing had been the work of a departed prophet and seer of his island, who, by those hieroglyphic marks, had written out on his body a complete theory of the heavens and the earth, and a mystical treatise on the art of attaining truth; so that Queequeg in his own proper person was a riddle to unfold; a wonderous work in one volume; but whose mysteries not even himself could read, though his own live heart beat against them; and these mysteries were therefore destined in the end to moulder away with the living parchment whereon they were inscribed, and so be unsolved to the last. And this thought it must have been which suggested to Ahab that wild exclamation of his, when one morning turning away from surveying poor Queequeg—'Oh, devilish tantalization of the gods!'" (Melville, *Moby Dick*, 367). Queequeg's tattoo artist is gone, departed, his promise a sealed letter lost in transit. He is the book that cannot be read, the other book buried in the depths of *Moby Dick* that holds its

future at bay. It is noteworthy that the exclamation ending this chapter of the novel does not differ greatly from the narrator's exclamation at the end of "Bartleby the Scrivener": "Ah, Bartleby! Ah, Humanity!"

17. Aristotle, *The Basic Works of Aristotle*, ed. Richard McKeon (New York: Random House, 1941), 826.

18. In his study of the concept of potentiality in educational discourse, Israel Scheffler also uses the example of the pianist in distinguishing between generic, but unavailable, potentiality and potentiality as the present capacity to do: "[One with generic potentiality] has now no *capacity to play* but he does now have another capacity, i.e. the *capacity to acquire the capacity to play*." Israel Scheffler, *Of Human Potential: An Essay in the Philosophy of Education* (New York: Routledge & Kegan Paul, 1985), 47.

19. See Aristotle, "De Anima [On the Soul]," in Aristotle, *The Basic Works*, 565, and Agamben, "On Potentiality," in *Potentialities*, 179.

20. In a passage from the *Metaphysics* that Agamben takes as the crux of his own theory of potentiality, Aristotle writes: "Impotentiality [*adynamia*] is a privation contrary to potentiality [*dynamis*]. Every potentiality is impotentiality of the same [potentiality] and with respect to the same [potentiality]." Agamben glosses this as follows: "'Impotentiality' does not mean here only absence of potentiality, not being able to do, but also and above all 'being able to not do,' being able to not exercise one's potentiality" Agamben, *Nudities*, 43; the translation of Aristotle is from the same text.

21. Giorgio Agamben, *The Coming Community*, trans. Michael Hardt (Minneapolis: University of Minnesota Press, 1993), 34. This point is repeated throughout Agamben's oeuvre.

22. Leland de la Durantaye describes Agamben as "*devastat*[ing] *the ground of presupposition* . . . . The *matter of language*, exposing the groundless presupposition of language, offers an experience of, an experiment in, a belonging that is without presupposition — 'the unpresupposable and unpresupposed principle' of which Agamben speaks, and which he calls in one of the essays from [*Potentialities*] 'pure destination.'" Leland de la Durantaye, "Agamben's Potential," *Diacritics* 30:2 (Summer 2000), 10. The referenced text can be found in Agamben, *Potentialities*, 113, emphasis in original.

23. Agamben, *Potentialities*, 179, emphasis in original.

24. Deleuze, *Essays Critical and Clinical*, 90.

25. McKenzie speculates that "*performance will be to the twentieth and twenty-first centuries what discipline was to the eighteenth and nineteenth, that is, an onto-historical formation of power and knowledge.*" Jon McKenzie, *Perform or Else: From Discipline to Performance* (New York: Routledge, 2001), 18, original emphasis. Indeed, discipline seems effectively absent from the office's operation as the narrator is unable to reprimand his employees for their delinquent behavior.

26. On November 10, 2011, twenty-seven Occupy Wall Street supporters presented a public reading of Herman Melville's 1853 short story "Bartleby, the Scrivener: A Story of Wall Street" at New York's Zuccotti Park. Several weeks beforehand, a "silent reading" of selections from the text was transmitted via private headphone to protesters at the park. At about the same time, the independent publishing company Melville House began offering what it called an

"Occupy Wall Street Bundle" with its printing of the story included in a canvas bag emblazoned with the fictional copyist's immortal words: "I would prefer not to."

27. Agamben, *The Coming Community*, 43. The project has much in common with contemporaneous Italian political theorists of the multitude endeavoring to articulate a post-Marxist vision of community that acknowledges a shift from imperialism to global empire. See Michael Hardt and Antonio Negri, *Multitude: War and Democracy in the Age of Empire* (New York: Penguin, 2004) for the broadest overview of this shift. Also Paolo Virno and Michael Hardt's edited collection *Radical Thought in Italy: A Potential Politics* (Minneapolis: University of Minnesota Press, 2006), which gathers together writings by a number of political thinkers in Italy surrounding these issues from the 1980s to 2000s.

28. This citational aspect of the performative has informed later elaborations by Judith Butler (as the authoritative power of discourse) and Jacques Derrida (as inescapable representation), among others. See Judith Butler, *Bodies That Matter*, and *Gender Trouble: Feminism and the Subversion of Identity* (New York: Routledge, 2006), and Jacques Derrida, *Limited Inc*, and *Writing and Difference*, trans. Alan Bass (Chicago: University of Chicago Press, 1978).

29. Austin, *How to Do Things*, 112.

30. The utterance establishes a boundary between the potential and the possible both in the sense of disrupting the utterance as "action" (via speech act theory and dramatism) and in terms of the theory of possible worlds proposed by analytic philosophers (see chapter 2, note 23). The formula presents the latter half of what linguists call a "counterfactual conditional statement" such as "If p happened, then q would happen." Such counterfactuals have proved fertile ground for analytic philosophers as a means toward describing relationships between different possibilities. The counterfactual expresses a possible world nearest to our own, one that, apart from the "if" statement p, operates according to the expectations of the actuality in which we exist. But Bartleby's formula dismantles the difference between these possible worlds, possessing and negating them all at once in a single common formula of indeterminacy. We could say that the various requests by the attorney amount to a number of p conditions that are, in turn, met with a uniform negative q statement. Regardless of *what [p] happened*, Bartleby's preference *not to [q] happen* would assert itself. Named events or actions have no consequence on the reluctant copyist. This accounts for one way of reading the "would" in the oft-repeated phrase, a manner that suggests a radical break with the causal relation between parts of language and the truth-values that ground the possible, as well as denying the authority of preexisting actuality in the determination of a future event. This "irrational" departure from the expected behavior of a possibility is precisely that which aggravates the narrator's doctrine of necessity, discussed at the beginning of the next chapter, "Beholding Potentiality."

31. Branka Arsić, *Passive Constitutions: 7 ½ Times Bartleby* (Stanford, CA: Stanford University Press, 2007), 140.

32. Deleuze, *Essays Critical and Clinical*, 73.

33. Agamben, *Potentialities*, 257.

34. As Jaworski has written, Bartleby "does not refuse, but neither does he

accept, he advances and then withdraws into this advance, barely exposing himself in a nimble retreat from speech." See Philippe Jaworski, "Desert and Empire: From 'Bartleby' to 'Benito Cereno,'" in Richard Chase, ed., *Herman Melville: A Collection of Critical Essays* (Englewood Cliffs, NJ: Prentice Hall, 1962), 151–59. Quoted in Deleuze, *Essays Critical and Clinical*, 71.

35. Moshé Feldenkrais and Richard Schechner, "Image, Movement, and Actor: Restoration of Potentiality," trans. Kelly Morris, *TDR: Tulane Drama Review* 10:3 (Spring 1966), 125. Thanks to Kris Salata for directing me to this source.

36. Martin Puchner, *Stage Fright: Modernism, Anti-Theatricality, and Drama* (Baltimore: Johns Hopkins University Press, 2011), 90.

37. André Lepecki, "Inscribing Dance" in his edited collection *Of the Presence of the Body: Essays on Dance and Performance Theory* (Middletown, CT: Wesleyan University Press, 2004), 124. The essay discusses how notation of dance in early eighteenth-century France, for example, presented a clear language of dance steps that often preceded, or even existed without, the body of a dancer as verification. Academics of the period would analyze the merit of conceptual dances that had never been performed based on the written depiction of the piece. For more on the early writing of dance and its ephemerality see, for example, Mark Franko, *Dance as Text: Ideologies of the Baroque Body* (New York: Cambridge University Press, 1993). In a publication from the 1970s Marcia Siegel wrote that dance "is an event that disappears in the very act of materializing," and Peggy Phelan would famously locate ephemerality as the ontology of performance more broadly speaking in the 1990s. See Marcia Siegel, *Dance at the Vanishing Point* (New York: Saturday Review Press, 1972) and Phelan, *Unmarked*.

38. Théron, press dossier for *Bartleby*, unpaginated. Various reviews and dramaturgical statements detailing the company's earlier work are available on the Théron website (www.didiertheron.com).

39. See Gilles Deleuze and Félix Guattari, *A Thousand Plateaus*, trans. Brian Massumi (Minneapolis: University of Minnesota, 1987).

40. Jullien, *In Praise of Blandness*, 49.

41. T. S. Eliot, *The Sacred Wood: Essays on Poetry and Criticism* (New York: Barnes & Noble, 1964), 100. Martin Puchner writes that "objective correlatives are what the theater demands" (Puchner, *Stage Fright*, 65).

42. See my article "The Rabbit and Its Double," *Theater* 37:2 (2007), 26–35, where I discuss a mass of stuffed rabbits filling the auditorium seats in a performance by Socìetas Raffaello Sanzio. Indeed, I would argue that this mass reproduction explains, at least in part, what can only be described as a contemporary obsession with the anthropomorphic rabbit as in, for example, films like David Lynch's *Inland Empire* (2006) and Richard Kelly's *Donnie Darko* (2001).

43. The accompanying electronic music by Gerome Nox underscores this unnerving distortion of the natural by taking concrete elements of the sonic landscape and twisting them into alien whispers and crackles that fill the air.

44. Théron proposed his version of *Bartleby* as a kind of answer to the first solo he choreographed for himself, *Autoportrait Raskolnikov*, based on the character from Dostoyevsky's *Crime and Punishment*. Both literary figures dissect intentional movement in a solitary existence, but Raskolnikov's indecision between possibilities never subsides into an ambivalence or indifference; the fig-

ure never stills itself, but shuttles rapidly back and forth from one intention to another, always in relation to a world outside himself.

45. Erin Manning, *Relationscapes: Movement, Art, Philosophy* (Cambridge, MA: MIT Press, 2009), 15.

46. "Even when we are still we are moving, we are not waiting for something, we are in action when we are still. . . . I think that it develops simply, first of all, by being conscious of a possibility of rest, not as rest, but as activity in inactivity, which is like a *koan*: two things going on, so that you are in a sense ready to go, but in a sense going all the time." Merce Cunningham, *The Dancer and the Dance: Merce Cunningham in Conversation with Jacqueline Lesschaeve* (New York: Marion Boyars, 1985), 129.

47. John Martin, *The Modern Dance* (New York: Dance Horizons, 1972), 6. Classical ballet utilizes movement on a clearly delineated plane of possibility, rather than experimenting on the limits of such possibilities. We see this plotting not only in the part-by-part arrangement of movement but also in the body of the dancer. Martin claims that the signal perversions of the ballet dancer's apparatus, namely the turning out of the hips and the elevation of the body (*en pointe*), were attempts to expand the possibilities of the human form along the coordinate axis of expansion and elevation. "When the entire leg is turned out from the hip we find that many more movements are possible" (22). Likewise, "The rising upon the points of the toes is a result of the endeavor to increase the dancer's range of movement in a vertical direction" (23).

48. Jacques Rivière, "Le Sacre du Printemps," in *Nijinsky Dancing* (New York: Knopf, 1975), 165. Quoted in André Lepecki's "Undoing the Fantasy of the (Dancing) Subject: 'Still Acts' in Jérôme Bel's Last Performance," in Steven De Belder, ed., *The Salt of the Earth: On Dance, Politics and Reality* (Brussels: VTI, 2001), 43.

49. Sally Banes, *Terpsichore in Sneakers: Post-modern Dance* (Boston: Houghton Mifflin, 1980), 189.

50. Ibid., 192–193.

51. See André Lepecki, *Exhausting Dance: Performance and the Politics of Movement* (New York: Routledge, 2006). The book looks primarily at a cluster of dancers in Europe who, beginning in the 1990s, revived and continued the minimalism of Judson Church dancers, frequently employing stillness and the extreme reduction of movement in their critique of dance's means of representation. Lepecki borrows the concept of the "still-act" from the Greek anthropologist and cultural critic C. Nadia Seremetakis's notion of stillness as an escape from historical time's progress and sedimentation. In *The Senses Still: Perception and Memory as Material Culture in Modernity* (Chicago: University of Chicago Press, 1996), Seremetakis speaks of a moving stillness as a form of repetition, a stillness that "acts" and remains acting over time.

52. Manning's *Relationscapes* considers preacceleration as the "incipiency of movement" in ways that clearly intersect with the discussion of stillness as potentiality proposed here.

53. Blau, *The Eye of Prey*, 181.

54. Roland Barthes, *Camera Lucida: Reflections on Photography*, trans. Richard Howard (New York: Hill & Wang, 1982), 10 and 14.

55. In what has become a signal aside for performance theorists, Barthes claims that in this respect photography is most closely related to the theatrical: "If Photography seems to me closer to the Theater [than painting], it is by way of a singular intermediary (and perhaps I am the only who sees it): by way of Death. . . . Photography is a kind of primitive theater, a kind of *Tableau Vivant*, a figuration of the motionless and made-up face beneath which we see the dead" (ibid., 31). Both the theater and photography present the mask of an image, while the face of death, the always "is no longer," peeks through.

56. Craig Owens, *Beyond Recognition: Representation, Power, and Culture* (Berkeley: University of California Press, 1992), 210.

57. Schneider, *Performing Remains*, 162.

58. See, for example, Bernth Lindfors, ed., *Africans on Stage: Studies in Ethnological Show Business* (Bloomington: Indiana University Press, 1999) and Paul Blanchard, Gilles Boëtsch, and Nanette Jacomijn Snoep, eds., *Human Zoos: The Invention of the Savage* (Paris: Actes Sud, 2012).

59. "Each *acting cycle* comprises three invariable stages: 1) Intention 2) Realization 3) Reaction. . . . The *reaction* is the attenuation of the volitional reflex after its realization mimetically and vocally, preparatory to the reception of a new intention (the transition to a new acting cycle)." Edward Braun, *Meyerhold: A Revolution in Theatre* (Iowa City: University of Iowa Press, 1998), 174. Meyerhold's parceling of action once again recalls the Austinian and Aristotelian three-part structure, but applies these distinctions to practicable, and in the case of his *etudes* from the 1920s repeatable, action.

60. Alma Law and Mel Gordon, eds., *Meyerhold, Eisenstein, and Biomechanics* (Jefferson, NC: McFarland, 1996), 169.

61. Henri Bergson, *Time and Free Will*, trans. F. L. Pogson (New York: Harper & Row, 1960), 11.

62. Many of Gordon's video pieces instantiate suspended states of potentiality. His *24 Hour Psycho* (1993), for example, disrupts the possible by slowing down the Hitchcock film so that it takes place over the course of a day, thereby saturating every frame of the film with the open-endedness of the gesture discussed here. His *Off-Screen* (1998) projects a closed theatrical curtain on a gallery wall, gently swaying with movement as something unseen passes behind its veil. See "Actualizing Potentiality" for a discussion of the offstage as a space of withheld potentiality and the curtain as its visible surrogate.

63. Giorgio Agamben, "Notes on Gesture," in *Means without End: Notes on Politics*, trans. Vincenzo Binetti and Cesare Casarino (Minneapolis: University of Minnesota Press, 2000), 51.

64. Agamben, *Means without End*, 56–57. The original sources for this material, quoted in Agamben's text, are as follows: Varro, *On the Latin Language*, trans. Roland G. Kent (Cambridge, MA: Harvard University Press, 1977), 245; and Aristotle, *The Nichomachean Ethics*, trans. Martin Ostwald (Indianapolis: Bobbs-Merrill Educational Publishing, 1983), 153.

65. Agamben, *Means without End*, 57.

66. Richard Blackmur, *Language as Gesture: Essays in Poetry* (New York: Har-

court, Brace, 1952), 2. Thanks to Christopher Grobe for bringing this work to my attention.

67. Giorgio Agamben, *The Idea of Prose*, trans. Michael Sullivan and Sam Whitsitt (New York: State University of New York Press, 1995), 41.

68. Bergson, *Creative Evolution*, 145–146.

69. Rayner, *To Act*, 47.

70. As Rayner writes of the play, "Action appears not in terms of a name that identifies intention, but as a fact, devoid of a justifying end point" (ibid., 46).

71. Such is the conception of the stutter, gag, or collapse explored in the late work of Paul de Man, who sees all these as consignments to an inevitable end, the ultimate resolution of death. Leland de la Durantaye has convincingly argued that Agamben's gag of potentiality offers an alternative to de Man. See de la Durantaye, "Agamben's Potential," 3–24.

72. The poem is available for reperformance on Wilding's website at http://faithwilding.refugia.net/waitingpoem.pdf (last accessed August 23, 2014)

73. First encountering the playwright's work in the early 1960s, Wilding worked as the associate producer of the Beckett Festival of Radio Plays from 1984 to 1988, which broadcast in the United States, Britain, Germany, and throughout Europe. See Wilding's website.

74. Judith Halberstam, *The Queer Art of Failure* (Durham, NC: Duke University Press, 2011), 144.

75. Agamben, *Means without End*, 59, my emphasis. The notion of a communication of communicability derives from Benjamin's essay "The Task of the Translator," which proclaims this revelation of the pure mediality of language to be the object of translation. See Walter Benjamin's "The Task of the Translator" in his *Selected Writings*, vol. 1, *1913–1926*, ed. Marcus Bullock and Michael W. Jennings (Cambridge, MA: Harvard University Press, 2004).

76. Agamben, *Remnants of Auschwitz*, 39. The relationship between potentiality and witnessing is discussed in more detail in the next chapter, "Beholding Potentiality."

77. See, for example, Bernard Knox, *Word and Action: Essays on the Ancient Theater* (Baltimore: Johns Hopkins University, 1986), 39–56.

78. Witold Gombrowicz, *Princess Ivona*, trans. Krystyna Griffith-Jones (London: Calder and Boyars, 1969).

79. In the first published version of the text Gombrowicz reduced Ivona's lines from twenty-five to seven. After the French translation of the text in 1965, he would further cut the character's speech until she was rendered entirely mute. See www.gombrowicz.net (last accessed on December 12, 2012).

80. Sarah Kofman, *The Enigma of Woman: Women in Freud's Writings* (Ithaca, NY: Cornell University Press, 1985), 48.

81. Samuel Beckett, *Waiting for Godot* (New York: Grove/Atlantic, 1987), 66.

82. The choreographer writes: "Dance is a physical experience which one 'tests' on oneself first and foremost. . . . In a solo, I am my own mental and physical experimental field." From Théron's website, www.didiertheron.com (accessed May 5, 2010).

CHAPTER 4

1. Friedrich Nietzsche, *Beyond Good and Evil: Prelude to a Philosophy of the Future*, ed. Rolf-Peter Horstmann and Judith Norman, trans. Judith Norman (Cambridge: Cambridge University Press, 2002), 69.

2. Robert Smithson, *The Collected Writings* (Cambridge, MA: MIT Press, 1996), 60.

3. I am referring to the way in which a language operates according to conventions common to those who partake of the same "game" or frame of reference. This common ground of possibilities determines a particular form of life. As Wittgenstein says, "To imagine a language is to imagine a life form." Ludwig Wittgenstein, *Philosophical Investigations*, trans. G. E. M. Anscombe (London: Blackwell, 2001), 7e.

4. One of several such considerations of possible courses of action occurs after the lawyer discovers Bartleby remaining within the office after hours: "I slowly went down stairs and out into the street, and while walking round the block, considered what I should next do in this unheard-of perplexity. Turn the man out by an actual thrusting I could not; to drive him away by calling him hard names would not do; calling in the police was an unpleasant idea; and yet, permit him to enjoy his cadaverous triumph over me,—this too I could not think of" (Melville, *Bartleby*, 24).

5. Bartleby's "infectiousness" extends beyond the office walls as well. Wandering through the streets of New York, the lawyer encounters a group of men wagering on whether a political official "will go" or not. At first he believes that they are referring to "his" Bartleby's assumed departure.

6. Nietzsche, *Beyond Good and Evil*, 69. I have expanded on this reading of Nietzsche's quote in relation to sensing the sense of sight in "Not Looking into the Abyss: The Potentiality to See," in *On Not Looking: The Paradox of Contemporary Visual Culture*, ed. Frances Guerin (New York: Routledge, 2015).

7. As Edwards's biographer Perry Miller writes, "The *Freedom of the Will* is the cornerstone of Edwards' fame; it is his most sustained intellectual achievement, the most powerful piece of sheer forensic argumentation in American literature." Perry Miller, *Jonathan Edwards* (Lincoln, NE: Bison Books, 2005), 251. It is quite clear that Melville's reference to Edwards concerns this text.

8. Arsić, *Passive Constitutions*, 38. My discussion of Edwards benefits greatly from Arsić's chapter on the intersections between the theologist and Bartleby.

9. The Lockean belief in a separation between will and action corresponds to a Calvinist frame of mind. Calvin saw a delay in the decision of the will to act, a gap in which reason determined the moral merit of an action or its refusal, while Edwards sought to eradicate this temporal delay. Perry Miller writes of Calvin: "The essential point of the distinction is the temporal sequence: the will must wait until the reason 'shall have pronounced'" (Miller, *Jonathan Edwards*, 253).

10. Edwards quoted in Miller, *Jonathan Edwards*, 254, and in Arsić, *Passive Constitutions*, 42.

11. Sang Hyun Lee, *The Philosophical Theology of Jonathan Edwards* (Princeton, NJ: Princeton University Press, 2000), 44.

12. According to Lee, Edwards extends this principle to the entirety of existence, by claiming that substances maintain solidity because of their disposition
to resist pressure. To a certain extent, then, all the world's substance acts, but
only according to its habitual possibilities of resistance, unless God intervenes
in a miraculous reinterpretation of what is possible.

13. This form of pure cause and effect determined from the start by God is
essentially an absolute passivity. Such is the critique that Joseph Priestley made
of Edwards in his *Doctrine of Philosophical Necessity Illustrated*. See Arsić, *Passive
Constitutions*, 49.

14. Michael Fried, *Art and Objecthood: Essays and Reviews* (Chicago: University of Chicago Press, 1988), 153. The antitheatrical bias that Fried invokes has
a long and storied history. See Jonas Barish, *The Anti-theatrical Prejudice* (Berkeley: University of California Press, 1981), and Tracy C. Davis and Thomas Postlewait, eds., *Theatricality* (Cambridge: Cambridge University Press, 2004).

15. The essay inspired a number of responses from critics championing the
theatrical and its turn toward the beholder. In his *Minimalism: Art and Polemics
in the Sixties*, Richard Meyer outlines subsequent critics and their readings of
Fried, with particular attention to Annette Michelson and Rosalind Krauss,
who read the movement as the culmination of a modernist tradition divergent
from Friedian/Greenbergian formalist abstraction. They would turn what Fried
deemed faults into new possibilities for practice and alternative genealogies of
modern art. See Richard Meyer, *Minimalism: Art and Polemics in the Sixties* (New
Haven: Yale University Press, 2001).

16. Amidst the vast array of literature responding to, or explicating, Fried's
argument, particularly significant responses include Thierry de Duve, "Performance Here and Now: Minimal Art, a Plea for a New Genre of Theatre," *Open
Letter* 5–6 (Summer–Fall 1983), 234–260; Hal Foster, "The Crux of Minimalism,"
in Howard Singerman, ed., *Individuals: A Selected History of Contemporary Art,
1945–1986* (New York: Abbeville Press, 1986); Rosalind Krauss, *Passages in Modern Sculpture* (Cambridge, MA: MIT Press, 1977); Robert Smithson's letter to
Artforum (discussed more fully below); and Fred Moten, *In the Break: The Aesthetics of the Black Radical Tradition* (Minneapolis: University of Minnesota Press,
2003); see also Jill Beaulieu, Mary Roberts, and Toni Ross, eds., *Refracting Vision:
Essays on the Writings of Michael Fried* (Seattle: University of Washington Press /
Power Publications, 2012). Meyer's *Minimalism* does an excellent job of histori-
cizing the many strands of work and criticism gathered under the term "minimalism."

17. Smithson, *The Collected Writings*, 60.

18. Theater theorist Nicholas Ridout has written that, for Fried, the theatricality of literalist objects hinges on the fact that they "turn the spectator into an
audience that thinks too much of itself, that exposes itself somehow to its own
gaze, that puts itself, improperly, upon the stage. . . . The objects turn themselves into you, and you into them." Nicholas Ridout, *Stage Fright, Animals, and
Other Theatrical Problems* (New York: Cambridge University Press, 2006), 9. Ridout persuasively argues that this acknowledges the face-to-face encounter at
the foundation of the theatrical event, where the event itself takes place in the
exchange between two people who are copresent with each other. I want to

push the object's claim further to say that, because it maintains the potentiality to see and to perform, the literalist object suspends such possibility for an exchange with a beholder. Refusing to participate in the games of representational possibility that we play in the theater, it instead requires that the beholder perform in the object's place.

19. Meyer, *Minimalism*, 3.

20. Meyer writes: "In fact, much minimal work does not conform to the Morris/Fried model" (ibid., 240).

21. Fried's brief mention of Artaud and Brecht as seeking the antitheatrical only poses more problems (Fried, *Art and Objecthood*, 163). The "antitheatrical" elements that he claims Artaud and Brecht utilize are derived from alternative or historical modes of theatrical performance (often popular or non-Western) that many would instead term overtly "theatrical" precisely because of their explicit acknowledgment of the viewing subject. Such moves toward quasi-participation hardly seem to eradicate the beholder.

22. In the years since the publication of *Art and Objecthood* Fried has distinguished between his writing as an art critic and as an art historian, while acknowledging strains of thought common to both. As he writes in "An Introduction to My Art Criticism," the text that opens his collected reviews and essays and looks back some thirty years to the criticism in question, "From the start the distinction between art criticism and art history seemed to me a matter of emphasis rather than of principle, and my understanding of contemporary art had implication for the questions I began to put to the past" (Fried, *Art and Objecthood*, 8).

23. In an essay on the painter Frank Stella, published the year before "Art Objecthood," Fried explicitly claims literalism as a development out of modernist painting: "It should be evident that what I think of as literalist sensibility is itself a product, or by-product, of the development of modernist painting itself—more accurately, of the increasingly explicit acknowledgment of the literal character of the support that has been central to that development" (ibid., 88). The more recent publication, *Why Photography Matters as Art as Never Before* (2008), appears to be a departure from his exclusive interest in the medium of painting, but ultimately claims that the importance of contemporary photography rests on the fact that many of its most famous recent practitioners take up these same issues of theatricality and the beholder that painting seems to have exhausted.

24. Michael Fried, *Manet's Modernism: Or the Face of Painting in the 1860s* (Chicago: University of Chicago Press, 1996), 326.

25. Ibid., 106.

26. Fried discusses this painting and Diderot's praise of the work in Michael Fried, *Absorption and Theatricality: Painting and Beholder in the Age of Diderot* (Chicago: University of Chicago Press, 1988), 55–57.

27. Ibid., 77.

28. Quoted from Denis Diderot's *Discours* in ibid., 94–95.

29. The theatrical convention of the fourth wall only developed in practice with the advent of French romanticism in the 1830s. Famously the scandal surrounding the first production of Victor Hugo's *Hernani* centered around the

fact that a character spent a portion of the first act with his back to the audience, thus refusing the neoclassical precept that an actor *address* the audience directly. With a single turn of the body, the play imagined an encompassing illusion that obscured the audience: the fourth wall. See Bert O. States, *Great Reckonings in Little Rooms: On the Phenomenology of Theater* (Berkeley: University of California Press, 1987), 191.

30. Michael Fried, *Courbet's Realism* (Chicago: University of Chicago Press, 1992), 17.

31. He summarizes this history as follows: "Put as briefly as possible, by 1860 the means and conventions by which French painting for more than a century had sought to establish the ontological illusion (in *Absorption and Theatricality* I called it a 'supreme fiction') that the beholder did not exist had come nearly to the end of their efficacy. In particular Courbet's project of quasi-corporeal merger with the painting on which he was working had become increasingly untenable for the artist himself (*The Quarry* of 1856 is perhaps the last work in which that project was fully in force), and in any case the conspicuous materiality of his pictures, along with their primary reference to the painter-beholder, meant that they failed to make themselves felt as neutralizing beholding generally" (Fried, *Manet's Modernism*, 404–405). Painting in response to Courbet's "project of quasi-corporeal merger with the painting," where the hand/brush of the painter is represented on the field of the painted, the subsequent work of Manet would announce the material presence of the painting while signaling the absence of the painted subject or model (Fried, *Manet's Modernism*, 344).

32. Miller, *Jonathan Edwards*, 329–330; also quoted on 148 of Fried's *Art and Objecthood*.

33. Edwards quoted in Miller, *Jonathan Edwards*, 298.

34. Zevi Adachiara, ed., *Sol LeWitt: Critical Texts* (Cologne, Germany: Buchhandlung Walther König, 1995), 124.

35. Fried, *Art and Objecthood*, 166.

36. I am grateful to Peggy Phelan for suggesting this connection.

37. "The next day I noticed that Bartleby did nothing but stand at his window in his dead-wall revery [*sic*]" (Melville, *Bartleby*, 20–21). Inverting a common metaphor and saying that "windows are eyes to the soul," one might say that this dead-wall reverie or blank stare implies a soul of pure uniform surface.

38. The narrator uses the word "pale" eleven times in the story: Nine times as description for the scrivener, once in reference to the plaster cast of Cicero, and once in reference to the window at which Bartleby stares. As suggested below, both the bust of Cicero and the blank window double Bartleby, so one could say that these many "pales" all refer back to the scrivener. Morris wrote in his essay "Notes on Sculpture, Part 1": "The more neutral hues that do not draw attention to themselves allow the maximum focus on those essential physical decisions [rather than the optical values associated with modernist painting] that inform sculptural works." Robert Morris, "Notes on Sculpture, Part 1," in Gregory Battcock, ed., *Minimal Art: A Critical Anthology* (Berkeley: University of California Press, 1995), 225.

39. See Rosenberg's "The American Action Painters," in Harold Rosenberg, *The Tradition of the New* (New York: Horizon Press, 1960).

40. This idealistic claim ignores the fact that the means of production have not been eradicated, but merely obscured. Much postminimalist work would delve into the consequences of outsourcing construction and the glorification of the untouchable surface, as well as the sociopolitical context implicated in the creation and reception of work.

41. "*At every moment the work itself is wholly manifest. . . .* It is this continuous and entire *presentness*, amounting, as it were, to the perpetual creation of itself, that one experiences as a kind of *instantaneousness*, as though if only one were infinitely more acute, a single infinitely brief instant would be long enough to see everything, to experience the work in all its depth and fullness, to be forever convinced by it" (Fried, *Art and Objecthood*, 167).

42. In *Chronophobia*, Pamela Lee looks at the question of temporality in relation to Fried's essay, noting how Fried's transcendent present is not a fixed guarantee, but a fleeting glance, much strived after, but rarely achieved. Lee argues that Fried's anxiety toward the literal derives at least in part from contemporaneous concerns with open-ended temporality apparent in much of the art of the sixties. See Pamela Lee, *Chronophobia: On Time in the Art of the 1960s* (Cambridge, MA: MIT Press, 2004), 39.

43. Fried continues, "Endlessness, being able to go on and on, even having to go on and on, is central to the concept of interest and to that of objecthood" (Fried, *Art and Objecthood*, 166). It is this Beckettian quality of "having to go on and on" that induces Fried to lament the fact that this endlessness is no different from the everyday, the passage of an endless life.

44. The reader has the distinct impression that Bartleby's existence in the office would ostensibly continue on indefinitely if it were not for the intervention of the narrator and his eventual relocation of his offices.

45. Fried, *Art and Objecthood*, 150.

46. Ibid., 162.

47. Ibid., 156.

48. Robert Morris, *Robert Morris: The Mind/Body Problem* (New York: Solomon R. Guggenheim Museum Press, 1994), 90.

49. "What we think of as stage presence is related to that aloneness, the nature of the performer who, in a primordial substitution or displacement, is born on the site of the other" (Blau, *The Eye of Prey*, 183).

50. "One way of describing what Smith *was* making might be something like a surrogate person—that is, a kind of statue" (Fried, *Art and Objecthood*, 156).

51. Ibid., 155.

52. Ibid., 163–164.

53. Ibid., 155, my emphasis.

54. Fried comes perhaps closest to this recognition in the final pages of *Why Photography Matters as Art as Never Before,* his study of contemporary photography. Turning again to Tony Smith's sculpture *Die,* the subject of much of his vitriol in "Art and Objecthood," he compares the theatricality of the Smith sculpture with a photograph by Jeff Wall. The success of the latter, he writes, stems in large part because it "is what it is regardless of the 'performance' of the viewer." Michael Fried, *Why Photography Matters as Art as Never Before* (New Haven: Yale University Press, 2008), 333.

55. Fried, *Art and Objecthood*, 42.

56. Much earlier in his career, when discussing Diderot's antitheatricality, Fried footnotes Rousseau's contemporaneous *Lettre sur les spectacles* (1758) as another detheatricalized mode of beholding. Rousseau, of course, advocated the beholder's sublimation within the performance-as-festival, urging artists to "make the beholders the spectacle; make them actors themselves, make each of them see himself and love himself in the others so that they will all be more closely united" (Fried, *Absorption and Theatricality*, 221). In the interests of brevity, Fried abdicates further conversation on the interplay between Rousseau and his own theoretical concepts.

57. Adrian Piper, *Out of Order, Out of Sight. Vol. 1, Selected Writings in Meta-Art: 1968-1992* (Cambridge, MA: MIT Press, 1999), 27.

58. We might think of Piper's *Mythic Being* (1973), where she dressed as a mustachioed young black male in an Afro wig and sunglasses and, for the most part, waited sentry-like around Harvard Square. Here, her literal potentiality was troublingly realized through a performed masculinity; the "aggression" projected onto this display of potentiality reads differently alongside the Law's inordinate and inexcusable history of violence against young black men.

59. Moten, *In the Break*, 235. Moten's final chapter of the book, "The Resistance of the Object: Adrian Piper's Theatricality," covers this ground with great eloquence and insight. As Piper put it in an essay from the same period, she became interested in the "passive capacity of [the] viewer" (Piper, *Out of Sight*, 37).

60. Fried, *Manet's Modernism*, 339.

61. Phelan, *Unmarked*, 21.

62. Jacques Lacan, *The Four Fundamental Concepts of Psychoanalysis: The Seminars of Jacques Lacan Seminar XI*, ed. Jacques-Alain Miller, trans. Alan Sheridan (New York: W.W. Norton, 1998), 95. See also Phelan, *Unmarked*, 19–21.

63. This transmutation of the beholder into the performer is not far removed from the sense of reversal that Phelan sees at play in performances that deliberately "unmark" the artist's body. Describing the exemplary work of performance artist Angelika Festa, whose blind and bound body refuses the demand to perform, Phelan writes: "The spectator has to play both parts—she has to become the spectator of her own performance because Festa will not fulfill the invitation her performance issues. . . . here the spectator becomes a kind of performer" (Phelan, *Unmarked*, 161). Phelan continues, describing what could be called the potentiality of the beholder: "The spectator's second 'performance' is a movement of accretion, excess, and the recognition of the plenitude of one's physical freedom in contrast to the confinement and pain of the performer's displayed body" (162–163). I want to explore the implications of the literal object's refusal to "fulfill the invitation" that the encounter presupposes and see how it inflects the role that beholder takes on.

64. "The object, not the beholder, must remain the center or focus of the situation, but the situation itself *belongs to* the beholder—it is his situation" (Fried, *Art and Objecthood*, 154).

65. She writes that "being 'closed' and oblivious to everything, Bartleby erases the economy between seeing and being seen, the very economy of wit-

nessing. For the witness both sees and exposes himself to the possibility of being seen. Bartleby, on the other hand, is sheer exposure—'being seen without seeing'—a non-witness'" (Arsić, *Passive Constitutions*, 144).

66. See Agamben, *Remnants of Auschwitz*, 39.

67. Primo Levi writes: "We, the survivors are not the true witnesses. . . . Those who did [experience all], those who saw the Gorgon, have not returned to tell about it or have returned mute. . . . We who were favored by fate tried, with more or less wisdom, to recount not only our fate but also that of the others, indeed of the drowned; but this was a discourse 'on behalf of third parties,' the story of things seen at close hand, not experienced personally. . . . We speak in their stead, by proxy." Primo Levi, *The Drowned and the Saved*, trans. Raymond Rosenthal (New York: Doubleday, 1989), 83–84. See also Giorgio Agamben in *Homo Sacer: Sovereign Power and Bare Life*, trans. Daniel Heller-Roazen (Stanford, CA: Stanford University Press, 1998). The question is also explored in Jean-François Lyotard's *The Differend: Phrases in Dispute*, trans. Georges Van Den Abbeele (Minneapolis: University of Minnesota Press, 1988) and Shoshana Felman and Dori Laub's *Testimony: Crises of Witnessing in Literature, Psychoanalysis, and History* (New York: Routledge, 1991).

68. Bartleby, too, plays at this game. At one point the narrator even explicitly calls Bartleby a kind of "spectator": "And here Bartleby makes his home; sole spectator of a solitude which he has seen all populous—a sort of innocent and transformed Marius brooding among the ruins of Carthage!" (17).

69. Fried describes their meeting and long-standing friendship in his "Introduction to My Art Criticism" in Fried, *Art and Objecthood*, 10. Cavell, too, is up front about his indebtedness to Fried in the treatments of modernist aesthetics that his work contains. See Stanley Cavell, *The World Viewed: Reflections on the Ontology of Film* (New York: Viking Press, 1971), xiv–xv.

70. The essay benefits from, and expands upon, the earlier piece of art criticism, as noted in a footnote that indexes several intersections between the two texts: "That the place of art is now pervasively threatened by the production of objects whose hold upon us is theatrical, and that serious modernist art survives only in its ability to defeat theater, are companion subjects of Michael Fried's 'Art and Objecthood'. . . . Its conjunction with what I am saying in this essay (even to the point of specific concepts, most notably that of 'presentness') is more exact than can be made clear in a summary, and will be obvious to anyone reading it" (Cavell, *The World Viewed*, 333).

71. Stanley Cavell, *Must We Mean What We Say?* (New York: Cambridge University Press, 2002), 320.

72. Ibid., 332. Or as he puts it in *The World Viewed*, "If you wander over and they address you in character, that will alter their future and so destroy them; and if the actors address you in person, that will suspend their characters" (155).

73. Cavell, "Knowing and Acknowledging," in *Must We Mean*, 257.

74. Cavell, *The World Viewed*, 123–124.

75. Cavell, *Must We Mean*, 333–334, my emphasis.

76. "Our condition has become one in which our natural mode of perception is to view, feeling unseen. We do not so much look at the world as look *out at it*,

from behind the self" (Cavell, *The World Viewed*, 102). This mimics Fried's claim in *Art and Objecthood* that "we are all literalists most or all of our lives."

77. Cavell, like Fried, does not interrogate the historicity of his crucial notion of the audience hiding in the darkened theater, for example, by ignoring the fact that while theaters in eighteenth-century Europe began to darken their auditorium, audiences only began sitting in truly unlit houses in the middle of the nineteenth century. While gas lighting was first used in 1816, it was not dependable and affordable enough for most theaters until many decades later. Prior to that, before the introduction of gas as a light source with variable intensity and the concomitant invention of the spotlight's precursor, the limelight, audience and performers alike shared a common diffuse light. Apart from the slight additional illumination of the footlights (candles or oil lamps at the foot of the stage) the audience would remain as visible as the actors. See Oscar Brockett, *History of the Theatre* (Needham Heights, MA: Allyn & Bacon, 1999), 373–374.

78. This separation is quite similar to the absorptive enclosure that Fried sees in painting and which Cavell, himself, takes up in clear reference to the art critic in his later text *The World Viewed* as what he calls "candidness" in both painting and the theater: "[The candid] must occur independently of me or any audience, it must be complete without me, in that sense *closed* to me. This is why candidness in acting was achieved by the actor's complete concentration within the character, absolutely denying any control of my awareness upon him" (Cavell, *The World Viewed*, 111).

79. Cavell describes his own performance as beholder in terms that strongly echo Fried's: "In response to minimal art I am deployed, dematerialized, unidentifiable; the moment is not grounded, but etherealized; the momentous is not defeated, but landscaped" (ibid., 117).

80. Ridout interprets Kostya's anxiety toward the black hole of the audience in compelling terms: "Stanislavski does not really specify what these 'sensations' might be, but points instead to their specific triggers, including a pleasant 'semi-isolation' in which the darkness above, behind and to either side of Kostya hems him in with some degree of comfort. At the same time these darknesses force him to attend to 'the public.' Again, it is not darkness as such that makes the 'hole' 'awful,' since darkness is now all around and comforting. Some particular awfulness is associated with the presence of a 'public' in the 'hole,' even though, at this moment, the public consists only of Tortsov and Kostya's fellow students" (Ridout, *Stage Fright*, 37).

81. Fried, *Art and Objecthood*, 167 and 166, respectively.

82. Smithson, "Letter to the Editor," in *The Collected Writings*, 60.

83. Cavell, *Must We Mean*, 338–339.

84. Fried, *Art and Objecthood*, 168.

85. See "Conversations on *the Natural Son*" and "On Dramatic Poetry" in *Diderot's Selected Writings*, ed. Leslie G. Crocker, trans. Derek Coltman (New York: Macmillan, 1966).

86. Peter Brooks, *The Melodramatic Imagination: Balzac, Henry James, Melodrama, and the Mode of Excess* (New Haven: Yale University Press, 1995), 15.

87. Ibid., 98.

88. Ibid., 66.

89. The opening line to the volume states that "the lover's discourse is today *of an extreme solitude."* Roland Barthes, *A Lover's Discourse: Fragments,* trans. Richard Howard (New York: Hill and Wang, 1979), 1.

90. Like Fried, Barthes refers to Diderot's writings on the *drame,* as in the following explication of the tableau as "pregnant moment": "By *imagining* an extreme (i.e., a definitive one; i.e., a definite one), I produce a fiction, I become an artist, I set a scene, I paint my exit; the Idea is *seen,* like the pregnant moment (pregnant = endowed with a strong, chosen meaning) of bourgeois drama" (ibid., 143). See also the figure "adorable!"

91. The theatricality of *A Lover's Discourse* could be productively read alongside Barthes's study of Jean Racine, a playwright who repeatedly stages the lover in exile from the offstage love. For example, "The blindness of the Racinian hero with regard to others is almost maniacal: everything in the world seems to seek him out personally, everything is distorted until it is no more than a narcissistic sustenance" (Barthes, *On Racine,* 34).

92. Barthes calls the formula "I love you" a "linguistic feint," recalling that Bartleby's side-stepping formula must also be said repeatedly to avow a preference. Saying "I love you," I become a kind of Bartleby holding fast to my preferences.

CHAPTER 5

1. Cornelius Castoriadis, *Figures of the Thinkable,* trans. Helen Arnold (Stanford, CA: Stanford University Press, 2007), 241.

2. Romeo Castellucci, program notes to *Genesi: From the Museum of Sleep* (1999), unpaginated.

3. Phelan, *Unmarked,* 146.

4. Said, *Beginnings,* 35. "In attempting to push oneself further and further back to what is only a beginning, a point that is stripped of every use but its categorization in the mind as beginning, one is caught in a tautological circuit of beginnings about to begin. This is the other kind of beginning, the one I called intransitive and conceptual. It is very much a creature of the mind, very much a bristling paradox, yet also very much a figure of thought that draws special attention to itself" (Said, 77). Or as Walter Benjamin puts it in *The Origin of German Tragic Drama,* "the term origin is not intended to describe the process by which the existent came into being, but rather to describe that which emerges from the process of becoming and disappearance. Origin is an eddy in the stream of becoming, and in its current it swallows the material involved in the process of genesis." Walter Benjamin, *The Origin of German Tragic Drama,* trans. John Osborne (London: Verso, 1990), 45.

5. Edward Gordon Craig, *On the Art of the Theatre* (New York: Theatre Arts Books, 1980), 46.

6. Craig encountered the Asphaleia system via Manfred Semper's *Handbuch der Architektur.* See Christopher Innes, *Edward Gordon Craig: A Vision of Theatre* (London: Routledge, 1998), 181.

7. Regarding the technical limitations of the Asphaleia system, Innes writes: "They could only be installed beneath a limited number of sections in the stage, their tempo of operation could not be varied, and they did not include the retractable walls, filling the space between a raised section and the floor, that formed the essence of Craig's visual concept" (ibid.).

8. Edward Craig, *Gordon Craig: The Story of His Life* (New York; Limelight Books, 1985), 316–317.

9. The marionettes "had a rhythmical movement and not a jerky one; had no need for wires to support them, nor did they speak through the nose of the hidden manipulator" (Gordon Craig, *Art of the Theatre*, 90). Olga Taxidou writes: "The actual technology creating movement is ignored altogether. It is too crude an activity to occupy a real artist. [The marionette] exemplifies a contradiction that runs throughout Craig's work." Olga Taxidou, *The Mask: A Periodical Performance* (London: Routledge, 1998), 36.

10. Craig, *Gordon Craig*, 235, my emphasis.

11. The "Primordial Soup" is a theory of the origin of life or moment when a prebiotic system becomes a biotic system, based on the notion that an electric shock could produce amino acids (organic compounds) out of a combination of gases. Essentially this supposes an origin of life out of the environment itself, figure out of a ground.

12. Quoted in Denis Bablet, *Edward Gordon Craig*, trans. Daphne Woodward (New York: Theatre Art Books, 1962), 121.

13. As related by his son, Edward Craig, this slow development of figure and ground in tandem was immediately apparent and attractive to the elder Craig when he was first introduced to the medium by his friend, the artist William Nicholson: "When Nicholson actually engraved on wood, [Gordon Craig] watched, spellbound, as the design slowly developed: the wood was cut away and a light pattern emerged on a dark ground, first in bold splashes by using a large tool, after which the minutest details were added with a small tool; one could then print a copy and go on altering the block until one achieved the desired result; then one could print, or have printed, hundreds of copies . . . thousands . . . The idea of starting with a black background and slowly introducing light was what captured [Gordon Craig's] imagination" (Edward Craig, *Gordon Craig*, 85).

14. See Hardt and Negri's *Multitude* and Paolo Virno, *A Grammar of the Multitude: For an Analysis of Contemporary Forms of Life*, trans. Isabella Bertoletti, James Cascaito, and Andrea Casson (New York: Semiotext(e), 2004).

15. As he writes in "The Art of the Theatre: The First Dialogue": "The Art of the Theatre has sprung from action—movement—dance" (Craig, *Art of the Theatre*, 139). He will also describe the essence of the modern theater as "the spirit of incessant *change*" in Edward Gordon Craig, *Scene* (London: Oxford University Press, 1922), 20.

16. *Crescita XII*'s sequel, *Crescita XIII*, staged the following week at the same festival, countered any notion that this mythic performance was divorced from its locale. Driven out in buses to the industrial outskirts of the old walled city, the audience entered an anonymous factory warehouse and watched workers building the various apparatuses of the theater used in *Crescita XII*. The white

cube sat in the rear of the warehouse, the unpainted wooden backside of the structure visible. The set as theatrical construction, as artifice, was brought to the fore.

17. "One can never extinguish everything. In the theater one never succeeds. . . . There will be no total darkness; the fire-exit signs stay lit, tiny bright spots that remind the mad idealist of the bounds of human community and the laws of protection. Darkness in the theater is utopian." Catherine Clément, *Syncope: The Philosophy of Rapture*, trans. Sally O'Driscoll and Dierdre M. Mahoney (Minneapolis: University of Minnesota Press, 1994), 23.

18. See also Adrian Kear, "The Memory of Promise: Theatre and the Ethic of the Future," in Judie Christie, Richard Gough, and Daniel Watt, eds., *A Performance Cosmology: Testimony from the Future, Evidence of the Past* (New York: Routledge, 2006).

19. Agamben, *Potentialities*, 179, emphasis in original.

20. Gilles Deleuze and Félix Guattari, *What Is Philosophy?*, trans. Hugh Tomlinson and Graham Birchill (New York: Columbia University Press, 1994), 118.

21. In *Absorption and Theatricality*, Fried remarks on the portraits of Chardin and Greuze in which a child is often shown engaged in a game as exemplary instances of absorption. His later reading of Douglas Gordon's *Zidane* film in *Why Photography Matters as Art as a Never Before* expands upon this same pairing of play and absorption, specifically in regards to the game of football (soccer). At the same time it is worth considering that here the boy is inside the literalist box. It is as if the literal object has been opened up and we can now see that the ominous presence that seemed to watch Fried so intently, to await his return, is now and has always been only a boy, a boy who is just as bored with the literal object as with the art critic. He, too, is there when we enter the space, resting on his ball and waiting—that "perpetual sentry in the corner of the room."

22. Walter Benjamin, "In the Sun," in Benjamin, *Selected Writings*, 2:665.

23. Gilles Deleuze writes of the potential of the event to open out into new futures, in that "the event is itself a splitting off from, or a breaking with causality; it is a bifurcation, a deviation with respect to laws, an unstable condition which opens up a new field of the possible." Gilles Deleuze, *Two Regimes of Madness: Texts and Interviews, 1975–1995*, trans. David Lapoujade, Ames Hodges, and Mike Taormina (New York: Semiotext(e), 2007), 233.

24. Nicholas Ridout suggests the same in his description of a closely related void-as-event, discussed in the last section of this chapter: "Surely this sound must have some utilitarian function: covering up an elaborate and noisy scene change, of course." Romeo Castellucci et al., *The Theatre of Societas Raffaello Sanzio* (New York: Routledge, 2007), 190.

25. Castellucci et al., *Societas Raffaello Sanzio*, 216.

26. Irish essayist and cartographer Tim Robinson writes of a quasi-Beckettian scene that resembles this instance: "Imagine oneself snatched out of the normal course of life and set down one knows not where, in utter darkness. Eventually one risks a step forward, out of one's perfect nescience, and finds firm footing. Another step, and then another, add to one's tentative belief that the ground underfoot, whatever its nature, is supportive. Each step is progressively less likely to bring one to the edge; in fact, one comes to imagine that there may not

be such an edge. Soon one is striding out confidently, towards the silently wait-ing precipice." Tim Robinson, *My Time in Space* (Dublin: Lilliput Press, 2001), 116.

27. Monty Hall's *Let's Make a Deal* (in various versions from 1963 onward) and other television game shows with live audiences are theatrical events of a peculiar breed. For audiences on set and at home, it is precisely the limited scope of potentiality harnessed by these events that inspires whatever attrac-tion they may hold.

28. Giuseppe Bartolucci, "The Post Avant-Garde: An Auto-Interview" in *TDR: The Drama Review* 22:1 (March 1978), 103–107. See Gabriella Giannachi and Nick Kaye's *Staging the Post-Avant-Garde: Italian Experimental Performance after 1970* (London: Peter Lang, 2002) for a more extended rehearsal of the vari-ous players in, and influences on, this scene. Giannachi and Kaye also devote a chapter to the work of the Socìetas Raffaello Sanzio from its inception in 1981 through the 1990s, from which my understanding of the company's early work benefits.

29. Mario Prosperi, "Contemporary Italian Theatre," *TDR: The Drama Review* 22:1 (March 1978), 19. See also Valentina Valentini's "In Search of Lost Stories: Italian Performance in the Mid-'80s. Three Interviews" in *TDR: The Drama Re-view* 32:3 (Autumn 1988), 109–125.

30. Giannachi and Kaye, *Staging the Post-Avant-Garde*, 140. See also Gabriella Calchi Novati, "Language under Attack: The Iconoclastic Theatre of Socìetas Raffaello Sanzio," *Theatre Research International* 34:1 (March 2009), 50–65.

31. Bennett, *Vibrant Matter*, 24.

32. Petra Kuppers discusses the ethics of the company's use of nonnormative bodies in her *Disability and Contemporary Performance: Bodies on Edge* (New York: Routledge, 2003), 77–80. Following the 1999 production of *Genesi: From the Mu-seum of Sleep* (discussed below), SRS has almost exclusively restricted its use of nonnormative bodies to the extremities of age—infancy and old age—and the animal body. The 2008 production of *Purgatorio* (also discussed below) is an exception, returning to the concrete indexicality of the nonnormative in casting an actor with an acute case of cerebral palsy.

33. For more on SRS's *Giuilio Cesare* see Dennis Kennedy's *Looking at Shake-speare: A Visual History of Twentieth Century Performance* (Cambridge: Cambridge University Press, 2001), 352–355, and Bridget Escolme's *Talking to the Audience: Shakespeare, Performance, Self* (New York: Routledge, 2005), 126–148. For discus-sion of a revision of the performance, see my essay "On Losing One's Voice: Two Performances from Romeo Castellucci's *e la volpe disse al corvo*," *Theatre Forum* 46 (Winter 2014), 37–46.

34. This is not to say that the earlier work of the company did not consider or display potentiality. See, for example, the 1989 piece *La discesa di Inanna* (*Inanna's Descent*), reviewed in Giannachi and Kaye, *Staging the Post-Avant-Garde*, 153.

35. See Lee Edelman, *No Future: Queer Theory and the Death Drive* (Durham, NC: Duke University Press, 2004).

36. Romeo Castellucci: "After iconoclasm and after artificial languages and after rhetorical languages we started to work on the language which par excel-

lence has a factual, creative power: the language of God which has a founding power. At least for nontheistic religion, as God speaks things happen and materialize" (quoted in Giannachi and Kaye, *Staging the Post-Avant-Garde*, 166).

37. Romeo Castellucci, program notes to *Genesi: From the Museum of Sleep*, unpaginated.

38. Curie's notebooks from the 1890s remain highly radioactive, so that researchers must wear protection before handling the documents. Mentioned in Bill Bryson, *A Short History of Nearly Everything* (New York: Broadway, 2004), 148.

39. Giannachi and Kaye, *Staging the Post-Avant-Garde*, 168.

40. As Romeo Castellucci says, "*Genesi* begins in the separation from 'matter' created in the 'doubling' of the 'first' word" (Giannachi and Kaye, *Staging the Post-Avant-Garde*, 166).

41. Allen S. Weiss has convincingly suggested that *To Have Done With the Judgment of God* represents Artaud's only realization of a Theater of Cruelty. See Allen S. Weiss, *Breathless: Sound Recording, Disembodiment, and the Transformation of Lyrical Nostalgia* (Middletown, CT: Wesleyan University Press, 2002).

42. "As soon as I speak, the words I have found (as soon as they are words) no longer belong to me, are originally *repeated* (Artaud desires a theater in which repetition is impossible)" (Derrida, *Writing and Difference*, 177). In one of many such instances arguing for unique and unrepeatable speech and gesture, Artaud writes that "an expression does not have the same value twice, does not live two lives; that all words, once spoken, are dead and function only at the moment when they are uttered, . . . a form, once it has served, cannot be used again and asks only to be replaced by another, and . . . the theater is the only place in the world where a gesture, once made, can never be made the same way twice." Antonin Artaud, *The Theatre and Its Double*, trans. Mary Caroline Richards (New York: Grove Press, 1958), 75.

43. Derrida, *Writing and Difference*, 181.

44. In the words of Allen S. Weiss, Bene's aesthetic procedure attempted "to work in the 'hollow' spaces of the text; to eliminate or 'subtract' the major dramatic structures of a play in order to reveal a revolutionary 'minor' discourse; to break open the representational system of both text and theatre." Allen S. Weiss, "In Memory: Carmelo Bene 1937–2002," *TDR: The Drama Review* 46:4 (Winter 2002), 8. Other characterizations of Bene also foreground the vocal aspect of his work. See, for example, Gautam Dasgupta, "The Director as Thinker: Carmelo Bene's *Otello*," *PAJ: A Journal of Performance and Art* 9:1 (1985), 12—16.

45. Pier Paolo Pasolini's "Manifesto for a New Theatre," trans. Thomas Simpson, *PAJ: A Journal of Performance and Art* 29:1 (2007), 138.

46. The full quote is as follows: "And the originality of his bearing, the totality of his methods, first appears to us as coming from the subtraction of the stable elements of power that will release a new potentiality of theater, an always unbalanced, nonrepresentative force." Gilles Deleuze, "One Less Manifesto," in Timothy Murray, ed., *Mimesis, Masochism, and Mime: The Politics of Theatricality in Contemporary French Thought* (Ann Arbor: University of Michigan Press, 1997), 242.

47. Deleuze also refers to this notion of constant variation as a "theater of

repetition"—meaning repetition with a difference rather than repetition of the same—that stands in opposition to the theater of representation: "In the theatre of repetition, we experience pure forces, dynamic lines in space which act without intermediary upon the spirit, and link it directly with nature and history, with a language which speaks before words, with gestures which develop before organized bodies, with masks before faces, with specters and phantoms before characters—the whole apparatus of repetition as a 'terrible power.'" Gilles Deleuze, *Difference and Repetition*, trans. Paul Patton (New York: Columbia University Press, 1994), 10.

48. Lorenzo Chiesa, "A Theatre of Subtractive Extinction: Bene without Deleuze," in Laura Cull, ed., *Deleuze and Performance* (Edinburgh: Edinburgh University Press, 2009), 72, my emphasis.

49. Deleuze famously described his approach to the history of philosophy as "a sort of buggery or (it comes to the same thing) immaculate conception. I saw myself as taking an author from behind and giving him a child that would be his own offspring, yet monstrous." Gilles Deleuze, *Negotiations, 1972–1990*, trans. Martin Joughin (New York: Columbia University Press, 1997), 6.

50. Romeo Castellucci, *Les Pèlerins de la Matière: Théorie et praxis du théâtre* (Besançon, France: Les Solitaires Intempestifs, 2001), 24.

51. Castellucci quoted in Giannachi and Kaye, *Staging the Post-Avant-Garde*, 145.

52. Friedrich Nietzsche, *"Twilight of the Idols" and "The Antichrist,"* trans. Thomas Common (Mineola, NY: Dover, 2004), 2.

53. W. J. T. Mitchell, *Iconology: Image, Text, Ideology* (Chicago: University of Chicago Press, 1987), 158 and 162, respectively.

54. This delineation of the classical and baroque presents problems both in terms of the generalization of a theoretical binary to describe varied tendencies across cultures and periods, and in regards to the qualities associated with each category. Rather than seeing classical stances as representations of the ideal figure in repose, perfectly balanced and symmetrically composed as in Wölflin's schema, Aby Warburg, for example, proposed that the Greek classical artists were interested in capturing gesture in motion. As Philippe-Alain Michaud remarks, "According to Warburg, what Renaissance artists derived from ancient forms was not an association between substance and immobility, a privilege granted the being over the becoming; on the contrary, they recognized in these forms a tension, a questioning of the ideal appearance of bodies in the visible world. Their works bear the stamp of a force that is not harmonious but contradictory, a force destabilizing the figure more than pulling it together." Philippe-Alain Michaud, *Aby Warburg and the Image in Motion* (Cambridge, MA: MIT Press, 2004), 28.

55. Castelluci, *Pèlerins*, 24, my translation.

56. Henri Focillon, *The Life of Forms in Art*, trans. George Kubler (New York: Zone Books, 1992), 80.

57. Heinrich Wölfflin, *Principles of Art History*, trans. M. D. Hottinger (New York: Dover, 1950), 127. This correlation is further accentuated in art historian Germain Bazin's description of the artist working under the sign of the baroque: "[The Baroque artist] longs to enter into the multiplicity of phenomena,

into the flux of things in their perpetual becoming—his compositions are dynamic and open and tend to expand outside their boundaries. . . . The Baroque artist's instinct for escape drives him to prefer 'forms that take flight' to those that are static and dense." Germain Bazin, *Baroque and Rococo Art*, trans. Jonathan Griffin (New York: Frederick A. Praeger, 1969), 6–7.

58. "The interesting thing [in the baroque] is the transition, how the free form disengages itself from the rigid" (Wölfflin, *Principles of Art History*, 153).

59. Romeo Castellucci quoted in Giannachi and Kaye, *Staging the Post-Avant-Garde*, 144.

60. The quotation continues as follows: ". . . making the simulacra function and raising a phantasm—the most innocent of all destructions, the destruction of Platonism." Gilles Deleuze, *The Logic of Sense*, trans. Constantin Boundas (New York: Columbia University Press, 1990), 266.

61. Castellucci et al., *Socìetas Raffaello Sanzio*, 26.

62. "On stage, the animal is comfortable (being not perfectible) in the confidence of its own body. . . . The device of technique cannot be used by the animal, as it already possesses the greatest device: to be alienated on stage, immobile, in an alert state." Romeo Castellucci, "The Animal Being on Stage," trans. Carolina Melis, Valentina Valetini, and Ric Allsopp, *Performance Research* 5:2 (2000), 23–28.

63. Castellucci et al., *Socìetas Raffaello Sanzio*, 190.

64. Focillon, *Life of Forms*, 58. As Romeo Castellucci writes, *Tragedia Endogonidia* "is in a process of becoming . . . every time it opens for an audience, it's a finished and complete production that supplies, within itself, the mechanism of endogonidial reproduction, a division of itself by itself, a sort of fall-out of spores, which provide for future and successive growth." Romeo Castellucci, "The Universal: The Simplest Place Possible," interview by Bonnie Marranca and Valentina Valentini, trans. Jane House, *PAJ: A Journal of Performance and Art* 26:2 (2004), 17–18. Or, as he describes the cycle elsewhere: "It was a process that developed irrespective of any preconceived plan. There wasn't time to plan. The development of *Tragedia* was like the growth of an organism, like an endocrinal potential" (Castellucci et al., *Socìetas Raffaello Sanzio*, 252–253).

65. This emphasizes the implicitly consanguine nature of all the company's work, so that the images and structures at play in the *Crescita* not only converse with the *Tragedia Endogonidia* episodes, but with other performances by SRS as well. This chapter traces the figure of the boy through some of his many appearances over the last decade of work, but even this single strand extends in directions that exceed the limits of this study.

66. In one of the statements published toward the beginning of the project, Romeo Castellucci would write that "every episode puts on stage its own ontogenesis and that is all it can do. An episode is closer to a series of pure and complete acts" (Castellucci et al., *Socìetas Raffaello Sanzio*, 31).

67. In the words of Edward Scheer, "For Artaud, organs are useless in terms of the production of vital energy (which is, after all, what bodies are for) and they sap the body's creative potential, forcing it to perform the menial tasks of biological *functions*." Edward Scheer, "I Artaud Bwo: The Uses of Artaud's *To have done with the judgement of god*," in Cull, *Deleuze and Performance*, 42. Scheer's

essay ends with a brief invocation of Scott Gibbons's sound design in SRS's *Genesi*, with its use of Artaud's *"to have done . . .,"* as a contemporary extension of the Theater of Cruelty.

68. Artaud, *Theatre and Its Double*, 27. Strikingly, Artaud distinguishes between a presupposed possibility, the kind of network of predetermined actions reproducing the actual, and "the virtuality of the possible," or potentiality. An even clearer articulation of such a virtuality appears in "the Alchemical Theater," in which we are told "alchemy and the theater are so to speak virtual arts, and do not carry their end—or their reality—within themselves" (Artaud, *Theatre and Its Double*, 48). Alchemy discovers materiality's potential to transubstantiate into another unrelated form, sundering elements from their determinate possibilities and qualities. The basest, heaviest of substances, lead, discovers its absolute potentiality in that most valuable (and in this sense, abstract) material, gold. Once this most extreme and impossible transformation is realized, as a temporary organ, one assumes that any other transformation in between would be available. Framed in this manner, alchemy becomes a succinct metaphor for the process of constant variation, wherein an actuality (the determinate object lead) is surrounded by a halo of virtualities (the potential to become any other substance).

69. Girard, *Violence and the Sacred*, 267.

70. Ostensibly, one can always have another spouse, but one cannot replace the relationship with a sibling or with a parent. See Judith Butler's *Antigone's Claim* (New York: Columbia University Press, 2002). Oedipus ensures that his children and his wife are irreplaceable.

71. Girard sees the structure of sacrificial substitution at work in a huge range of sites and, in more recent years, has used the theory to justify the sanctity of Christianity as the true religion. I find this a highly problematic proposition.

72. Peter Galison's "Image of the Self," in Lorraine Daston, ed., *Things That Talk: Object Lessons from Art and Science* (New York: Zone Books, 2004), 257.

73. "Verlag Hans Huber [the company that prints the plates] is so concerned about the quality of their reproduction that it will only use the same antique printing presses that stamped out the first edition of the cards in 1921" (ibid.). Furthermore, the reproduction of the ten plates was strictly controlled by copyright until the turn of the millennium, preventing publication in any capacity (book, journal, Internet, or otherwise).

74. As Peter Galison writes, "If the blots suggested even a shard of human design, certain patients would seize on that fragment, losing their own ability to speak from within. For this reason, nothing was more important to Rorschach than creating and reproducing cards that would register as undesigned designs, unpainted paintings. . . . In order for the subject to speak, the card, and the card's author, had to find a perfect silence" (ibid., 271).

75. In 1936 Lawrence Frank would explicitly attach the process of the Rorschach test to the notion of projection, claiming that the manner in which a subject organized the field of the "undesigned design" reflected his or her organization of the perceptual world (ibid., 289–290). The possible images that the subject recognized in the blot corresponded to the possibilities surrounding his or her everyday action and living.

76. The woman, Lavinia Bertotti, sings variations on Thomas Tallis's "Lamentations (of Jeremiah)" and John Dowland's "Lachrimae."

77. Deleuze, *Difference and Repetition*, 28. Brian Massumi describes the same concept: "Before the flash there is only potential, in a continuum of intensity: a *field* of charged particles. The triggering of the charge is a movement immanent to the field of potential, by which it plays out the consequences of its own intensity. The movement involves the field in its entirety. It is non-local, belonging directly to the dynamic relation *between* a myriad of charged particles. The flash of lightning expresses this non-local relation. Expression is always fundamentally of a *relation*, not a subject. In the expression, process and product are one." Brian Massumi, *A Shock to Thought: Expression after Deleuze and Guattari* (New York: Routledge, 2002), xxiv.

78. Because of the unique nature of their original sites, both *Inferno* and *Paradiso* required revision in future stagings. The latter was completely reconceptualized into a different performance-installation.

79. Romeo Castellucci, *Inferno Purgatorio Paradiso*, trans. Valentina Guidi (Cesena, Italy: Stampa Litografia CILS Cooperativa Sociale, 2008), unpaginated.

80. Richard K. Fenn, *The Persistence of Purgatory* (Cambridge: Cambridge University Press, 1995), 3.

81. In terms of church doctrine, purgatory was invented in 1274, but Dante's depiction of *Purgatorio* from the early fourteenth century constitutes the most extensive and influential of many early imaginative renderings. See Stephen Greenblatt, *Hamlet in Purgatory* (Princeton, NJ: Princeton University Press, 2002).

82. Stéphane Mosès, *The Angel of History: Rosenzweig, Benjamin, Scholem*, trans. Barbara Harshav (Stanford, CA: Stanford University Press, 2008), 108.

83. "When I say 'Alice becomes larger,' I mean that she becomes larger than she was. Certainly, she is not bigger and smaller at the same time. She is larger now; she was smaller before. But it is at the same moment that one becomes larger than one was and smaller than one becomes. This is the simultaneity of a becoming whose characteristic is to elude the present. Insofar as it eludes the present, becoming does not tolerate the separation or the distinction of before and after, or of past and future. It pertains to the essence of becoming to move and to pull in both directions at once; Alice does not grow without shrinking, and vice versa. Good sense affirms that in all things there is a determinable sense or direction (*sens*); but paradox is the affirmation of both senses or directions at the same time" (Deleuze, *The Logic of Sense*, 1).

84. *Hey Girl!*, a shorter portrait piece that Castellucci staged in 2006, ruminates on the famous passage from *Romeo and Juliet*. See my discussion of the piece in Meiling Cheng and Gabrielle Cody, eds., *Reading Contemporary Performance: Theatricality Across Genres* (New York: Routledge, 2015).

85. Castellucci intended for the machine to fill the lens with blackness by the end of the scene, but the ink itself was often too fickle to operate in this clean and strictly defined manner. Instead, in most of the performances a smaller iris of transparency remains as the disk spins on, slowly closing on itself as more and more ink gathers. The material asserts its own life. From personal conversation with Romeo Castellucci, October 2009.

86. Focillon, *Life of Forms*, 66. He continues describing the nature of these ornamental curves, claiming that "although [the ornament] welcomes both men and animals into its system, it yields nothing to them—it incorporates them. New images are constantly being composed on the same figures" (67).

87. In addition to his abandoned production of *The Minister's Black Veil* and *The Four Seasons Restaurant*, discussed below, Castellucci includes his production *On the concept of the face: regarding the Son of God* (2010) as part of the cycle.

88. Simone Weil, *Gravity and Grace*, trans. A. Willis (Lincoln: University of Nebraska Press, 1997), 81. Anne Carson quotes Simone Weil in her *Decreation: Poetry, Essays, Opera* (New York: Knopf, 2005), 167.

89. Asked why he canceled future performances of the production, Castellucci stated: "I believe that Hawthorne's subject is very dense and it can't be dealt with directly, but it isn't over. . . . It's a story that has totally invaded me, that possesses me." From "Conversation between Christina Tilmann of the Berliner Festspiele and Romeo Castellucci" in Duisburg, August 15, 2012. Unpublished text (courtesy of the Berliner Festspiele and Socìetas Raffaello Sanzio).

90. On the ephemerality of sound, see Walter J. Ong, *Orality and Literacy: The Technologizing of the Word* (New York: Methuen, 1982), 32.

91. In conversation with Romeo Castellucci, September 2014. The performance vocabulary of the Noh theater has remained essentially unchanged for more than five hundred years.

92. *Giudizio Possibilità Esssere (Judgment Possibility Essence)*, a standalone outgrowth of *The Four Seasons Restaurant* that focuses on the Hölderlin section alone, extends this connection by interrupting the play with an obscure Nordic folk song and dance accompanied by projected images of pristine alpine landscapes.

93. I will attempt a description. At the conclusion of *The Death of Empedocles* the curtain draws a black veil over the white chamber. Then, countering its logic of opening and closing, the curtain begins to recede upstage into the empty chamber to reveal a dead horse, lying on its side. In place of an ejected sandal, we find Empedocles's steed; earlier in the performance the recorded sound of the philosopher atop a galloping horse had circled the stage, pulling all the young women's attention. The curtain closes and then opens again on the empty white chamber. Slowly, the white room folds back on itself, the walls fly out and the black creeps up: the white cube becomes a black hole. Smoke descends now in great plumes, as if Etna were spewing its hot winds overhead. A great and amorphous cloud swells midair. Sudden brief flashes of huge light make the smoke a blinding white smear on the eye, leaving a shadow hovering over the retina in the afterglow. When the curtain descends again, the flashes of light cut a thin line of brilliant white into the darkened theater from under its fringe. Something is back there, exerting a vast pressure. A Schubert lied rises in lament under the occasional jabs of static sound, a song of mourning with its lyrics caught in surtitles on the black masking: "Do not leave me. No no no. I implore you. I implore you." The last of these appeals is repeated in smaller and smaller text until it is indiscernible. Receding further and further, it stages another withdrawal.

94. Artaud, *Theatre and Its Double*, 13.

95. Castellucci et al., *Socìetas Raffaello Sanzio*, 259. See also Nicholas Ridout's "Regarding Theatre: Thoughts on Recent Work by Simon Vincenzi and Romeo Castellucci," *Theatre Journal* 66 (October 2014), 427–436.

96. Artaud, *Theatre and Its Double*, 79.

97. For a materialist reading of the company's work see Nicholas Ridout's "Make-Believe: Societas Raffaello Sanzio do Theatre," in Joe Kelleher and Nicholas Ridout, eds., *Contemporary Theatres in Europe: A Critical Companion* (New York: Routledge, 2006), 175–187.

98. "The Second Coming" by W. B. Yeats in *Michael Robartes and the Dancer* (Dundrum, Ireland: Chuala Press, 1920).

CHAPTER 6

1. *Let us think of these things always. Let us speak of them never.* Performance by Every House Has a Door (2010). Unpublished script, courtesy of Matthew Goulish. Lin Hixson directed the piece in collaboration with two Chicago-based artists, Stephen Fiehn and Matthew Goulish (the cofounder, alongside Hixson, of Every house has a door), and two artists from Zagreb, Selma Banich and Mislav Cavajda.

2. Franco "Bifo" Berardi, *After the Future*, ed. Gary Genosko and Nicholas Thoburn (Berkeley: AK Press, 2011), 125.

3. Bert O. States, "Phenomenology of the Curtain Call," *Hudson Review* 34:3 (Autumn 1981), 371.

4. "Translated into theatrical terms, dark matter refers to the invisible dimension of theater that escapes visual detection, even though its effects are felt everywhere in performance." Andrew Sofer, *Dark Matter: Invisibility in Drama, Theater, and Performance* (Ann Arbor: University of Michigan Press, 2013), 3.

5. The Socìetas Raffaello Sanzio borrowed the image of the raised hand from the pictogram of "universal greeting" that was designed by Carl Sagan to announce the existence of humanity to extraterrestrial life and, simultaneously but unintentionally, to say farewell to humanity. The pictogram was affixed to the first spacecraft to leave the solar system, the *Pioneer 10* (1972) and *Pioneer 11* (1973) space probes. For the SRS, it acted as a kind of visual formula for the cycle.

6. Tim Flannery, *The Eternal Frontier: An Ecological History of North America and Its People* (New York: Grove Press, 2001), 337.

7. Thanks to Aaron C. Thomas for pointing me to Santa Catalina island.

8. See Naomi Klein, *The Shock Doctrine: The Rise of Disaster Capitalism* (New York: Picador, 2008).

9. Richard Slotkin, *Regeneration through Violence: The Mythology of the American Frontier, 1600–1860* (Norman: University of Oklahoma Press, 2000).

10. Jane Tompkins, *West of Everything: The Inner Life of Westerns* (New York: Oxford University Press, 1992), 75.

11. Robert Venturi, Steven Izenour, and Denise Scott Brown, *Learning from Las Vegas: The Forgotten Symbolism of Architectural Form* (Cambridge, MA: MIT Press, 1977), 34.

12. C. W. E. Bigsby, *A Critical Introduction to Twentieth-Century American Drama*, vol. 3, *Beyond Broadway* (New York: Cambridge University Press, 1985), 223–224.

13. Here I am grateful to Paul Rae for sharing his text "Performance and Finance Capital," presented at *ASTR 2011: Economies of Theatre*, Montreal, Canada, November 2011.

14. Carol Martin, "What Did They Do to My Country! An Interview with Rachel Chavkin," *TDR: The Drama Review* 54:4 (Winter 2010), 108.

15. Kear, "The Memory of Promise," 149.

16. Franz Kafka, *Amerika: The Missing Person*, trans. Mark Harman (New York: Schocken, 2008), 267. Kafka titled the novel *The Missing Person*, but Max Brod retitled it *America* in his first German edition of the book, published three years after the author's death in 1927 (see "Translator's Preface," xvii).

17. Ibid., 268.

18. Benjamin, *Selected Writings*, 2:814. Benjamin's text retains the traditional spelling of the state. This idea of the theater as a site for the redemption of the past guides the work of the New York–based theater company Nature Theatre of Oklahoma. Its monumental *Life and Times* project (five episodes lasting twelve hours at writing, with five more in store), stages the verbatim personal account of a company member's life from birth to present.

19. Adam Kirsch, "America, 'Amerika,'" *New York Times*, January 2, 2009.

20. Kafka, *Amerika*, xxv.

21. Ibid., 272.

22. Francis Alÿs and Russell Ferguson, *The Politics of Rehearsal* (Göttingen: Stiedl, 2009), 13.

Bibliography

Adachiara, Zevi, ed. *Sol LeWitt: Critical Texts*. Cologne, Germany: Buchhandlung Walther König, 1995.

Agamben, Giorgio. *The Coming Community*. Translated by Michael Hardt. Minneapolis: University of Minnesota Press, 1993.

Agamben, Giorgio. *Homo Sacer: Sovereign Power and Bare Life*. Translated by Daniel Heller-Roazen. Stanford, CA: Stanford University Press, 1998.

Agamben, Giorgio. *The Idea of Prose*. Translated by Michael Sullivan and Sam Whitsitt. New York: State University of New York Press, 1995.

Agamben, Giorgio. *Means without End: Notes on Politics*. Translated by Vincenzo Binetti and Cesare Casarino. Minneapolis: University of Minnesota Press, 2000.

Agamben, Giorgio. *Nudities*. Translated by David Kishik and Stefan Pedatella. Stanford, CA: Stanford University Press, 2011.

Agamben, Giorgio. *Potentialities: Collected Essays in Philosophy*. Translated by Daniel Heller-Roazen. Stanford, CA: Stanford University Press, 1999.

Agamben, Giorgio. *Remnants of Auschwitz: The Witness and the Archive*. Translated by Daniel Heller-Roazen. New York: Zone Books, 2002.

Alÿs, Francis, and Russell Ferguson. *The Politics of Rehearsal*. Göttingen: Stiedl, 2009.

Aristotle. *The Basic Works of Aristotle*. Edited by Richard McKeon. New York: Random House, 1941.

Aristotle. *The Nichomachean Ethics*. Translated by Martin Ostwald. Indianapolis: Bobbs-Merrill Educational Publishing, 1983.

Aristotle. *Poetics*. Translated by Gerald Else. Ann Arbor: University of Michigan, 1967.

Arsić, Branka. *Passive Constitutions: 7 ½ Times Bartleby*. Stanford, CA: Stanford University Press, 2007.

Artaud, Antonin. *The Theatre and Its Double*. Translated by Mary Caroline Richards. New York: Grove Press, 1958.

Auslander, Philip. "Digital Liveness: A Historico-Philosophical Perspective." *PAJ: A Journal of Performance and Art* 34:3 (September 2012), 3–11.

Auslander, Philip. *Liveness: Performance in a Mediatized Culture*. New York: Routledge, 1999.

Austin, J. L. *How to Do Things with Words*. Cambridge, MA: Harvard University Press, 2003.

Bablet, Denis. *Edward Gordon Craig*. Translated by Daphne Woodward. New York: Theatre Art Books, 1962.

Banes, Sally. *Terpsichore in Sneakers: Post-modern Dance*. Boston: Houghton Mifflin, 1980.

Barish, Jonas. *The Anti-theatrical Prejudice*. Berkeley: University of California Press, 1981.

Barthes, Roland. *Camera Lucida: Reflections on Photography*. Translated by Richard Howard. New York: Hill & Wang, 1982.

Barthes, Roland. *A Lover's Discourse: Fragments*. Translated Richard Howard. New York: Hill and Wang, 1979.

Barthes, Roland. *On Racine*. Translated by Richard Howard. New York: PAJ Publications, 1983.

Barthes, Roland. *The Responsibility of Forms: Critical Essays on Music, Art, and Representation*. Translated by Richard Howard. Berkeley: University of California Press, 1985.

Bartolucci, Giuseppe. "The Post Avant-Garde: An Auto-Interview." *TDR: The Drama Review* 22:1 (March 1978), 103–107.

Bazin, Germain. *Baroque and Rococo Art*. Translated by Jonathan Griffin. New York: Frederick A. Praeger, 1969.

Beaulieu, Jill, Mary Roberts, and Toni Ross, eds. *Refracting Vision: Essays on the Writings of Michael Fried*. Seattle: University of Washington Press / Power Publications, 2012.

Becker, Daniel Levin. *Many Subtle Channels: In Praise of Potential Literature*. Cambridge, MA: Harvard University Press, 2012.

Beckett, Samuel. *Waiting for Godot*. New York: Grove/Atlantic, 1987.

Benjamin, Walter. *The Origin of German Tragic Drama*. Translated by John Osborne. London: Verso, 1990.

Benjamin, Walter. *Selected Writings*. Vol. 1, *1913–1926*. Edited by Marcus Bullock and Michael W. Jennings. Cambridge, MA: Harvard University Press, 2004.

Benjamin, Walter. *Selected Writings*. Vol. 2, *1927–1934*. Edited by Michael W. Jennings, Howard Eiland, and Gary Smith. Cambridge, MA: Harvard University Press, 1999.

Bennett, Jane. *Vibrant Matter: A Political Ecology of Things*. Durham, NC: Duke University Press, 2010.

Bentley, Eric. *Theatre of War: Comments on 32 Occasions*. New York: Viking Press, 1972.

Berardi, Franco "Bifo." *After the Future*. Edited by Gary Genosko and Nicholas Thoburn. Berkeley: AK Press, 2011.

Bergson, Henri. *Creative Evolution*. Translated by Arthur Mitchell. New York: Dover Publications, 1998.

Bergson, Henri. *Introduction to Metaphysics*. Translated by T. E. Hulme. Indianapolis: Hackett, 1999.

Bergson, Henri. *Matter and Memory*. Translated by N. M. Paul and W. S. Palmer. New York: Zone Books, 1990.

Bergson, Henri. *Time and Free Will*. Translated by F. L. Pogson. New York: Harper & Row, 1960.

Bernard, Tristan. *Contes, Répliques et Bon Mots*. Paris: Livre club de libraire, 1964.

Bigsby, C. W. E. *A Critical Introduction to Twentieth-Century American Drama.* Vol. 3, *Beyond Broadway.* New York: Cambridge University Press, 1985.

Blackmur, Richard. *Language as Gesture: Essays in Poetry.* New York: Harcourt, Brace, 1952.

Blanchard, Paul, Gilles Boëtsch, and Nanette Jacomijn Snoep, eds. *Human Zoos: The Invention of the Savage.* Paris: Actes Sud, 2012.

Blau, Herbert. *The Eye of Prey: Subversions of the Postmodern.* Bloomington: Indiana University Press, 1987.

Blau, Herbert. *Take Up the Bodies: Theatre at the Vanishing Point.* Urbana: University of Illinois Press, 1982.

Bloch, Ernst. *The Principle of Hope.* Vol. 1. Translated by Neville Plaice, Stephen Plaice, and Paul Knight. Cambridge, MA: MIT Press, 1995.

Bloch, Ernst, and Theodor W. Adorno. "Something's Missing: A Discussion between Ernst Bloch and Theodor Adorno on the Contradictions of Utopian Longing." In *The Utopian Function of Art and Literature: Selected Essays,* translated by Jack Zipes and Frank Mecklenburg. Cambridge, MA: MIT Press, 1988.

Brantley, Ben. "Finding Appalling Sense in a Giddy Anarchy." *New York Times,* February 1, 1999. Accessed October 8, 2014. http://www.nytimes.com/1999/02/01/theater/theater-review-finding-appalling-sense-in-a-giddy-anarchy.html.

Braun, Edward. *Meyerhold: A Revolution in Theatre.* Iowa City: University of Iowa Press, 1998.

Brecht, Bertolt. *Brecht on Theatre: The Development of an Aesthetic.* Edited and Translated by John Willett. New York: Hill & Wang, 1964.

Brockett, Oscar. *History of the Theatre.* Needham Heights, MA: Allyn & Bacon, 1999.

Brook, Peter. *The Empty Space.* New York: Simon & Schuster, 1996.

Brooks, Peter. *The Melodramatic Imagination: Balzac, Henry James, Melodrama, and the Mode of Excess.* New Haven: Yale University Press, 1995.

Bruder, Melissa, Lee Michael Cohn, Madeleine Olnek, Nathaniel Pollack, Robert Previtio, Scott Zigler, and David Mamet. *A Practical Handbook for the Actor.* New York: Vintage, 1986.

Bryson, Bill. *A Short History of Nearly Everything.* New York: Broadway, 2004.

Büchner, Georg. *Georg Büchner: Complete Plays and Prose.* Translated by Carl Richard Mueller. New York: Hill & Wang, 1963.

Burian, Peter. "Myth into *Mythos*: The Shaping of Tragic Plot." In *The Cambridge Companion to Greek Tragedy,* edited by P. E. Easterling. New York: Cambridge University Press, 1997.

Burke, Kenneth. *A Grammar of Motives.* Berkeley: University of California Press, 1969.

Butler, Judith. *Antigone's Claim.* New York: Columbia University Press, 2002.

Butler, Judith. *Bodies That Matter: On the Discursive Limits of "Sex."* New York: Routledge, 1993.

Butler, Judith. *Gender Trouble: Feminism and the Subversion of Identity.* New York: Routledge, 2006.

Cage, John. *Silence: Lectures and Writings by John Cage.* Middletown, CT: Wesleyan University Press, 1961.

Caldarone, Marina, and Maggie Lloyd-Williams. *Actions: The Actors' Thesaurus*. New York: Drama Publishers, 2004.

Carlson, Marvin. *The Haunted Stage: The Theater as Memory Machine*. Ann Arbor: University of Michigan Press, 2003.

Carnicke, Sharon Marie. *Stanislavsky in Focus: An Acting Master for the Twenty-First Century*. New York: Routledge, 1998.

Carson, Anne. *Decreation: Poetry, Essays, Opera*. New York: Knopf, 2005.

Castellucci, Romeo. "The Animal Being on Stage." Translated by Carolina Melis, Valentina Valetini, and Ric Allsopp. *Performance Research* 5:2 (2000), 23–28.

Castellucci, Romeo. "Conversation between Christina Tilmann of the Berliner Festspiele and Romeo Castellucci." Duisburg, August 15, 2012. Unpublished text.

Castellucci, Romeo. Program for *Genesi: From the Museum of Sleep*. 1999.

Castellucci, Romeo. *Inferno Purgatorio Paradiso*. Translated by Valentina Guidi. Cesena, Italy: Stampa Litografia CILS Cooperativa Sociale, 2008.

Castellucci, Romeo. *Les Pèlerins de la Matière: Théorie et praxis du théâtre*. Besançon, France: Les Solitaires Intempestifs, 2001.

Castellucci, Romeo. "The Universal: The Simplest Place Possible." Interview by Bonnie Marranca and Valentina Valentini. Translated by Jane House. *PAJ: A Journal of Performance and Art* 26:2 (2004), 16–25.

Castellucci, Romeo, Claudia Castellucci, Chiara Guidi, Nicholas Ridout, and Joe Kelleher. *The Theatre of Socìetas Raffaello Sanzio*. New York: Routledge, 2007.

Castoriadis, Cornelius. *Figures of the Thinkable*. Translated by Helen Arnold. Stanford, CA: Stanford University Press, 2007.

Cavell, Stanley. *Must We Mean What We Say?* New York: Cambridge University Press, 2002.

Cavell, Stanley. *The World Viewed: Reflections on the Ontology of Film*. New York: Viking Press, 1971.

Cheng, Meiling and Gabrielle Cody, eds. *Reading Contemporary Performance: Theatricality Across Genres*. New York: Routledge, 2015.

Churchill, Caryl. *Blue Heart*. New York: TCG Publications, 1997.

Clément, Catherine. *Syncope: The Philosophy of Rapture*. Translated by Sally O'Driscoll and Dierdre M. Mahoney. Minneapolis: University of Minnesota Press, 1994.

Craig, Edward. *Gordon Craig: The Story of His Life*. New York: Limelight Books, 1985.

Craig, Edward Gordon. *On the Art of the Theatre*. New York: Theatre Arts Books, 1980.

Craig, Edward Gordon. *Scene*. London: Oxford University Press, 1922.

Cull, Laura, ed. *Deleuze and Performance*. Edinburgh: Edinburgh University Press, 2009.

Cunningham, Merce. *The Dancer and the Dance: Merce Cunningham in Conversation with Jacqueline Lesschaeve*. New York: Marion Boyars, 1985.

Dasgupta, Gautam. "The Director as Thinker: Carmelo Bene's *Otello*." *PAJ: A Journal of Performance and Art* 9:1 (1985), 12–16.

Davis, Tracy C., and Thomas Postlewait, eds. *Theatricality*. Cambridge: Cambridge University Press, 2004.

de Duve, Thierry. "Performance Here and Now: Minimal Art, A Plea for a New Genre of Theatre." *Open Letter 5–6* (Summer–Fall 1983), 234–260.

De Landa, Manuel. *Intensive Science and Virtual Philosophy*. London: Bloomsbury Academic, 2005.

Deleuze, Gilles. *Bergsonism*. Translated by Hugh Tomlinson and Barbara Habberjam. New York: Zone Books, 1990.

Deleuze, Gilles. *Difference and Repetition*. Translated by Paul Patton. New York: Columbia University Press, 1994.

Deleuze, Gilles. *Essays Critical and Clinical*. Translated by Daniel Smith and Michael Greco. Minneapolis: University of Minnesota Press, 1997.

Deleuze, Gilles. *The Logic of Sense*. Translated by Constantin Boundas. New York: Columbia University Press, 1990.

Deleuze, Gilles. *Two Regimes of Madness: Texts and Interviews, 1975–1995*. Translated by David Lapoujade, Ames Hodges, and Mike Taormina. New York: Semiotext(e), 2007.

Deleuze, Gilles, and Félix Guattari. *A Thousand Plateaus*. Translated by Brian Massumi. Minneapolis: University of Minnesota Press, 1987.

Deleuze, Gilles, and Félix Guattari. *What Is Philosophy?* Translated by Hugh Tomlinson and Graham Birchill. New York: Columbia University Press, 1994.

Derrida, Jacques. *Limited Inc*. Translated by Jeffrey Mehlman and Samuel Weber. Evanston, IL: Northwestern University Press, 1988.

Derrida, Jacques. "The Purveyor of Truth." Translated by Willis Domingo, James Hulbert, and Moshe Ron. *Yale French Studies* 52 (1975), 31–113.

Derrida, Jacques. *Writing and Difference*. Translated by Alan Bass. Chicago: University of Chicago Press, 1978.

Dewey, John. *Reconstruction in Philosophy*. New York: Beacon Press, 1948.

Diderot, Denis. *Diderot's Selected Writings*. Edited by Leslie G. Crocker. Translated by Derek Coltman. New York: Macmillan, 1966.

Dolan, Jill. *Utopia in Performance: Finding Hope at the Theater*. Ann Arbor: University of Michigan Press, 2005.

Donnellan, Declan. *The Actor and the Target*. New York: TCG Publications, 2006.

Durantaye, Leland de la. "Agamben's Potential." *Diacritics* 30:2 (Summer 2000), 3–24.

Eco, Umberto. *The Open Work*. Translated by Ann Cancogni. Cambridge, MA: Harvard University Press, 1989.

Edelman, Lee. *No Future: Queer Theory and the Death Drive*. Durham, NC: Duke University Press, 2004.

Eliot, T. S. *The Sacred Wood: Essays on Poetry and Criticism*. New York: Barnes & Noble, 1964.

Eno, Will. *Flu Season and Other Plays*. New York: TCG Publications, 2006.

Escolme, Bridget. *Talking to the Audience: Shakespeare, Performance, Self*. New York: Routledge, 2005.

Feldenkrais, Moshé, and Richard Schechner. "Image, Movement, and Actor:

Restoration of Potentiality." Translated by Kelly Morris. *TDR: Tulane Drama Review* 10:3 (Spring 1966), 112–126.

Felman, Shoshana. *The Literary Speech Act: Don Juan with J.L. Austin, or Seduction in Two Languages*. Translated by Catherine Porter. Stanford, CA: Stanford University Press, 2003.

Felman, Shoshana, and Dori Laub. *Testimony: Crises of Witnessing in Literature, Psychoanalysis, and History*. New York: Routledge, 1991.

Fenn, Richard K. *The Persistence of Purgatory*. Cambridge: Cambridge University Press, 1995.

Fischer-Lichte, Erika. *The Transformative Power of Performance: A New Aesthetics*. Translated by Saskya Iris Jain. New York: Routledge, 2008.

Flannery, Tim. *The Eternal Frontier: An Ecological History of North America and Its People*. New York: Grove Press, 2001.

Focillon, Henri. *The Life of Forms in Art*. Translated by George Kubler. New York: Zone Books, 1992.

Foster, Hal. "The Crux of Minimalism." In *Individuals: A Selected History of Contemporary Art, 1945–1986*, edited by Howard Singerman. New York: Abbeville Press, 1986.

Foucault, Michel. *Discipline and Punish: The Birth of the Prison*. Translated by Alan Sheridan. New York: Vintage, 1995.

Franko, Mark. *Dance as Text: Ideologies of the Baroque Body*. New York: Cambridge University Press, 1993.

Fried, Michael. *Absorption and Theatricality: Painting and Beholder in the Age of Diderot*. Chicago: University of Chicago Press, 1988.

Fried, Michael. *Art and Objecthood: Essays and Reviews*. Chicago: University of Chicago Press, 1988.

Fried, Michael. *Courbet's Realism*. Chicago: University of Chicago Press, 1992.

Fried, Michael. *Manet's Modernism: Or the Face of Painting in the 1860s*. Chicago: University of Chicago Press, 1996.

Fried, Michael. *Why Photography Matters as Art as Never Before*. New Haven: Yale University Press, 2008.

Galison, Peter. "Image of the Self." In *Things That Talk: Object Lessons from Art and Science*, edited by Lorraine Daston. New York: Zone Books, 2004.

Genet, Jean. *The Blacks: A Clown Show*. Translated by Bernard Frechtman. New York: Grove Press, 1984.

Giannachi, Gabriella, and Nick Kaye. *Staging the Post-Avant-Garde: Italian Experimental Performance after 1970*. London: Peter Lang, 2002.

Girard, René. *Violence and the Sacred*. Translated by Patrick Gregory. Baltimore: Johns Hopkins University Press, 1979.

Gombrowicz, Witold. *Princess Ivona*. Translated by Krystyna Griffith-Jones. London: Calder and Boyars, 1969.

Greenblatt, Stephen. *Hamlet in Purgatory*. Princeton, NJ: Princeton University Press, 2002.

Grosz, Elizabeth. *Architecture from the Outside: Essays on Virtual and Real Space*. Cambridge, MA: MIT Press, 2001.

Halberstam, Judith. *The Queer Art of Failure*. Durham, NC: Duke University Press, 2011.

Hardt, Michael, and Paolo Virno, eds. *Radical Thought in Italy: A Potential Politics*. Minneapolis: University of Minnesota Press, 2006.

Hardt, Michael, and Antonio Negri. *Multitude: War and Democracy in the Age of Empire*. New York: Penguin, 2004.

Hansen, Mark. *New Philosophy for New Media*. Cambridge, MA: MIT Press, 2006.

Hays, Michael. "Drama and Dramatic Theory: Peter Szondi and the Modern Theater." *Boundary 2* 11:3 (Spring 1983), 69–81.

Hume, David. *An Enquiry Concerning Human Understanding*. Edited by L. A. Selby-Bigge. London: Oxford University Press, 1967.

Innes, Christopher. *Edward Gordon Craig: A Vision of Theatre*. London: Routledge, 1998.

Ionesco, Eugène. "Notes on Theatre." In *Twentieth-Century Theatre: A Sourcebook*, edited by Richard Drain. New York: Routledge, 1995.

Jacob, François. *The Possible and the Actual*. Seattle: University of Washington Press, 1982.

Jannarone, Kimberly. *Artaud and His Doubles*. Ann Arbor: University of Michigan Press, 2010.

Jauss, Hans Robert. *Toward an Aesthetic of Reception*. Translated by Timothy Bahti. Minneapolis: University of Minnesota Press, 1982.

Jaworski, Philippe. "Desert and Empire: From 'Bartleby' to 'Benito Cereno'." In *Herman Melville: A Collection of Critical Essays*, edited by Richard Chase. Englewood Cliffs, NJ: Prentice Hall, 1962.

Jullien, François. *The Great Image Has No Form, or On the Nonobject through Painting*. Translated by Jane Marie Todd. Chicago: University of Chicago Press, 2012.

Jullien, François. *In Praise of Blandness: Proceeding from Chinese Thought and Aesthetics*. Translated by Paula M. Varsano. Stanford, CA: Stanford University Press, 2004.

Jullien, François. *The Propensity of Things: Toward a History of Efficacy in China*. Translated by Janet Lloyd. Cambridge, MA: Zone Books, 1999.

Kafka, Franz. *Amerika: The Missing Person*. Translated by Mark Harman. New York: Schoken, 2008.

Kaye, Nick. "Live Art: Definition and Documentation." *Contemporary Theatre Review* 2:2 (1994), 1–7.

Kear, Adrian. "The Memory of Promise: Theatre and the Ethic of the Future." In *A Performance Cosmology: Testimony from the Future, Evidence of the Past*, edited by Judie Christie, Richard Gough, and Daniel Watt. New York: Routledge, 2006.

Kelleher, Joe, and Nicholas Ridout, eds. *Contemporary Theatres in Europe: A Critical Companion*. New York: Routledge, 2006.

Kennedy, Dennis. *Looking at Shakespeare: A Visual History of Twentieth Century Performance*. Cambridge: Cambridge University Press, 2001.

Kermode, Frank. *The Sense of an Ending: Studies in the Theory of Fiction*. New York: Oxford University Press, 2000.

Kirsch, Adam. "America, 'Amerika.'" *New York Times*, January 2, 2009.

Kirstein, Lincoln. *Nijinsky Dancing*. New York: Knopf, 1975.

Klein, Naomi. *The Shock Doctrine: The Rise of Disaster Capitalism*. New York: Picador, 2008.

Knox, Bernard. *Word and Action: Essays on the Ancient Theater*. Baltimore: Johns Hopkins University, 1986.

Kofman, Sarah. *The Enigma of Woman: Women in Freud's Writings*. Ithaca, NY: Cornell University Press, 1985.

Krauss, Rosalind. *Passages in Modern Sculpture*. Cambridge, MA: MIT Press, 1977.

Kuppers, Petra. *Disability and Contemporary Performance: Bodies on Edge*. New York: Routledge, 2003.

Lacan, Jacques. *Écrits: A Selection*. Translated by Bruce Fink. New York: W.W. Norton, 2002.

Lacan, Jacques. *The Four Fundamental Concepts of Psychoanalysis: The Seminars of Jacques Lacan Seminar XI*. Edited by Jacques-Alain Miller. Translated by Alan Sheridan. New York: W.W. Norton, 1998.

Langer, Susanne K. *Feeling and Form*. New York: Scribner, 1953.

Law, Alma, and Mel Gordon, eds. *Meyerhold, Eisenstein, and Biomechanics*. Jefferson, NC: McFarland, 1996.

Lee, Pamela. *Chronophobia: On Time in the Art of the 1960s*. Cambridge, MA: MIT Press, 2004.

Lee, Sang Hyun. *The Philosophical Theology of Jonathan Edwards*. Princeton, NJ: Princeton University Press, 2000.

Lepecki, André. *Exhausting Dance: Performance and the Politics of Movement*. New York: Routledge, 2006.

Lepecki, André, ed. *Of the Presence of the Body: Essays on Dance and Performance Theory*. Middletown, CT: Wesleyan University Press, 2004.

Lepecki, André. "Undoing the Fantasy of the (Dancing) Subject: 'Still Acts' in Jérôme Bel's Last Performance." In *The Salt of the Earth: On Dance, Politics and Reality*, edited by Steven De Belder. Brussels: VTI, 2001.

Levi, Primo. *The Drowned and the Saved*. Translated by Raymond Rosenthal. New York: Doubleday, 1989.

Lindfors, Bernth, ed. *Africans on Stage: Studies in Ethnological Show Business*. Bloomington: Indiana University Press, 1999.

Loux, Michael J., ed. *The Possible and the Actual: Readings in the Metaphysics of Modality*. Ithaca, NY: Cornell University Press, 1979.

Lucian. *The Works of Lucian of Samosata*. Translated by H. W. Fowler and F. G Fowler. Oxford: Clarendon Press, 1905.

Lyotard, Jean-François. *The Differend: Phrases in Dispute*. Translated by Georges Van Den Abbeele. Minneapolis: University of Minnesota Press, 1988.

Manning, Erin. *Relationscapes: Movement, Art, Philosophy*. Cambridge, MA: MIT Press, 2009.

Martin, Carol. "What Did They Do to My Country! An Interview with Rachel Chavkin." *TDR: The Drama Review* 54:4 (Winter 2010), 99–117.

Martin, John. *The Modern Dance*. New York: Dance Horizons, 1972.

Massumi, Brian. *A Shock to Thought: Expression after Deleuze and Guattari*. New York: Routledge, 2002.

Mathews, Harry, and Alastair Brotchie. *The Oulipo Compendium*. London: Atlas Press, 1998.

McKenzie, Jon. *Perform or Else: From Discipline to Performance*. New York: Routledge, 2001.

Melville, Herman. *"Bartleby the Scrivener" and "Benito Cereno"*. New York: Dover, 1990.

Melville, Herman. *Moby Dick*. Edited by Herschel Parker and Harrison Hayford. New York: W.W. Norton, 2002.

Merlin, Bella. *Beyond Stanislavsky: A Psycho-physical Approach to Actor Training*. New York: Routledge, 2001.

Michaud, Philippe-Alain. *Aby Warburg and the Image in Motion*. Cambridge, MA: MIT Press, 2004.

Miller, Perry. *Jonathan Edwards*. Lincoln, NE: Bison Books, 2005.

Mitchell, W. J. T. *Iconology: Image, Text, Ideology*. Chicago: University of Chicago Press, 1987.

Morris, Robert. "Notes on Sculpture, Part 1." In *Minimal Art: A Critical Anthology*, edited by Gregory Battcock. Berkeley: University of California Press, 1995.

Morris, Robert. *Robert Morris: The Mind/Body Problem*. New York: Solomon R. Guggenheim Museum Press, 1994.

Mosès, Stéphane. *The Angel of History: Rosenzweig, Benjamin, Scholem*. Translated by Barbara Harshav. Stanford, CA: Stanford University Press, 2008.

Moten, Fred. *In the Break: The Aesthetics of the Black Radical Tradition*. Minneapolis: University of Minnesota Press, 2003.

Motte, Warren F., Jr., trans. and ed. *Oulipo: A Primer of Potential Literature*. Lincoln: University of Nebraska Press, 1986.

Mullarkey, John. *Bergson and Philosophy*. Edinburgh: Edinburgh University Press, 1999.

Mullarkey, John, ed. *The New Bergson*. New York: Manchester University Press, 1999.

Muñoz, José Esteban. *Cruising Utopia: The Then and There of Queer Futurity*. New York: NYU Press, 2009.

Murray, Timothy, ed. *Mimesis, Masochism, and Mime: The Politics of Theatricality in Contemporary French Thought*. Ann Arbor: University of Michigan Press, 1997.

Nietzsche, Friedrich. *Beyond Good and Evil: Prelude to a Philosophy of the Future*. Edited by Rolf-Peter Horstmann and Judith Norman. Translated by Judith Norman. Cambridge: Cambridge University Press, 2002.

Nietzsche, Friedrich. *On the Genealogy of Morals*. Translated by Walter Kaufmann. New York: Vintage, 1969.

Nietzsche, Friedrich. *"Twilight of the Idols" and "The Antichrist"*. Translated by Thomas Common. Mineola, NY: Dover, 2004.

Novati, Gabriella Calchi. "Language under Attack: The Iconoclastic Theatre of Societas Raffaello Sanzio." *Theatre Research International* 34:1 (March 2009), 50–65.

Ong, Walter J. *Orality and Literacy: The Technologizing of the Word*. New York: Methuen, 1982.

Orgel, Stephen. *The Jonsonian Masque*. Cambridge, MA: Harvard University Press, 1965.

Owens, Craig. *Beyond Recognition: Representation, Power, and Culture*. Berkeley: University of California Press, 1992.

Pasolini, Pier Paolo. "Manifesto for a New Theatre." Translated by Thomas Simpson. *PAJ: A Journal of Performance and Art* 29:1 (2007), 126–138.

Phelan, Peggy. *Unmarked: The Politics of Representation*. New York: Routledge, 1993.

Phelan, Peggy. "Seven Not So Easy Pieces: Marina Abramovic's Re-Do's." Paper presented at the Guggenheim Museum, New York, April 7, 2005.

Piper, Adrian. *Out of Order, Out of Sight. Vol. 1, Selected Writings in Meta-Art: 1968-1992*. Cambridge, MA: MIT Press, 1999.

Plato. *Plato: The Collected Dialogues*. Edited by Edith Hamilton and Huntington Cairns. Princeton, NJ: Princeton University Press, 1961.

Prosperi, Mario. "Contemporary Italian Theatre." *TDR: The Drama Review* 22:1 (March 1978), 49–62.

Puchner, Martin. *Stage Fright: Modernism, Anti-Theatricality, and Drama*. Baltimore: Johns Hopkins University Press, 2011.

Puleston, Dennis. *Blue Water Vagabond: Six Years' Adventure at Sea*. New York: Doubleday, Doran, 1939.

Quigley, Austin E. *The Modern Stage and Other Worlds*. New York: Routledge, 1985.

Rancière, Jacques. *The Politics of Aesthetics*. Translated by Gabriel Rockhill. New York: Continuum, 2004.

Rayner, Alice. *To Act, To Do, To Perform: Drama and the Phenomenology of Action*. Ann Arbor: University of Michigan Press, 1994.

Read, Alan. *Theatre, Intimacy and Engagement: The Last Human Venue*. New York: Palgrave Macmillan, 2008.

Reason, Matthew. *Documentation, Disappearance and the Representation of Live Performance*. New York: Palgrave Macmillan, 2006.

Ridout, Nicholas. "Regarding Theatre: Thoughts on Recent Work by Simon Vincenzi and Romeo Castellucci." *Theatre Journal* 66 (October 2014), 427–436.

Ridout, Nicholas. *Stage Fright, Animals, and Other Theatrical Problems*. New York: Cambridge University Press, 2006.

Roach, Joseph. *The Player's Passion: Studies in the Science of Acting*. Ann Arbor: University of Michigan Press, 2007.

Robinson, Tim. *My Time in Space*. Dublin: Lilliput Press, 2001.

Rosenberg, Harold. *The Tradition of the New*. New York: Horizon Press, 1960.

Sack, Daniel. "Not Looking into the Abyss: The Potentiality to See." In *On Not Looking: The Paradox of Contemporary Visual Culture*, edited by Frances Guerin. New York: Routledge, 2015.

Sack, Daniel. "On Losing One's Voice: Two Performances from Romeo Castellucci's *e la volpe disse al corvo*." *Theatre Forum* 46 (Winter 2014), 37–46.

Sack, Daniel. "The Rabbit and Its Double." *Theater* 37:3 (2007), 27–36.

Said, Edward. *Beginnings: Intentions and Methods*. New York: Columbia University Press, 2004.

Schechner, Richard. *Between Theatre and Anthropology*. Philadelphia: University of Pennsylvania Press, 1985.

Scheffler, Israel. *Of Human Potential: An Essay in the Philosophy of Education*. New York: Routledge & Kegan Paul, 1985.

Schlegel, August Wilhelm von. "Lectures on Dramatic Art and Literature." In *Dramatic Theory and Criticism: Greeks to Grotowski*, edited by Bernard F. Dukore. New York: Harcourt Brace Jovanovich, 1974.

Schneider, Rebecca. "Lithic Liveness and Agential Theatricality." Presentation at the Annual Conference of the American Society for Theatre Research, Baltimore, MD, November 22, 2014.

Schneider, Rebecca. *Performing Remains: Art and War in the Times of Theatrical Reenactment*. New York: Routledge, 2011.

Scott, James C. *Seeing Like a State: How Certain Schemes to Improve the Human Condition Have Failed*. New Haven: Yale University Press, 1999.

Seely, Hart. *Pieces of Intelligence: The Existential Poetry of Donald H. Rumsfeld*. New York: Free Press, 2003.

Seremetakis, C. Nadia. *The Senses Still: Perception and Memory as Material Culture in Modernity*. Chicago: University of Chicago Press, 1996.

Serres, Michel. *Angels: A Modern Myth*. Translated by Francis Cowper. Paris: Flammarion, 1997.

Serres, Michel. *Genesis*. Translated by Genevieve James and James Nielson. Ann Arbor: University of Michigan Press, 1997.

Siegel, Marcia. *Dance at the Vanishing Point*. New York: Saturday Review Press, 1972.

Slotkin, Richard. *Regeneration through Violence: The Mythology of the American Frontier, 1600–1860*. Norman: University of Oklahoma Press, 2000.

Smithson, Robert. *The Collected Writings*. Cambridge, MA: MIT Press, 1996.

Sofer, Andrew. *Dark Matter: Invisibility in Drama, Theater, and Performance*. Ann Arbor: University of Michigan Press, 2013.

Sofer, Andrew. *The Stage Life of Props*. Ann Arbor: University of Michigan Press, 2003.

Spinoza, Baruch. *The Ethics and Selected Letters*. Translated by Samuel Shirley. Indianapolis: Hackett, 1982.

Stanislavsky, Konstantin. *An Actor Prepares*. Translated by Elizabeth Hapgood. New York: Theatre Arts Books, 1964.

States, Bert O. *Great Reckonings in Little Rooms: On the Phenomenology of Theater*. Berkeley: University of California Press, 1987.

States, Bert O. "Phenomenology of the Curtain Call." *Hudson Review* 34:3 (Autumn 1981), 371–380.

States, Bert O. *The Pleasure of the Play*. Ithaca, NY: Cornell University Press, 1994.

Stein, Gertrude. *Last Operas and Plays*. Baltimore: John Hopkins University Press, 1995.

Stein, Gertrude. *Look at Me Now and Here I Am: Writings and Lectures, 1911–1945*. New York: Penguin, 1967.

Steiner, George. *The Death of Tragedy*. New York: Faber and Faber, 1996.

Steiner, George. *Grammars of Creation*. New Haven: Yale University Press, 2001.

Sophocles. *Oedipus*. Translated by F. Storr. Cambridge, MA: Harvard University Press, 1912.

Szondi, Peter. *Theory of Modern Drama*. Translated by Michael Hays. Minneapolis: University of Minnesota Press, 1987.

Taxidou, Olga. *The Mask: A Periodical Performance*. London: Routledge, 1998.

Thèron, Didier. http://www.didiertheron.com. Accessed May 5, 2010.

Thoreau, Henry David. *Walden.* New York: Houghton Mifflin, 1906.

Tompkins, Jane. *West of Everything: The Inner Life of Westerns.* New York: Oxford University Press, 1992.

Toro, Fernando. *Theatre Semiotics: Text and Staging in Modern Theatre.* Translated by Mario Valdez. Toronto: University of Toronto Press, 1995.

Turner, Victor. *From Ritual to Theatre: The Human Seriousness of Play.* New York: PAJ Books, 2001.

Uexküll, Jakob von. *A Foray in the World of Animals and Humans.* Translated by Joseph D. O'Neill. Minneapolis: University of Minnesota Press, 2010.

Valentini, Valentina. "In Search of Lost Stories: Italian Performance in the Mid-'80s. Three Interviews." *TDR: The Drama Review* 32:3 (Autumn 1988), 109–125.

Varro. *On the Latin Language.* Translated by Roland G. Kent. Cambridge, MA: Harvard University Press, 1977.

Venturi, Robert, Steven Izenour, and Denise Scott Brown. *Learning from Las Vegas: The Forgotten Symbolism of Architectural Form.* Cambridge, MA: MIT Press, 1977.

Virilio, Paul. *The Original Accident.* Translated by Julie Rose. Cambridge: Polity, 2007.

Virno, Paolo. *A Grammar of the Multitude: For an Analysis of Contemporary Forms of Life.* Translated by Isabella Bertoletti, James Cascaito, and Andrea Casson. New York: Semiotext(e), 2004.

Walton, J. Michael. *Euripides: Our Contemporary.* Berkeley: University of California Press, 2009.

Weil, Simone. *Gravity and Grace.* Translated by A. Willis. Lincoln: University of Nebraska Press, 1997.

Weiss, Allen S. *Breathless: Sound Recording, Disembodiment, and the Transformation of Lyrical Nostalgia.* Middletown, CT: Wesleyan University Press, 2002.

Weiss, Allen S. "In Memory: Carmelo Bene 1937–2002." *TDR: The Drama Review* 46:4 (Winter 2002), 8–10.

Wilding, Faith. "Waiting Poem." http://faithwilding.refugia.net/waitingpoem.pdf. Accessed August 23, 2014.

Wittgenstein, Ludwig. *Philosophical Investigations.* Translated by G. E. M. Anscombe. London: Blackwell, 2001.

Wölfflin, Heinrich. *Principles of Art History.* Translated by M. D. Hottinger. New York: Dover, 1950.

Yeats, W. B. *Michael Robartes and the Dancer.* Dundrum, Ireland: Chuala Press, 1920.

Žižek, Slavoj. "The Empty Wheelbarrow." http://www.lacan.com/zizekempty.htm. Accessed October 13, 2014.

Žižek, Slavoj. "What Rumsfeld Doesn't Know That He Knows about Abu Ghraib." http://www.lacan.com/zizekrumsfeld.htm. Accessed October 13, 2014.

Žižek, Slavoj. *Iraq: The Borrowed Kettle.* New York: Verso, 2005.

Index